A DYNAMIC THEORY
OF PERSONALITY

Selected Papers

BY
KURT LEWIN, Ph.D.

TRANSLATED BY
DONALD K. ADAMS, Ph.D.
Duke University

AND

KARL E. ZENER, Ph.D.
Duke University

McGRAW-HILL BOOK COMPANY, Inc.
NEW YORK AND LONDON

COPYRIGHT, 1935, BY THE
McGRAW-HILL BOOK COMPANY, INC.

ISBN 07-0-37451-1

11 12 13 - MUMU - 7

PREFACE

The present book is a collection of originally independent articles which were written at different times and for quite different occasions. Hence, the reader will find some of the fundamental ideas recurring throughout the book. The selection has been made in order to give a picture of the fields thus far studied, the psychology of the person and of the environment, and at the same time to indicate their connections with the various applied fields, especially child psychology, pedagogy, psychopathology, characterology, and social psychology.

Only a few years ago one could observe, at least among German psychologists, a quite pessimistic mood. After the initial successes of experimental psychology in its early stages, it seemed to become clearer and clearer that it would remain impossible for experimental method to press on beyond the psychology of perception and memory to such vital problems as those with which psychoanalysis was concerned. Weighty "philosophical" and "methodological" considerations seemed to make such an undertaking a priori impossible. The first positive experiments in this direction seemed only to confirm the belief that the experimental psychology of will, emotion, and character was condemned to rest content with surface facts and to leave all deeper problems to schools and speculation, incapable of experimental test.

Working in this field I felt that I had begun a task methodologically and technically sound and necessary, the broader elaboration of which could not be expected for decades. Nevertheless it soon became clear that though these problems are difficult, they are by no means impossible to solve. One had only to clear out a number of hoary philosophical prejudices and to set his scientific goal high enough to arrive at explanation and prediction. Today it can no longer be doubted that the questions set, for example, by psychoanalysis are readily accessible to experimental clarification if only appropriate methods and concepts are employed. Indeed, it seems somewhat easier to advance to dynamic laws in the field of needs and emotions than in the psychology of perception. My visit to American universities during the last year has shown me that, in spite of all the differences of historical background, the belief in these possibilities is giving rise to many experiments. The relations to psychopathology and to comparative psychology give promise of becoming especially fruitful. Naturally I know how near the beginning we stand. But the development seems to be proceeding much more rapidly than I had hoped. The reason for this is, above all, the historical position of psychology, which is ripe for a "Galileian" mode of thought.

I have been asked whether I approve of the name "topological psychology" for this type of research. I have no objection to it so long as the following points are emphasized. I am convinced that psychology is today in a position to grow beyond the "schools" in the old sense of the word. To contribute to this growth is a major goal of our work which uses, so far as possible, the language of mathematics. For this language is less equivocal than any other and at the same time "objective" and "unspeculative," since it expresses only the structural order of things and events. However, I do not limit myself to concepts of topology. Furthermore, the use of mathematical language is only an expression of a more general "constructive" method whose chief characteristic is its greater ability to bridge the gap between theory and particular fact. Nevertheless, topology remains the basic mathematical discipline for the presentation of dynamics in the whole field of psychology, and I am more and more convinced that it will become, beyond this, a solid framework for a dynamic sociology.

Doctors D. K. Adams and Karl Zener have undertaken the great labor of translating the articles into English. Only those who know the difficulties of this sort of translation in scientifically new fields will appreciate the extent to which I am indebted to them.   KURT LEWIN.

ITHACA, NEW YORK,
    March, 1935.

TRANSLATORS' PREFACE

Several of the terms used in this translation may be better understood if the German terms which they are designed to translate are indicated. The adjectives *psychisch* and *seelisch* have both been translated "psychic" or "psychical" because it seems to us that events, processes, and structures that are properly called psychical do not become *psychological* until they have been operated upon in some way by the science of psychology or by psychologists. An ambiguity is thus avoided which could give rise to unnecessary misunderstandings and which, in the case of physics, has done so. Thus the expression "the physical world" is ambiguous because it may mean "the material world of experience" or "the world of physics," two radically different things.

The word *Seele* has been translated, with much misgiving, by "mind." We had thought to translate it by "soul," in the belief that the time was ripe for a reintroduction of the latter word into the technical English terminology of psychology. It seemed impossible that there should be any confusion of the psychological "soul," deduced as it is from concrete behavior, with the "soul" of theology, the properties of which cannot be derived from or tested by concrete behavior. But a sampling of opinion among American psychologists was against the use of this more accurate translation. It is consequently necessary to point out that "mind" as here used ("the totality of psychical systems") is not to be taken in any narrowly intellectualistic sense but rather in a meaning approximating that of McDougall. In his later papers Lewin uses the term *psychologische Person* (translated by "psychological person") in what seems to be essentially the same sense as *Seele* in the earlier articles.

Other translations which might require comment are explained either in the text itself or in notes.

Acknowledgment is due Professor Murchison, Director, and the Clark University Press for permission to reprint Chapters I and III, which originally appeared in the *Journal of General Psychology*, Volume 5, pages 141–177, and in Murchison's *Handbook of Child Psychology*, respectively.

The monograph *Die psychologische Situation bei Lohn und Strafe* (Chapter IV of this book) was first published by Hirzel of Leipzig in 1931. The "Theorie des Schwachsinns" (Chapter VII of this book) was published in *Hommage au Dr. Decroly* by Les Usines reunies Scheerders van Kerchove a St.-Nicholas-W., Belgium in 1933. "Erziehung zur Realität" (Chapter V of this book) was published in *Die Neue Erziehung* in 1931. We have to thank the publishing house of Julius Springer, Berlin, for permission to translate the portion of *Vorsatz, Wille und Bedürfnis* which appears in Chapter II and for the use of most of the figures in Chapter VIII. The latter have been redrawn after certain of those in the long series of articles edited by Professor Lewin in the *Psychologische Forschung*. We also wish to thank Mr. Charles E. Stuart for generous assistance in preparing the drawings.

D. K. ADAMS.

K. E. ZENER.

DURHAM, NORTH CAROLINA,

CONTENTS

A DYNAMIC THEORY
OF PERSONALITY

CHAPTER I

THE CONFLICT BETWEEN ARISTOTELIAN AND GALILEIAN MODES OF THOUGHT IN CONTEMPORARY PSYCHOLOGY[1]

In the discussion of several urgent problems of current experimental and theoretical psychology I propose to review the development of the concepts of physics, and particularly the transition from the Aristotelian to the Galileian mode of thought. My purpose is not historical; rather do I believe that certain questions, of considerable importance in the reconstruction of concepts in present-day psychology, may be clarified and more precisely stated through such a comparison, which provides a view beyond the difficulties of the day.

I do not intend to infer by deduction from the history of physics what psychology ought to do. I am not of the opinion that there is only one empirical science, namely, physics; and the question whether psychology, as a part of biology, is reducible to physics or is an independent science may here be left open.

Since we are starting from the point of view of the researcher, we shall, in our contrast of Aristotelian and Galileian concept formation, be less concerned with personal nuances of theory in Galileo and Aristotle than with certain ponderable differences in the modes of thought that determined the actual research of the medieval Aristotelians and of the post-Galileian

[1] *Jour. Gen. Psychol.*, 1931, **5,** 141–177, edited by Carl Murchison.

physicists. Whether some particular investigator had previously shown the later sort of thinking in respect to some special point or whether some very modern speculations of the relativity theory should accord in some way with Aristotle's is irrelevant in the present connection.

In order to provide a special setting for the theoretical treatment of the dynamic problems, I shall consider first the general characteristics of Aristotelian and Galileian physics and of modern psychology.

GENERAL CHARACTER OF THE TWO MODES OF THOUGHT

In Physics

If one asks what the most characteristic difference between "modern" post-Galileian and Aristotelian physics is, one receives, as a rule, the following reply, which has had an important influence upon the scientific ideals of the psychologist: the concepts of Aristotelian physics were anthropomorphic and inexact. Modern physics, on the contrary, is quantitatively exact, and pure mathematical, functional relations now occupy the place of former anthropomorphic explanations. These have given to physics that abstract appearance in which modern physicists are accustomed to take special pride.

This view of the development of physics is, to be sure, pertinent. But if one fixes one's attention less upon the style of the concepts employed and more upon their actual functions as instruments for understanding the world, these differences appear to be of a secondary nature, consequences of a deeplying difference in the conception of the relation between the world and the task of research.

Aristotelian Concepts.

Their Valuative Character. As in all sciences, the detachment of physics from the universal matrix of philosophy and practice was only gradually achieved. Aristotelian physics is full of concepts which today are considered not only as specifically biological, but preeminently as valuative concepts. It abounds in specifically normative concepts taken from ethics, which occupy a place between valuative and nonvaluative concepts: the highest forms of motions are circular and rectilinear, and they occur only in heavenly movements, those of the stars; the earthly sublunar world is endowed with motion of inferior types. There are similar valuative differences between causes: on one side there are the good or, so to speak, authorized forces of a body which come from its tendency toward perfection ($\tau\acute{\epsilon}\lambda os$), and on the other side the disturbances due to chance and to the opposing forces ($\beta\acute{\iota}\alpha$) of other bodies.

This kind of classification in terms of values plays an extraordinarily important part in medieval physics. It classes together many things with very slight or unimportant relation and separates things that objectively are closely and importantly related.

It seems obvious to me that this extremely "anthropomorphic" mode of thought plays a large role in psychology, even to the present day. Like the distinction between earthly and heavenly, the no less valuative distinction between "normal" and "pathological" has for a long time sharply differentiated two fields of psychological fact and thus separated the phenomena which are fundamentally most nearly related.

No less important is the fact that value concepts completely dominate the conceptual setting of the special problems, or have done so until very recently. Thus, not till lately has psychology begun to investigate the structural (Gestalt) relations concerned in perception, thus replacing the concept of optical illusion, a concept which, derived not from psychological but from epistemological categories, unwarrantedly lumps together all these "illusions" and sets them apart from the other phenomena of psychological optics. Psychology speaks of the "errors" of children, of "practice," of "forgetting," thus classifying whole groups of processes according to the value of their products, instead of according to the nature of the psychological processes involved. Psychology is, to be sure, beyond classifying events *only* on the basis of value when it speaks of disturbances, of inferiority and superiority in development, or of the quality of performance on a test. On all sides there are tendencies to attack actual psychological processes. But there can hardly be any doubt that we stand now only at the beginning of this stage, that the same transitional concepts that we have seen in the Aristotelian physics to lie between the valuative and the nonvaluative are characteristic of such antitheses as intelligence and feeble-mindedness or drive and will. The detachment of the conceptual structure of psychology from the utilitarian concepts of pedagogy, medicine, and ethics is only partly achieved.

It is quite possible, indeed I hold it to be probable, that the utility or performance concepts, such as a "true" cognition versus an "error," may later acquire a legitimate sense. If that is the case, however, an "illusion" will have to be characterized not epistemologically but biologically.

Abstract Classification. When the Galileian and post-Galileian physics disposed of the distinction between heavenly and earthly and thereby extended the field of natural law enormously, it was not due solely to the exclusion of value concepts, but also to a changed interpretation of classification. For Aristotelian physics the membership of an object in a given class was of critical importance, because for Aristotle the class defined the essence or essential nature of the object and thus determined its behavior in both positive and negative respects.

This classification often took the form of paired opposites, such as cold and warm, dry and moist, and compared with present-day classification had a rigid, absolute character. In modern quantitative physics dichotomous classifications have been entirely replaced by continuous gradations. Substantial concepts have been replaced by functional concepts.

Here also it is not difficult to point out the analogous stage of development in contemporary psychology. The separation of intelligence, memory, and impulse bears throughout the characteristic stamp of Aristotelian classification; and in some fields, for example, in the analysis of feelings (pleasantness and

---

[1] E. CASSIRER, *Substanzbegriff und Funktionsbegriff, Untersuchungen über die Grundfragen der Erkenntniskritik*, B. Cassirer, Berlin, 1910.

unpleasantness), or of temperaments,[1] or of drives,[2] such dichotomous classifications as Aristotle's are even today of great significance. Only gradually do these classifications lose their importance and yield to a conception which seeks to derive the same laws for all these fields, and to classify the whole field on the basis of other, essentially functional, differences.

The Concept of Law. Aristotle's classes are abstractly defined as the sum total of those characteristics which a group of objects have in common. This circumstance is not merely a characteristic of Aristotle's logic, but largely determines his conception of *lawfulness* and *chance*, which seems to me so important to the problems of contemporary psychology as to require closer examination.

For Aristotle those things are lawful, conceptually intelligible, which occur *without exception*. Also, and this he emphasizes particularly, those are lawful which occur *frequently*. Excluded from the class of the conceptually intelligible as mere chance are those things which occur only *once*, individual events as such. Actually since the behavior of a thing is determined by its essential nature, and this essential nature is exactly the abstractly defined class (*i.e.*, the sum total of the common characteristics of a whole group of objects), it follows that each event, as a particular event, is chance, undetermined. For in these Aristotelian classes individual differences disappear.

The real source of this conception may lie in the fact that for Aristotelian physics not all physical processes possess the lawful character ascribed to them by post-Galileian physics. To the young science of physics the universe it investigated appeared to contain as much that was chaotic as that was lawful. The lawfulness, the intelligibility of physical processes was still narrowly limited. It was really present only in certain processes, for example, the courses of the stars, but by no means in all the transitory events of the earth. Just as for other young sciences, it was still a question for physics, whether physical

[1] R. SOMMER, Über Persönlichkeitstypen, *Ber. Kong. f. exper. Psychol.*, 1925.
[2] LEWIN, *Die Entwicklung der experimentellen Willenspsychologie und die Psychotherapie*, S. Hirzel, Leipzig, 1929.

processes were subject to law and if so how far. And this circumstance exercised its full effect on the formation of physical concepts, even though in philosophical principle the idea of general lawfulness already existed. In post-Galileian physics, with the elimination of the distinction between lawful and chance events, the necessity also disappeared of proving that the process under consideration was lawful. For Aristotelian physics, on the contrary, it was necessary to have criteria to decide whether or not a given event was of the lawful variety. Indeed the regularity with which similar events occurred in nature was used essentially as such a criterion. Only such events, as the celestial, which the course of history proves to be regular, or at least frequent, are subject to law; and only in so far as they are frequent, and hence more than individual events, are they conceptually intelligible. In other words, the ambition of science to understand the complex, chaotic, and unintelligible world, its faith in the ultimate decipherability of this world, were limited to such events as were certified by repetition in the course of history to possess a certain persistence and stability.

In this connection it must not be forgotten that Aristotle's emphasis on frequency (as a further basis for lawfulness, besides absolute regularity) represents, relative to his predecessors, a tendency toward the extension and concrete application of the principle of lawfulness. The "empiricist," Aristotle, insists that not only the regular but the frequent is lawful. Of course, this only makes clearer his antithesis of individuality and law, for the individual event as such still lies outside the pale of the lawful and hence, in a certain sense, outside the task of science. Lawfulness remains limited to cases in which events recur and classes (in Aristotle's abstract sense) reveal the essential nature of the events.

This attitude toward the problem of lawfulness in nature, which dominated medieval physics and from which even the opponents of Aristotelian physics, such as Bruno and Bacon, escaped only gradually, had important consequences in several respects.

As will be clear from the preceding text, this concept of lawfulness had throughout a quasi-statistical character. Lawfulness was considered as equivalent to the highest degree of generality, as that which occurs very often in the same way, as the extreme case of regularity, and hence as the perfect antithesis of the infrequent or of the particular event. The statistical determination of the concept of lawfulness is still clearly marked in Bacon, as when he tries to decide through his *tabula praesentia* whether a given association of properties is real (essential) or fortuitous. Thus he ascertains, for example, the numerical frequency of the cases in which the properties warm and dry are associated in everyday life. Less mathematically exact, indeed, but no less clear is this statistical way of thinking in the whole body of Aristotelian physics.

At the same time—and this is one of the most important consequences of the Aristotelian conception—regularity or particularity was understood entirely in *historical* terms.

The complete freedom from exceptions, the "always" which is found also in the later conceptions of physical lawfulness, still has here its original connections with the frequency with which similar cases have occurred in the actual, historical course of events in the everyday world. A crude example will make this clearer: light objects, under the conditions of everyday life, relatively frequently go up; heavy objects usually go down. The flame of the fire, at any rate under the conditions known to Aristotle, almost always goes upward. It is these frequency rules, within the limits of the climate, mode of life, etc., familiar to Aristotle, that determine the nature and tendency to be ascribed to each class of objects and lead in the present instance to the conclusion that flames and light bodies have a tendency upward.

Aristotelian concept formation has yet another immediate relation to the geographically-historically given, in which it resembles, as do the valuative concepts mentioned above, the thinking of primitive man and of children.

When primitive man uses different words for "walking," depending upon its direction, north or south, or upon the sex of the walker, or upon whether the latter is going into or out of a house,[1] he is employing a reference to the historical situation that is quite similar to the putatively absolute descriptions (upward or downward) of Aristotle, the real significance of which is a sort of geographic characterization, a place definition relative to the earth's surface.[2]

The original connection of the concepts with the "actuality," in the special sense of the given historic-geographic circumstances, is perhaps the most important feature of Aristotelian physics. It is from this almost more even than from its teleology that his physics gets its general anthropomorphic character. Even in the minute particulars of theorizing and in the actual conduct of research it is always evident not only that physical and normative concepts are still undifferentiated, but that the formulation of problems and the concepts that we would today distinguish, on the one hand, as historic[3] and, on the other, as nonhistoric or systematic are inextricably interwoven. (Incidentally, an analogous confusion exists in the early stages of other sciences, for example in economics.)

From these conceptions also the attitude of Aristotelian physics toward lawfulness takes a new direction. So long as lawfulness remained limited to such processes as occurred repeatedly in the same way, it is evident not only that the young physics still lacked the courage to extend the principle to all physical phenomena, but also that the concept of lawfulness

---

[1] L. Lévy-Bruhl, *La Mentalité primitive*, Alcan, Paris, 1922, (5th ed., 1927).

[2] In the following pages we shall frequently have to use the term "historic-geographic." This is not in common usage, but it seems to me inaccurate to contrast historic and systematic questions. The real opposition is between "type" (of object, process, situation) and "occurrence." And for concepts that deal with occurrence, the reference to absolute geographic space-coordinates is just as characteristic as that to absolute time-coordinates by means of dates.

At the same time, the concept of the geographic should be understood in such a general sense as to refer to juxtaposition, correlative to historical succession, and as to be applicable to psychical events.

[3] There is no term at present in general use to designate nonhistoric problem formulations. I here employ the term "systematic," meaning thereby, not "ordered," but collectively nonhistoric problems and laws such as those which form the bulk of present-day physics (see p. 12).

still had a fundamentally historic, a temporally particular significance. Stress was laid not upon the general validity which modern physics understands by lawfulness, but upon the events in the historically given world which displayed the required stability. The highest degree of lawfulness, beyond mere frequency, was characterized by the idea of always, eternal (ἀεί as against ἐπὶ τὸ πολύ). That is, the stretch of historic time for which constancy was assumed was extended to eternity. General validity of law was not yet clearly distinguished from eternity of process. Only permanence, or at least frequent repetition, was proof of more than momentary validity. Even here in the idea of eternity, which seems to transcend the historical, the connection with immediate historic actuality is still obvious, and this close connection was characteristic of the "empiricist" Aristotle's method and concepts.

Not only in physics but in other sciences—for example, in economics and biology—it can be clearly seen how in certain early stages the tendency to empiricism, to the collection and ordering of facts, carries with it a tendency to historical concept formation, to excessive valuation of the historical.

Galileian Physics.

From the point of view of this sort of empiricism the concept formation of Galileian and post-Galileian physics must seem curious and even paradoxical.

As remarked above, the use of mathematical tools and the tendency to exactness, important as they are, cannot be considered the real substance of the difference between Aristotelian and Galileian physics. It is indeed quite possible to recast in mathematical form the essential content of, for example, the dynamic ideas of Aristotelian physics (see page 16). It is conceivable that the development of physics could have taken the form of a mathematical rendition of Aristotelian concepts such as is actually taking place in psychology today. In reality, however, there were only traces of such a tendency, such as Bacon's quasi-statistical methods, mentioned above.

The main development took another direction and proved to be a change of content rather than a mere change of form.

The same considerations apply to the exactness of the new physics. It must not be forgotten that in Galileo's time there were no clocks of the sort we have today, that these first became possible through the knowledge of dynamics founded upon Galileo's work.[1] Even the methods of measurement used by Faraday in the early investigations of electricity show how little exactness, in the current sense of precision to such and such a decimal place, had to do with these critical stages in the development of physics.

The real sources of the tendency to quantification lie somewhat deeper, namely in a new conception by the physicist of the nature of the physical world, in an extension of the demands of physics upon itself in the task of understanding the world, and in an increased faith in the possibility of their fulfillment. These are radical and far-reaching changes in the fundamental ideas of physics, and the tendency to quantification is simply one of their expressions.

Homogenization. The outlook of a Bruno, a Kepler, or a Galileo is determined by the idea of a comprehensive, all-embracing unity of the physical world. The same law governs the courses of the stars, the falling of stones, and the flight of birds. This homogenization of the physical world with respect to the validity of law deprives the division of physical objects into rigid abstractly defined classes of the critical significance it had for Aristotelian physics, in which membership in a certain conceptual class was considered to determine the physical nature of an object.

Closely related to this is the loss in importance of logical dichotomies and conceptual antitheses. Their places are taken by more and more fluid transitions, by gradations which deprive the dichotomies of their antithetical character and represent in logical form a transition stage between the class concept and the series concept.[2]

[1] E. MACH, *Die Mechanik in ihrer Entwicklung*, Leipzig, 1921.
[2] E. CASSIRER, *op. cit.*

Genetic Concepts. This dissolution of the sharp antitheses of rigid classes was greatly accelerated by the coeval transition to an essentially functional way of thinking, to the use of conditional-genetic concepts. For Aristotle the immediate perceptible appearance, that which present-day biology terms the *phenotype*, was hardly distinguished from the properties that determine the object's dynamic relations. The fact, for example, that light objects relatively frequently go upward sufficed for him to ascribe to them an upward tendency. With the differentiation of phenotype from *genotype* or, more generally, of descriptive from conditional-genetic[1] concepts and the shifting of emphasis to the latter, many old class distinctions lost their significance. The orbits of the planets, the free falling of a stone, the movement of a body on an inclined plane, the oscillation of a pendulum, which if classified according to their phenotypes would fall into quite different, indeed into antithetical classes, prove to be simply various expressions of the same law.

Concreteness. The increased emphasis upon the quantitative which seems to lend to modern physics a formal and abstract character is not derived from any tendency to logical formality. Rather, the tendency to a full description of the concrete actuality, even that of the particular case, was influential, a circumstance which should be especially emphasized in connection with present-day psychology. The particular object in all departments of science not only is determined in kind and thereby qualitatively, but it possesses each of its properties in a special intensity or to a definite degree. So long as one regards as important and conceptually intelligible only such properties of an object as are common to a whole group of objects, the individual differences of degree remain without scientific relevance, for in the abstractly defined classes these differences more or less disappear. With the mounting aspirations of research toward an understanding of actual events and particular cases, the task of describing the differences

[1] LEWIN, *Gesetz und Experiment in der Psychologie*, Weltkreis verlag, Berlin-Schlachtensee, 1927.

of degree that characterized individual cases had necessarily
to increase in importance and finally required actual quantitative determination.

It was the increased desire, and also the increased ability,
to comprehend concrete particular cases, and to comprehend
them fully, which, together with the idea of the homogeneity
of the physical world and that of the continuity of the properties
of its objects, constituted the main impulse to the increasing
quantification of physics.

Paradoxes of the New Empiricism.   This tendency toward the
closest possible contact with actuality, which today is usually
regarded as characteristic and ascribed to an antispeculative
tendency, led to a mode of concept formation diametrically
opposed to that of Aristotle, and, surprisingly enough, involved
also the direct antithesis of his "empiricism."

The Aristotelian concepts show, as we have seen above, an
immediate reference to the historically given reality and to the
actual course of events.   This immediate reference to the
historically given is lacking in modern physics.   The fact, so
decisively important for Aristotelian concepts, that a certain
process occurred only once or was very frequently or invariably
repeated in the course of history, is practically irrelevant to
the most essential questions of modern physics.[1]   This circumstance is considered fortuitous or merely historical.

The law of falling bodies, for example, does not assert that
bodies very frequently fall downward.   It does not assert that
the event to which the formula $s = \frac{1}{2}gt^2$ applies, the "free
and unimpeded fall" of a body, occurs regularly or even frequently in the actual history of the world.   Whether the event
described by the law occurs rarely or often has nothing to
do with the law.   Indeed, in a certain sense, the law refers only
to cases that are never realized, or only approximately realized,
in the actual course of events.   Only in experiment, that is,
under artificially constructed conditions, do cases occur which
approximate the event with which the law is concerned.   The

[1] So far as it is not immediately concerned with an actual "History of the
Heavens and the Earth" or a geography.

propositions of modern physics, which are often considered to be antispeculative and empirical, unquestionably have in comparison with Aristotelian empiricism a much less empirical, a much more constructive character than the Aristotelian concepts based immediately upon historical actuality.

In Psychology

Here we are confronted by questions which, as problems of actual research and of theory, have strongly influenced the development of psychology and which constitute the most fundamental grounds of its present crisis.

The concepts of psychology, at least in certain decisive respects, are thoroughly Aristotelian in their actual content, even though in many respects their form of presentation has been somewhat civilized, so to speak. The present struggles and theoretical difficulties of psychology resemble in many ways, even in their particulars, the difficulties which culminated in the conquest over Aristotelian ways of thinking in physics.

Aristotelian Concepts.

Fortuitousness of the Individual Case. The concept formation of psychology is dominated, just as was that of Aristotelian physics, by the question of regularity in the sense of frequency. This is obvious in its immediate attitude toward particular phenomena as well as in its attitude toward lawfulness. If, for example, one show a film of a concrete incident in the behavior of a certain child, the first question of the psychologist usually is: "Do all children do that, or is it at least common?" And if one must answer this question in the negative the behavior involved loses for that psychologist all or almost all claim to scientific interest. To pay attention to such an "exceptional case" seems to him a scientifically unimportant bit of folly.

The real attitude of the investigator toward particular events and the problem of individuality is perhaps more clearly expressed in this actual behavior than in many theories. The individual event seems to him fortuitous, unimportant, scientifically indifferent. It may, however, be some extraordinary event, some tremendous experience, something that has critically determined the destiny of the person involved, or the appearance of an historically significant personality. In such a case it is customary to emphasize the "mystical" character of all individuality and originality, comprehensible only to "intuition," or at least not to science.

Both of these attitudes toward the particular event lead to the same conclusion: that that which does not occur repeatedly lies outside the realm of the comprehensible.

Lawfulness as Frequency. The esteem in which frequency is held in present-day psychology is due to the fact that it is still considered a question whether, and if so how far, the psychical world is lawful, just as in Aristotelian physics this esteem was due to a similar uncertainty about lawfulness in the physical world. It is not necessary here to describe at length the vicissitudes of the thesis of the lawfulness of the psychic in philosophical discussion. It is sufficient to recall that even at present there are many tendencies to limit the operation of law to certain "lower" spheres of psychical events. For us it is more important to note that the field which is considered lawful, not in principle, but in the actual research of psychology—even of experimental psychology—has only been extended very gradually. If psychology has only very gradually and hesitantly pushed beyond the bounds of sensory psychology into the fields of will and affect, it is certainly due not only to technical difficulties, but mainly to the fact that in this field actual repetition, a recurrence of the same event, is not to be expected. And this repetition remains, as it did for Aristotle, to a large extent the basis for the assumption of the lawfulness or intelligibility of an event.

As a matter of fact, any psychology that does not recognize lawfulness as inherent in the nature of the psychical, and hence in all psychical processes, even those occurring only once, must have criteria to decide, like Aristotelian physics, whether or not it has in any given case to deal with lawful phenomena.

And, again, just as in Aristotelian physics, frequency of recurrence is taken as such a criterion. It is evidence of the depth and momentum of this connection (between repetition and lawfulness) that it is even used to define experiment, a scientific instrument which, if it is not directly opposed to the concepts of Aristotelian physics, has at least become significant only in relatively modern times.[1] Even for Wundt repetition inhered in the concept of experiment. Only in recent years has psychology begun to give up this requirement, which withholds a large field of the psychical from experimental investigation.

But even more important perhaps than the restriction of experimental investigation is the fact that this extravagant valuation of repetition (*i.e.*, considering frequency as the criterion and expression of lawfulness) dominates the formation of the concepts of psychology, particularly in its younger branches.

Just as occurs in Aristotelian physics, contemporary child psychology regards as characteristic of a given age, and the psychology of emotion as characteristic of a given expression, that which a group of individual cases have in common. This abstract Aristotelian conception of the class determines the kind and dominates the procedure of classification.

Class and Essence. Present-day child psychology and affect psychology also exemplify clearly the Aristotelian habit of considering the abstractly defined classes as the essential nature of the particular object and hence as an explanation of its behavior. Whatever is common to children of a given age is set up as the fundamental character of that age. The fact that three-year-old children are quite often negative is considered evidence that negativism is inherent in the nature of three-year-olds, and the concept of a negativistic age or stage is then regarded as an explanation (though perhaps not a complete one) for the appearance of negativism in a given particular case!

Quite analogously, the concept of drives—for example, the hunger drive or the maternal instinct—is nothing more than the

[1] The Greeks, of course, *knew* of experiment.

abstract selection of the features common to a group of acts that are of relatively frequent occurrence. This abstraction is set up as the essential reality of the behavior and is then in turn used to explain the frequent occurrence of the instinctive behavior, for example, of the care of infant progeny. Most of the explanations of expression, of character, and of temperament are in a similar state. Here, as in a great many other fundamental concepts, such as that of ability, talent, and similar concepts employed by the intelligence testers, present-day psychology is really reduced to explanation in terms of Aristotelian essences, a sort of explanation which has long been attacked as faculty psychology and as circular explanation, but for which no other way of thinking has been substituted.

Statistics. The classificatory character of its concepts and the emphasis on frequency are indicated methodologically by the commanding significance of statistics in contemporary psychology. The statistical procedure, at least in its commonest application in psychology, is the most striking expression of this Aristotelian mode of thinking. In order to exhibit the common features of a given group of facts, the average is calculated. This average acquires a representative value, and is used to characterize (as mental age) the properties of "the" two-year-old child. Outwardly, there is a difference between contemporary psychology, which works so much with numbers and curves, and the Aristotelian physics. But this difference, characteristically enough, is much more a difference in the technique of execution than in the actual content of the concepts involved. Essentially, the statistical way of thinking, which is a necessary consequence of Aristotelian concepts, is also evident in Aristotelian physics, as we have already seen. The difference is that, owing to the extraordinary development of mathematics and of general scientific method, the statistical procedure of psychology is clearer and more articulate.

All the efforts of psychology in recent years toward exactness and precision have been in the direction of refinement and extension of its statistical methods. These efforts are quite justified in so far as they indicate a determination to achieve an adequate comprehension of the full reality of mental life. But they are really founded, at least in part, on the ambition to demonstrate the scientific status of psychology by using as much mathematics as possible and by pushing all calculations to the last possible decimal place.

This formal extension of the method has not changed the underlying concepts in the slightest: they are still thoroughly Aristotelian. Indeed, the mathematical formulation of the method only consolidates and extends the domination of the underlying concepts. It unquestionably makes it more difficult to see the real character of the concepts and hence to supplant them with others; and this is a difficulty with which Galileian physics did not have to contend, inasmuch as the Aristotelian mode of thought was not then so intrenched and obscured in mathematics (see page 9).

Limits of Knowledge. Exceptions. Lawfulness is believed to be related to regularity and considered the antithesis of the individual case. (In terms of the current formula, lawfulness is conceived as a correlation approaching $r = \pm 1$.) So far as the psychologist agrees at all to the validity of psychological propositions, he regards them as only regularly valid, and his acceptance of them takes such a form that one remains aware of a certain distinction between mere regularity and full lawfulness; and he ascribes to biological and, above all, to psychological propositions (in contrast to physical) only regularity. Or else lawfulness is believed to be only the extreme case of regularity,[1] in which case all differences (between lawfulness and regularity) disappear in principle while the necessity of determining the degree of regularity still remains.

---

[1] As is well known, the concept of possible exceptions and the merely statistical validity of laws has very recently been revived in physical discussion. Even if this view should finally be adopted, it would not in any way mean a return to Aristotelian concepts. It suffices here to point out that, even in that event, it would not involve setting apart within the physical world a class of events on the basis of its degree of lawfulness, but the whole physical universe would be subject only to a statistical lawfulness. On the relation of this statistical view to the problem of precision of measurement, see Lewin, *Gesetz und Experiment in der Psychologie* Weltkreisverlag, Berlin, 1927.

The fact that lawfulness and individuality are considered antitheses has two sorts of effect on actual research. It signifies in the first place a limitation of research. It makes it appear hopeless to try to understand the real, unique, course of an emotion or the actual structure of a particular individual's personality. It thus reduces one to a treatment of these problems in terms of mere averages, as exemplified by tests and questionnaires. Anyone to whom these methods appear inadequate usually encounters a weary skepticism or else a maudlin appreciation of individuality and the doctrine that this field, from which the recurrence of similar cases in sufficient numbers is excluded, is inaccessible to scientific comprehension and requires instead sympathetic intuition. In both cases the field is withdrawn from experimental investigation, for qualitative properties are considered as the direct opposite of lawfulness. The manner in which this view is continually and repeatedly advanced in the discussion of experimental psychology resembles, even to its particulars, the arguments against which Galileian physics had to struggle. How, it was urged at that time, can one try to embrace in a single law of motion such qualitatively different phenomena as the movements of the stars, the flying of leaves in the wind, the flight of birds, and the rolling of a stone downhill. But the opposition of law and individual corresponded so well with the Aristotelian conception and with the primitive mode of thinking which constituted the philosophy of everyday life that it appears often enough in the writings of the physicists themselves, not, however, in their physics but in their philosophy.[1]

The conviction that it is impossible wholly to comprehend the individual case as such implies, in addition to this limitation, a certain laxity of research: it is satisfied with setting forth mere regularities. The demands of psychology upon the stringency of its propositions go no farther than to require a validity "in

---

[1] To avoid misunderstanding, the following should be emphasized: when we criticize the opposition of individual and law, as is customary in psychology, it does not mean that we are unaware of the complex problems of the concept of individuality.

general," or "on the average," or "as a rule." The "complexity" and "transitory nature" of life processes make it unreasonable, it is said, to require complete, exceptionless, validity. According to the old saw that "the exception proves the rule," *psychology does not regard exceptions as counter-arguments so long as their frequency is not too great.*

The attitude of psychology toward the concept of lawfulness also shows clearly and strikingly the Aristotelian character of its mode of thought. It is founded on a very meager confidence in the lawfulness of psychological events and has for the investigator the added charm of not requiring too high a standard of validity in his propositions or in his proofs of them.

Historic-geographic Concepts. For the view of the nature of lawfulness and for the emphasis upon repetition which we have seen to be characteristic of Aristotelian physics, in addition to the motives which we have just mentioned, the immediate reference to the concerned actuality in the historic-geographic sense was fundamental. Likewise, and this is evidence of the intimacy in which these modes of thought are related, present-day psychology is largely dominated by the same immediate reference to the historic-geographic datum. The historical bent of psychological concepts is again not always immediately obvious as such, but is bound up with nonhistoric, systematic concepts and undifferentiated from them. This quasi-historical set forms, in my opinion, the central point for the understanding and criticism of this mode of concept formation.

Although we have criticized the statistical mode of thought, the particular formulas used are not ultimately important to the questions under discussion. It is not the fact that an arithmetic mean is taken, that one adds and divides, that is the object of the present critique. These operations will certainly continue to be used extensively in the future of psychology. The critical point is not that statistical methods are applied, but how they are applied and, especially, what cases are combined into groups.

In contemporary psychology the reference to the historic-geographic datum and the dependence of the conclusions upon frequency of actual occurrence are striking. Indeed, so far as immediate reference to the historic datum is concerned, the way in which the nature of the one-, two-, or three-year-old child is arrived at through the calculation of statistical averages corresponds exactly to Bacon's collection of the given cases of dryness in his *tabulae praesentiae*.   To be sure, there is a certain very crude concession made in such averages to the requirements of nonhistoric concepts: patently pathological cases, and sometimes even cases in which an unusual environment is concerned, are usually excluded.   Apart from this consideration, the exclusion of the most extreme abnormalities, the determination of the cases to be placed in a statistical group is essentially on historic-geographic grounds. For a group defined in historic-geographic terms, perhaps the one-year-old children of Vienna or New York in the year 1928, averages are calculated which are doubtless of the greatest significance to the historian or to the practical school man, but which do not lose their dependence upon the accidents of the historic-geographic given even though one go on to an average of the children of Germany, of Europe, or of the whole world, or of a decade instead of a year. *Such an extension of the geographic and historic basis does not do away with the specific dependence of this concept upon the frequency with which the individual cases occur within historically-geographically defined fields.*

Mention should have been made earlier of that refinement of statistics which is founded upon a restriction of the historic-geographic basis, such as a consideration of the one-year-old children of a proletarian quarter of Berlin in the first years after the War. Such groupings usually are based on the qualitative individuality of the concrete cases as well as upon historic-geographic definitions. But even such limitations really contradict the spirit of statistics founded on frequency. Even they signify methodologically a certain shift to the concrete particulars.   Incidentally, one must not forget that even in the extreme case of such refinement, perhaps in the statistical investigation of the only child, the actual definition is in terms of historic-geographic or at best of sociological categories;

that is, according to criteria which combine into a single group cases that psychologically are very different or even antithetical. Such statistical investigations are consequently unable as a rule to give an explanation of the dynamics of the processes involved.

The immediate reference to the historically given actuality which is characteristic of Aristotelian concept formation is evident also in the discussion of experiment and nearness to life conditions. Certainly one may justly criticize the simple reaction experiments, the beginnings of the experimental psychology of the will, or the experiments of reflexology on the ground of their wide divergence from the conditions of life. But this divergence is based in large part upon the tendency to investigate such processes as do not present the individual peculiarities of the particular case but which, as "simple elements" (perhaps the simplest movements), are common to all behavior, or which occur, so to speak, in everything. In contrast to the foregoing, approximation to life conditions is often demanded of, for example, the psychology of will. By this is usually meant that it should investigate those cases, impossible to produce experimentally, in which the most important decisions of life are made. And here also we are confronted by an orientation toward the historically significant. It is a requirement which, if transferred to physics, would mean that it would be incorrect to study hydrodynamics in the laboratory; one must rather investigate the largest rivers in the world. Two points then stand out: in the field of theory and law, the high valuation of the historically important and disdain of the ordinary; in the field of experiment, the choice of processes which occur frequently (or are common to many events). Both are indicative in like measure of that Aristotelian mixing of historical and systematic questions which carries with it for the systematic the connection with the abstract classes and the neglect of the full reality of the concrete case.

Galileian Concept Formation.

Opposed to Aristotelian concept formation, which I have sought briefly to characterize, there is now evident in psychology a development which appears occasionally in radical or apparently radical tendencies, more usually in little half steps, sometimes falling into error (especially when it tries most exactly to follow the example of physics), but which on the whole seems clearly and irresistibly to be pushing on to modifications that may ultimately mean nothing less than a transition from Aristotelian to Galileian concept formation.

No Value Concepts.   No Dichotomies.   Unification of Fields. The most important general circumstances which paved the way for Galileian concepts in physics are clearly and distinctly to be seen in present-day psychology.

The conquest over *valuative*, anthropomorphic classifications of phenomena on bases other than the nature of the mental process itself (see page 3) is not by any means complete, but in many fields, especially in sensory psychology, at least the chief difficulties are past.

As in physics, the grouping of events and objects into paired opposites and similar logical dichotomies is being replaced by groupings with the aid of serial concepts which permit of continuous variation, partly owing simply to wider experience and the recognition that transition stages are always present.

This has gone furthest in sensory psychology, especially in psychological optics and acoustics, and lately also in the domain of smell.   But the tendency toward this change is also evident in other fields, for example, in that of feeling.

Freud's doctrine especially—and this is one of its greatest services—has contributed largely to the abolition of the boundary between the normal and the pathological, the ordinary and the unusual, and hereby furthered the *homogenization* (see page 10) of all the fields of psychology.   This process is certainly still far from complete, but it is entirely comparable to that introduced in modern physics by which heavenly and earthly processes were united.

Also in child and animal psychology the necessity is gradually disappearing of choosing between two alternatives—regarding the child as a little adult and the animal as an undeveloped inferior human, or trying to establish an unbridgeable gap between the child and adult, animal and man. This homogenization is becoming continually clearer in all fields, and it is not a purely philosophical insistence upon some sort of abstract fundamental unity but influences concrete research in which differences are fully preserved.

Unconditional General Validity of Psychological Laws. The clearest and most important expression of increasing homogeneity, besides the transition from class to serial concepts, is the fact that the validity of particular psychological laws is no longer limited to particular fields, as it was once limited to the normal human adult on the ground that anything might be expected of psychopathics or of geniuses, or that in such cases the same laws do not hold. It is coming to be realized that every psychological law must hold without exception.

In actual content, this transition to the concept of strict exceptionless lawfulness signifies at once the same final and all-embracing homogenization and harmonization of the whole field that gave to Galileian physics its intoxicating feeling of infinite breadth, because it does not, like the abstract class concepts, level out the rich variety of the world and because a single law embraces the whole field.

Tendencies toward a homogeneity based upon the exceptionless validity of its laws have become evident in psychology only very recently, but they open up an extraordinarily wide perspective.[1]

---

[1] The association psychology contains an attempt at this sort of homogeneity, and it has really been of essential service in this direction. Similarly, in our time reflexology and behaviorism have contributed to the homogenization of man and animal and of bodily and mental. But the Aristotelian view of lawfulness as regularity (without which it would have been impossible to support the law of association) brought this attempt to nothing. Consequently, the experimental association psychology, in its attempt at the end of the nineteenth century to derive the whole mental life from a single law, displayed the circular and at the same time abstract character that is typical of the speculative early stages of a science, and of Aristotelian class concepts.

Indeed, it seems almost as if, because of the great importance of frequency and repetition for Aristotelian methodological concepts, the law of association was designed to make use of these as the actual content of psychological principles, inasmuch as frequent repetition is regarded as the most important cause of mental phenomena.

The investigation of the laws of structure—particularly the experimental investigation of wholes—has shown that the same laws hold not only within different fields of psychological optics but also in audition and in sensory psychology in general. This in itself constitutes a large step in the progress toward homogeneity.

Further, the laws of optical figures and of intellectual insight have turned out to be closely related. Important and similar laws have been discovered in the experimental investigation of behavioral wholes, of will processes, and of psychological needs. In the fields of memory and expression, psychological development appears to be analogous. In short, the thesis of the general validity of psychological laws has very recently become so much more concrete, particular laws have shown such capacity for fruitful application to fields that at first were qualitatively completely separated, that the thesis of the homogeneity of psychic life in respect to its laws gains tremendously in vigor and is destroying the boundaries of the old separated fields.[1]

Mounting Ambitions. Methodologically also the thesis of the exceptionless validity of psychological laws has a far-reaching significance. It leads to an extraordinary increase in the demands made upon proof. It is no longer possible to take exceptions lightly. They do not in any way "prove the rule," but on the contrary are completely valid disproofs, even though they are rare, indeed, so long as one single exception is demonstrable. The thesis of general validity permits of no exceptions in the entire realm of the psychic, whether of child or adult, whether in normal or pathological psychology.

---

[1] For this section compare especially M. Wertheimer, Untersuchungen zur Lehre von der Gestalt, II, *Psychol. Forsch.*, 1923, 4, 301–350, W. Köhler, *Gestalt Psychology*, Liveright, New York, 1929. K. Koffka, *The Growth of the Mind: An Introduction to Child Psychology* (trans. by R. M. Ogden), Harcourt, Brace, New York; Kegan Paul, London, 1924, (2d ed., 1928), and Lewin, *Vorsatz, Wille und Bedürfnis, mit Vorbemerkungen über die psychischen Kräfte und Energien und die Struktur der Seele*, Springer, Berlin, 1926. A review of the special researches is found in W. Köhler, Gestaltprobleme und Anfänge einer Gestalttheorie, *Jahresber. d. ges. Physiol.*, 1924.

On the other hand, the thesis of exceptionless validity in psychological laws makes available to investigation, especially to experiment, such processes as do not frequently recur in the same form, as, for example, certain affective processes.

From the Average to the Pure Case. A clear appreciation of this circumstance is still by no means habitual in psychology. Indeed, from the earlier, Aristotelian point of view the new procedure may even seem to conceal the fundamental contradiction we have mentioned above. One declares that one wants to comprehend the full concrete reality in a higher degree than is possible with Aristotelian concepts and yet considers this reality in its actual historical course and its given geographical setting as really accidental. The general validity, for example, of the law of movement on an inclined plane is not established by taking the average of as many cases as possible of real stones actually rolling down hills, and then considering this average as the most probable case.[1] It is based rather upon the frictionless rolling of an ideal sphere down an absolutely straight and hard plane, that is, upon a process that even the laboratory can only approximate and which is most improbable in daily life. One declares that one is striving for general validity and concreteness, yet uses a method which, from the point of view of the preceding epoch, disregards the historically given facts and depends entirely upon individual accidents, indeed upon the most pronounced exceptions.

How physics arrives at this procedure, which strikes the Aristotelian views of contemporary psychology as doubly paradoxical, begins to become intelligible when one envisages the necessary methodological consequences of the change in the ideas of the extent of lawfulness. When lawfulness is no longer limited to cases which occur regularly or frequently

---

[1] In psychology it is asserted, often with special emphasis, that one obtains, perhaps from the construction of baby tests, a representation of the "general human," because those processes are selected which occur most frequently in the child's daily life. Then one may expect with sufficient probability that the child will spontaneously display similar behavior in the test.

but is characteristic of every physical event, the necessity disappears of demonstrating the lawfulness of an event by some special criterion, such as its frequency of occurrence. Even a particular case is then assumed, without more ado, to be lawful. Historical rarity is no disproof, historical regularity no proof of lawfulness. For the concept of lawfulness has been quite detached from that of regularity; the concept of the complete absence of exceptions to laws is strictly separated from that of historical constancy (the "forever" of Aristotle).[1]

Further, the content of a law cannot then be determined by the calculation of averages of historically given cases. For Aristotle the nature of a thing was expressed by the characteristics common to the historically given cases. Galileian concepts, on the contrary, which regard historical frequency as accident, must also consider it a matter of chance which properties one arrives at by taking averages of historical cases. If the concrete event is to be comprehended and the thesis of lawfulness without exception is to be not merely a philosophical maxim but determinative of the mode of actual research, there must be another possibility of penetrating the nature of an event, some other way than that of ignoring all individual peculiarities of concrete cases. The solution of this problem may only be obtained by the elucidation of the paradoxical procedures of Galileian method through a consideration of the problems of dynamics.

[1] The contrast between Aristotelian and Galileian views of lawfulness and the difference in their methods may be briefly tabulated as follows:

	For Aristotle	For Galileo
1. The regular is	lawful	lawful
The frequent is	lawful	lawful
The individual case is	chance	lawful
2. Criteria of lawfulness are	regularity frequency	not required
3. That which is common to the historically occurring cases is	an expression of the nature of the thing	an accident, only historically conditioned

Dynamics

Changes in the Fundamental Dynamic Concepts of Physics

The dynamic problems of physics were really foreign to the Aristotelian mode of thought. The fact that dynamic problems had throughout such great significance for Galileian physics permits us to regard dynamics as a characteristic consequence of the Galileian mode of thought.[1] As always, it involved not merely a superficial shift of interest, but a change in the content of the theories. Even Aristotle emphasized "becoming," as compared with his predecessors. It is perhaps more correct to say that in the Aristotelian concepts statics and dynamics are not yet differentiated. This is due especially to certain fundamental assumptions.

Teleology and Physical Vectors.

A leading characteristic of Aristotelian dynamics is the fact that it explained events by means of concepts which we today perceive to be specifically biological or psychological: *every object tends, so far as not prevented by other objects, toward perfection*, toward the realization of its own nature. This nature is for Aristotle, as we have already seen, that which is common to the class of the object. So it comes about that the class for him is at the same time the concept and the goal (τέλος) of an object.

This teleological theory of physical events does not show only that biology and physics are not yet separated. It indicates also that the dynamics of Aristotelian physics resembles in essential points the animistic and artificial mode of thought of primitive man, which views all movement as life and makes artificial manufacture the prototype of existence. For, in the case of manufactured things, the maker's idea of the object is, in one sense, both the cause and the goal of the event.

Further, for Aristotelian concepts the *cause* of a physical event was very closely related to psychological "drives": the object strives toward a certain goal; so far as movement is

[1] E. Mach, *The Science of Mechanics* (Eng. trans., 2d ed., rev.), Chicago, 1902.

concerned, it tends toward the place appropriate to its nature. Thus heavy objects strive downward, the heavier the more strongly, while light objects strive upward.

It is customary to dismiss these Aristotelian physical concepts by calling them anthropomorphic. But perhaps it would be better, when we consider that the same fundamental dynamic ideas are today completely dominant in psychology and biology, to examine the actual content of the Aristotelian theses as far as possible independently of the style of their presentation.

It is customary to say that teleology assumes a direction of events toward a goal, which causal explanation does not recognize, and to see in this the most essential difference between teleological and causal explanation. But this sort of view is inadequate, for the causal explanation of modern physics uses directed quantities, mathematically described vectors. Physical force, which is defined as "the cause of a physical change," is considered a directed, vectorial factor. In the employment of vectorial factors as the foundation of dynamics there is thus no difference between the modern and the Aristotelian view.

The real difference lies rather in the fact that *the kind and direction of the physical vectors in Aristotelian dynamics are completely determined in advance by the nature of the object concerned.* In modern physics, on the contrary, *the existence of a physical vector always depends upon the mutual relations of several physical facts*, especially upon the relation of the object to its environment.[1]

Significance of the Whole Situation in Aristotelian and Galileian Dynamics.

For Aristotelian concepts, the environment plays a part only in so far as it may give rise to "disturbances," forced modifications of the processes which follow from the nature of the object concerned. The vectors which determine an object's movements are completely determined by the object. That is,

---

[1] Naturally this applies also to internal causes, which involve the mutual relation of the parts of a physical system.

they do not depend upon the relation of the object to the environment, and they belong to that object once for all, irrespective of its surroundings at any given time. The tendency of light bodies to go up resided in the bodies themselves; the downward tendency of heavy objects was seated in those objects. In modern physics, on the contrary, not only is the upward tendency of a lighter body derived from the relation of this body to its environment, but the weight itself of the body depends upon such a relation.

This decisive revolution comes to clear expression in Galileo's classic investigations of the law of falling bodies. The mere fact that he did not investigate the heavy body itself, but the process of "free falling or movement on an inclined plane," signifies a transition to concepts which can be defined only by reference to a certain sort of situation (namely, the presence of a plane with a certain inclination or of an unimpeded vertical extent of space through which to fall). The idea of investigating free falling, which is too rapid for satisfactory observation, by resorting to the slower movement upon an inclined plane presupposes that the dynamics of the event is no longer related to the isolated object as such, but is seen to be dependent upon the whole situation in which the event occurs.

Galileo's procedure, in fact, includes a penetrating investigation of precisely the situation factors. The slope of the inclined plane, that is, the proportion of height to length, is defined. The list of situations involved (free falling, movement on an inclined plane, and horizontal movement) is exhausted and, through the varying of the inclination, classified. The dependence of the essential features of the event (for example, its velocity) upon the essential properties of the situation (the slope of the plane) becomes the conceptual and methodological center of importance.

This view of dynamics does not mean that the nature of the object becomes insignificant. The properties and structure of the object involved remain important also for the Galileian theory of dynamics. But the situation assumes as much importance as the object. *Only by the concrete whole which comprises the object and the situation are the vectors which determine the dynamics of the event defined.*

In carrying out this view, Galileian physics tried to characterize the individuality of the total situation concerned as concretely and accurately as possible.   This is an exact reversal of Aristotelian principles.   The dependence of an event upon the situation in which it occurs means for the Aristotelian mode of thought, which wants to ascertain the general by seeking out the like features of many cases, nothing more than a disturbing force.   The changing situations appear as something fortuitous that disturbs and obscures the essential nature. It was therefore valid and customary to exclude the influence of the situation as far as possible, to abstract from the situation, in order to understand the essential nature of the object and the direction of its goal.

Getting Rid of the Historical Bent.

The actual investigation of this sort of vectors obviously presupposes that the processes involved occur with a certain regularity or frequency (see page 6).   For otherwise an exclusion of the differences of the situation would leave no similarities.   If one starts from the fundamental concepts of Aristotelian dynamics, the investigation of the dynamics of a process must be more difficult—one might think here of emotion in psychology—the more it depends upon the nature of the situation concerned.   The single event becomes thereby unlawful in principle because there is no way of investigating its dynamics.

The Galileian method of determining the dynamics of a process is directly opposed to this procedure.   Since the dynamics of the process depends not only upon the object but also, primarily, upon the situation, it would be nonsensical to try to obtain general laws of processes by excluding the influence of the situations as far as possible.   It becomes silly to bring in as many different situations as possible and regard only those factors as generally valid that are observed under all circumstances, in any and every situation.   It must, on the contrary, become important to comprehend the whole situation involved, with all its characteristics, as precisely as possible.

The step from particular case to law, from "this" event to "such" an event, no longer requires the confirmation by historical regularity that is characteristic of the Aristotelian mode of thought. This step to the general is automatically and immediately given by the principle of the exceptionless lawfulness of physical events.[1] What is now important to the investigation of dynamics is not to abstract from the situation, but to hunt out those situations in which the determinative factors of the total dynamic structure are most clearly, distinctly, and purely to be discerned. *Instead of a reference to the abstract average of as many historically given cases as possible, there is a reference to the full concreteness of the particular situations.*

We cannot here examine in great detail why not all situations are equally useful for the investigation of dynamics, why certain situations possess a methodological advantage, and why as far as possible these are experimentally set up. Only one circumstance, which seems to me very seldom to be correctly viewed and which has given rise to misunderstandings that have had serious consequences for psychology, requires elucidation.

We have seen above how Galileian concepts separated the previously undifferentiated questions of the historical course of events on one side and of the laws of events on the other. They renounced in systematic problems the immediate reference to the historic-geographic datum. That the procedure instituted does not, as might at first appear, contradict the empirical tendency toward the comprehension of the full reality may already be clear from our last consideration: the Aristotelian immediate relation to the historically regular and its average really means giving up the attempt to understand the particular, always situation-conditioned event. When this immediate relation is completely abandoned, when the place of historic-geographic constancy is taken by the position of the particular

---

[1] It is impossible here to go more fully into the problem of induction. (Cf. Lewin, *Gesetz und Experiment in der Psychologie.*)

in the whole situation, and when (as in experimental method) it is just the same whether the situation is frequent and permanent or rare and transitory, only then does it become possible to undertake the task of understanding the real, always ultimately unique, event.

The Meaning of the Process Differential.

Methodologically there may seem to result here another theoretical difficulty which can perhaps be better elucidated

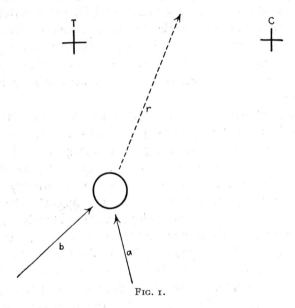

FIG. I.

by a simple example than by general discussion. In order that the essentials may be more easily seen, I choose an example not from familiar physics but from problematical psychology. If one attempt to trace the behavior of a child to psychical field forces, among other things—the justification for this thesis is not here under discussion—the following objection might easily be raised. A child stands before two attractive objects (say a toy *T* and a piece of chocolate *C*), which are in different places (see Fig. I). According to this hypothesis, then, there exist field forces in these directions (*a* and *b*). The proportional strength of the forces is indifferent, and it does not matter whether the physical law of the parallelogram of forces is applicable to psychical field forces or not. So far, then, as a resultant of these two forces is formed, it must take a direction (*r*) which leads neither to *T* nor to *C*. The child would then, so one might easily conclude according to this theory, reach neither *T* nor *C*.[1]

In reality such a conclusion would be too hasty, for even if the vector should have the direction *r* at the moment of starting, that does not mean that the actual process permanently retains this direction. Instead, *the whole situation changes with the process*, thus changing also, in both strength and direction, the vectors that at each moment determine the dynamics. Even if one assumes the parallelogram of forces and in addition a constant internal situation in the child, the actual process, because of this changing in the situation, will always finally bring the child to one or the other of the attractive objects (Fig. 2).[2]

What I would like to exhibit by this example is this: if one tries to deduce the dynamics of a process, particularly the vectors which direct it, from the actual event, one is compelled to resort to process differentials. In our example, one can regard only the process of the first moment, not the whole course, as the immediate expression of the vector present in the beginning of the situation.

The well-known fact that all, or at least most, physical laws are differential laws[3] does not seem to me, as is often supposed, to prove that physics endeavors to analyze everything into the smallest "elements" and to consider these elements in the most perfect possible isolation. It proceeds rather from the circumstance that physics since Galileo no longer regards the historic course of a process as the immediate expression of the vectors

[1] I am neglecting here the possibility that one of the field forces entirely disappears.

[2] Even if the distances of the attractive objects and the strength of their attractions were equal, the resulting conflict situation would lead to the same result, owing to the lability of the equilibrium.

[3] H. POINCARE, *La Science et l'hypothèse*, Paris, 1916.

determinative of its dynamics. For Aristotle, the fact that the movement showed a certain total course was proof of the existence of a tendency to that course, for example, toward a perfect circular movement. Galileian concepts, on the contrary, even in the course of a particular process, separate the quasi-historical from the factors determining the dynamics. They refer to the whole situation in its full concrete individuality, to the state of the situation at every moment of time.

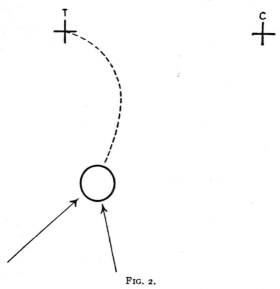

Fig. 2.

Further, for Galileian concepts, the forces, the physical vectors which control the situation, are proved by the resulting process. However, it is valid to exclude the quasi-historical in order to get the pure process, and therefore necessary to comprehend the type of process by recourse to the process differential, because only in the latter, and hence unmixed, is it expressed. This recourse to the process differential thus arises not, as is usually supposed, from a tendency to reduce all events to their "ultimate elements," but as a not immediately obvious complementary expression of the tendency to derive the dynamics from the relation of the concrete particular to the concrete whole situation and to ascertain as purely and as unmixed with historic factors as possible the type of event with which this total situation is dynamically related.

Experimentally also it is important to construct such situations as will actually yield this pure event, or at least permit of its conceptual reconstruction.

Methodological.

It remains to examine more closely the logical and methodological consequences of this mode of thought. Since law and individual are no longer antitheses, nothing prevents relying for proof upon historically unusual, rare, and transitory events, such as most physical experiments are. It becomes clear why it is very illuminating, for systematic concepts, to produce such cases, even if not exactly for the sake of their rarity itself.

The tendency to comprehend the actual situation as fully and concretely as possible, even in its individual peculiarities, makes the most precise possible qualitative and quantitative determination necessary and profitable. But it must not be forgotten that only this task, and not numerical precision for its own sake, gives any point or meaning to exactness.

Some of the most essential services to knowledge of the quantitative, and in general of the mathematical, mode of representation are (1) the possibility of using continuous transitions instead of dichotomies in characterization, thereby greatly refining description, and (2) the fact that with such functional concepts it is possible to go from the particular to the general without losing the particular in the general and thereby making impossible the return from the general to the particular.

Finally, reference should be made to the method of approximation in the description of objects and situations, in which the continuous, functional mode of thought is manifest.

Fundamental Dynamic Concepts in Psychology

The dynamic concepts of psychology today are still thoroughly Aristotelian,[1] and indeed the same internal relations

---

[1] The same holds, incidentally, for biology, which I cannot here especially examine, although I regard psychology in general as a field of biology.

and motives seem to me here displayed, even to the details.

Aristotelian Ideas: Independence of the Situation; Instinct.

In content, which is easiest to exhibit and indeed hardly requires exposition, psychological dynamics agrees most completely with Aristotelian concepts: it is teleology in the Aristotelian sense. The traditional mistake of regarding causal explanation as an explanation without the use of directed forces has notably retarded the progress of dynamics, since psychological dynamics, like physical, cannot be understood without the use of vector concepts. It is not the fact that directed quantities are employed in psychological dynamics that gives it its Aristotelian character, but the fact that the process is ascribed to vectors connected with the object of investigation, for example, with the particular person, and *relatively independent of the situation.*

The concept of instinct in its classical form is perhaps the most striking example of this. The instincts are the sum of those vectors conditioned by predispositions which it is thought must be ascribed to an individual. The instincts are determined essentially by finding out what actions occur most frequently or regularly in the *actual life* of the individual or of a group of like individuals. That which is *common* to these frequent acts (*e.g.*, food getting, fighting, mutual aid) is regarded as the *essence* or essential nature of the processes. Again, completely in the Aristotelian sense, these abstract class concepts are set up as at once the goal and the cause of the process. And indeed the instincts obtained in this way, as averages of historical actuality, are regarded as the more fundamental the more abstract the class concept is and the more various the cases of which the average is taken. It is thought that in this way, and only in this way, those "accidents" inherent in the particular case and in the concrete situation can be overcome. For the aim that still completely dominates the procedure of psychology in large fields is founded upon its effort to free itself of the connection to specific situations.

Intrinsic Difficulties and Unlawfulness.

The whole difference between the Aristotelian and Galileian modes of thought becomes clear as soon as one sees what consequences, for a strict Galileian view of the concept of law, follow from this close and fixed connection of the instinct to the individual "in itself." In that case the instinct (*e.g.*, the maternal) must operate continually without interruption; just as the explanation of negativism by the "nature" of the three-year-old child entails for Galileian concepts the consequence that all three-year-old children must be negative the whole day long, twenty-four hours out of the twenty-four.

The general Aristotelian set of psychology is able to dodge these consequences. It is satisfied, even for proof of the existence of the vectors which should explain the behavior, to depend upon the concept of regularity. In this way it avoids the necessity of supposing the vector to be existent in every situation. On the basis of the strict concept of law it is possible to disprove the hypothesis, for example, of the existence of a certain instinct by demonstrating its nonexistence in given concrete cases. Aristotelian concepts do not have to fear such disproofs, inasmuch as they can answer all references to concrete particular cases by falling back on mere statistical validity.

Of course these concepts are thereby also unable to explain the occurrence of a particular case, and by this is meant not the behavior of an abstractly defined "average child," but, for example, the behavior of a certain child at a certain moment. The Aristotelian bent of psychological dynamics thus not only implies a limitation of explanation to such cases as occur frequently enough to provide a basis for abstracting from the situation, but leaves literally any possibility open in any particular case, even of frequent events.

Attempts at Self-correction: the Average Situation.

The intrinsic difficulties for dynamics which the Aristotelian mode of thought brings with it, namely, the danger of destroying the explanatory value of the theory by the exclusion of the situation, are constantly to be observed in contemporary psychology and lead to the most singular hybrid methods and to attempts to include the concept of the situation somehow. This becomes especially clear in the attempts at quantitative determination.   When, for example, the question is raised and an attempt made to decide experimentally how the strengths of various drives in rats (perhaps hunger, thirst, sex, and mother love) compare with each other, such a question (which corresponds to asking in physics which is stronger, gravitation or electromotive force) has meaning only if these vectors are ascribed entirely to the rat and regarded as practically independent of the concrete whole situation, independent of the condition of the rat and its environment at the moment.   Such a fixed connection is, of course, ultimately untenable, and one is compelled at least in part to abandon this way of thinking. Thus the first step in this direction consists in taking account of the *momentary condition of the drive* with regard to its state of satiation: the various possible degrees of strength of the several drives are ascertained, and their maximal strengths are compared.

It is true, of course, that the Aristotelian attitude is really only slightly ameliorated thereby.   The curve expresses the statistical average of a large number of cases, which is not binding for an individual case; and, above all, this mode of thought applies the vector independently of the structure of the situation.

To be sure, it is not denied that the situation essentially determines the instinctive behavior in the actual particular case, but in these problems, as in the question of the child's spontaneous behavior in the baby tests, it is evident that no more is demanded of a law than a behavioral average.   The law thus applies to an average situation.   It is forgotten that there just is no such thing as an "average situation" any more than an average child.

Practically, if not in principle, the reference to the concept of an "optimal" situation goes somewhat further.   But even here the concrete structure of the situation remains indeterminate: only a maximum of results in a certain direction is required.

In none of these concepts however are the two fundamental faults of the Aristotelian mode of thought eliminated: the vectors determining the dynamics of the process are still attributed to the isolated object, independently of the concrete whole situation; and only very slight demands are made upon the validity of psychological principles and the comprehension of the concrete actuality of the individual single process.

This holds true even for the concepts immediately concerned with the significance of the situation. As mentioned before, the question at the center of the discussion of the situation is, quite in the Aristotelian sense, how far the situation can hinder (or facilitate). The situation is even considered as a constant object and the question is discussed: which is more important, heredity or environment? Thus again, on the basis of a concept of situation gotten by abstraction, a dynamic problem is treated in a form which has none but a statistical historical meaning. The heredity or environment discussion also shows, even in its particulars, how completely these concepts separate object and situation and derive the dynamics from the isolated object itself.

The role of the situation in all these concepts may perhaps be best exhibited by reference to certain changes in painting. In medieval painting at first there was, in general, no environment, but only an empty (often a golden) background. Even when gradually an environment did appear it usually consisted in nothing more than presenting, beside the one person, other persons and objects. Thus the picture was at best an assembling of separate persons in which each had really a separate existence.

Only later did the space itself exist in the painting: it became a whole situation. At the same time this situation as a whole became dominant, and each separate part, so far indeed as separate parts still remain, is what it is (*e.g.*, in such an extreme as Rembrandt) only in and through the whole situation.

Beginnings of a Galileian Mode of Thought.

Opposed to these Aristotelian fundamental ideas of dynamics there are now signs in psychology of the beginnings of a Galileian mode of thought. In this respect the concepts of sensory psychology are farthest advanced.

At first, even in sensory psychology, explanations referred to isolated single perceptions, even to single isolated elements of these perceptions. The developments of recent years have brought about, at first slowly but then more radically, a revolution in the fundamental dynamic ideas by showing that the dynamics of the processes are to be deduced, not from the single elements of the perception, but from its whole structure. For it is impossible by a consideration of the elements to define what is meant by *figure* in the broader sense of the word. Rather, the whole dynamics of sensory psychological processes depends upon the ground[1] and beyond it upon the structure of the whole surrounding field. The dynamics of perception is not to be understood by the abstract Aristotelian method of excluding all fortuitous situations, but—this principle is penetrating today all the fields of sensory psychology—only by *the establishment of a form of definite structure in a definite sort of environment.*

Recently the same fundamental ideas of dynamics have been extended beyond the special field of perception and applied in the fields of higher mental processes, in the psychology of instinct, will, emotion, and expression, and in genetic psychology. The sterility, for example, of the always circular discussion of heredity or environment and the impossibility of carrying through the division, based upon this discussion, of the characteristics of the individual begin to show that there is something radically wrong with their fundamental assumptions. A mode of thought is becoming evident, even though only gradually, which, corresponding somewhat to the biological concept of phenotype and genotype, tries to determine the

---

[1] E. Rubin, *Visuellwahrgenommene Figuren*, Gyldenalske, Copenhagen, 1921.

predisposition, not by excluding so far as possible the influence of the environment, but by accepting in the concept of disposition its necessary reference to a group of concretely defined situations.

Thus in the psychological fields most fundamental to the whole behavior of living things the transition seems inevitable to a Galileian view of dynamics, which derives all its vectors not from single isolated objects, but from the mutual relations of the factors in the concrete whole situation, that is, essentially, from the momentary condition of the individual and the structure of the psychological situation. *The dynamics of the processes is always to be derived from the relation of the concrete individual to the concrete situation*, and, so far as internal forces are concerned, from the mutual relations of the various functional systems that make up the individual.

The carrying out of this principle requires, to be sure, the completion of a task that at present is only begun: namely, the providing of a workable representation of a concrete psychological situation according to its individual characteristics and its associated functional properties, and of the concrete structure of the psychological person and its internal dynamic facts. Perhaps the circumstance that a technique for such a concrete representation, not simply of the physical but of the psychological situation, cannot be accomplished without the help of topology, the youngest branch of mathematics, has contributed to keeping psychological dynamics, in the most important fields of psychology, in the Aristotelian mode of thought. But more important than these technical questions may be the general substantial and philosophical presuppositions: too meager scientific courage in the question of the lawfulness of the psychical, too slight demands upon the validity of psychological laws, and the tendency, which goes hand in hand with this leaning toward mere regularity, to specifically historic-geographic concepts.

The accidents of historical processes are not overcome by excluding the changing situations from systematic consideration, but only by taking the fullest account of the individual nature of the concrete case. *It depends upon keeping in mind that general validity of the law and concreteness of the individual case are not antitheses, and that reference to the totality of the concrete whole situation must take the place of reference to the largest possible historical collection of frequent repetitions.* This means methodologically that the importance of a case, and its validity as proof, cannot be evaluated by the frequency of its occurrence. Finally, it means for psychology, as it did for physics, a transition from an abstract classificatory procedure to an essentially concrete constructive method.

That psychology at present is not far from the time when the dominance of Aristotelian concepts will be replaced by that of the Galileian mode of thought seems to me indicated also by a more external question of psychological investigation.

It is one of the characteristic signs of the speculative early stage of all sciences that schools, representative of different systems, oppose each other in a way and to an extent that is unknown, for example, in contemporary physics. When a difference of hypotheses occurs in contemporary physics there still remains a common basis that is foreign to the schools of the speculative stage. This is only an external sign of the fact that the concepts of that field have introduced a method that permits step-by-step approximation to understanding. Thereby results a continuous progress of the science which is constantly more narrowly limiting the consequences for the whole structure of differences between various physical theories.

There seems to me much to indicate that even the development of the schools in contemporary psychology is bringing about a transition to a similar sort of constant development, not only in sensory psychology but throughout the entire field.

CHAPTER II

ON THE STRUCTURE OF THE MIND[1]

On the Causes of Psychical Events

The relations to which theory has heretofore looked in experimental psychology, when seeking the causes of a psychical event, belong almost exclusively to one quite specific type of relation. This is a real connection which one may designate as *adhesion* of any sort of object or collection of objects or processes. The fact that certain single objects are connected with each other, or that a whole event sticks together in the sense of adhesion, is given as the cause of a psychical event.

The most pronounced case of such a type of connection is presented by the association between two psychical objects in the sense of the old association theory. The objects *a* and *b* have entered into an association by reason of earlier contiguity. And this association phenomenon is claimed to be the cause of the fact that on the occurrence of experience *a*, experience *b* results.

But even when experience is not regarded as the cause of the association and forces are assumed which do not obey the laws of association, such as the determining tendency[2] or any sort of natural coherence,[3] the following fundamental type is still retained: *the stimulus possesses an adhesion with certain reactions*. And this adhesion is regarded as the cause of the course of the event.

---

[1] An excerpt from *Vorsatz, Wille und Bedürfnis, mit Vorbemerkungen über die psychischen Kräfte und Energien und die Struktur der Seele*, pp. 21–39. For use of the word "mind" see translators' note.

[2] N. ACH, *Über den Willensakt und das Temperament*, Quelle u. Meyer, Leipzig, 1910.

[3] G. E. MÜLLER, *Komplextheorie und Gestalttheorie*, Vanderhoeck u. Ruprecht, Göttingen, 1923.

In psychology these couplings were conceived for the most part as mechanically rigid connections in the sense of an association of individual stimulations with established reactions. In opposition to this, the idea is beginning to gain ground that usually we have to do not with rigid connections of distinct pieces or elements but with temporally extended wholes (of the type, for example, of a melody), the moments or phases of which can be explained only by the whole. Recently a deplorable misconception of the fundamental ideas of Gestalt theories has sometimes occurred. This misconception may be stated as follows: The cause of the process b is not to be seen in its rigid coupling with the preceding independent event a. Rather, if a forms a dependent moment of a more comprehensive whole, it carries that whole with it. Thus, indeed, no chain-like coupling of member to member, but the connections of the parts in the whole, is regarded as the "cause" of the event.[1]

The experimental investigation of habits (association) has shown that the couplings created by habit are never, as such, the motor of a psychical event.[2] Such a conception is also erroneous when the essential fact of the process of habit formation and of practice is taken to be, not the formation of piecemeal associations, but the re-formation and new formation of definite action unities. Rather, certain psychical energies, that is, tense psychical systems which derive, as a rule, from the pressure of will or of a need, are always the necessary condition of the occurrence—in whatever way—of the psychical event. It hardly requires special mention that this does not mean that on the one side there are psychical Gestalten, and on the other psychical energies without any definite psychical locus.

Sometimes the habit, for example in "compulsive habits," may with the waxing of the needs breed new psychical energies. Sometimes it may bring about access to energies which have not theretofore been available to the act involved; when in drug

[1] Thus, there is still no reference to any such thing as the tensions in a dynamic whole.

[2] LEWIN, *Zeitschr. f. Psychol.*, 1917, **77**, 212–247; *Psychol. Forsch.*, 1922, **1**, 191–302; 1922, **2**, 65–140. SĪGMAR, Über die Hemmung bei der Realisation eines Willensaktes, *Arch. f. d. ges. Psychol.*, 1925, **52**, 92.

addicts, for example, originally single and occasional pleasurable experiences are "absorbed into the vital needs,"[1] and ever broader and deeper strata of the person are drawn into this addiction.

In the case, however, of a mere "habit of execution"[2] (that is, the fusion, formation, or re-formation of certain actions) it is in principle impossible to regard them as the cause (in any full sense) of the psychical events.[3]

These propositions, first valid for habit and association, can be generalized to every kind of coupling. For *connections are never causes of events*, wherever and in whatever form they may occur. Rather, in order that the bound or coupled complex move, in other words that a process occur (and this holds also for purely machine systems), energy capable of doing work

---

[1] E. Joël and F. Fränkel, Zur Pathologie der Gewöhnung, II in *Therapie der Gegenwart*, 1926, **67,** 60. Further: *Der Kokainismus*, Springer, Berlin, 1924. Cf. also W. McDougall, *Social Psychology*, Methuen, London, 1908.

[2] Lewin, *loci cit.*

[3] That one must assume further factors besides associations as the causes of psychical events has long been said. Among experimental investigations which have advanced in this direction, should be mentioned, above all, those of Ach (*op. cit.*) and Poppelreuter (Über die Ordnung des Vorstellungslaufes, *Arch. f.d. ges. Psychol.* 1913, **3,** 371). Selz (*Die Gesetze des geordneten Denkverlaufs*, Spemann, Stuttgart, 1913, and *Zur Psychologie des produktiven Denkens und des Irrtums*, Cohen, Bonn, 1922) exhibited the significance of nonassociative forces, the determining tendencies, chiefly in the field of particular intellectual processes. He also remarked that "even in investigations of memory the existing determinations can by no means always be neglected" (*op., cit.,* pp. 283–290). To be sure, as late as 1920 the same author in a polemic against attacks from the side of association psychology (Komplextheorie und Gestalttheorie, *Zeitschr. f. Psychol,* 1920, **83,** 215), expressly remarks, for example, that the actualization of complexes of knowledge "can also occur without a determination directed upon them," which together with a number of other statements seems to me unequivocally to mean that association as one possible cause of psychological events cannot be denied. Since Selz recently (Zur Psychologie der Gegenwart, *Zeitschr. f. Psychol.,* **99,** 166 ff.) refers to the above and similar sentences in raising questions of priority I should like merely to remark without going into these questions that I should be very glad if I might interpret these references to mean that Selz, in any event at present, regards the fundamental thesis of my work as experimentally proven: namely, that not only must other causes of psychical events be recognized besides association but that association presents in principle no motor for psychical events.

must be set free. *One must therefore inquire of every psychical event whence the causal energies come.*

To say that couplings are not to be regarded as sources of energy is by no means to say that there are no couplings, or that their presence or absence is unimportant. They are, indeed, not sources of energy for events, but the form of the event depends in large degree upon them. Thus, for example, the re-formation of certain common action unities plays a very important role. (To be sure, if we are to advance to laws, the practice must be given up of subsuming every case in which an earlier occurrence can be established under the concept of "experience." Instead of this senseless conglomerate, a number of phenomena will have to be distinguished which obey laws of very different nature: the enriching or changing of the fund of knowledge; the learning and practicing of tasks of different kinds; and, of essentially different nature, the process which one may characterize as fixation of impulses or needs.)

When the concept of energy is used here and when later those of force, of tension, of systems, and others are employed, the question may be left quite open as to whether or not one should ultimately go back to physical forces and energies. In any event, these concepts are, in my opinion, general logical fundamental concepts of all dynamics (even though their treatment in logic is usually very much neglected). They are in no way a special possession of physics but are seen, for example, in economics (although up to the present less precisely developed), without requiring the assumption that therefore one must derive economics in some way from physics.

Quite independently, then, of the question of the ultimate derivability of psychology from physics, the treatment of causal dynamic problems compels psychology to employ the fundamental concepts of dynamics, not, as frequently in the past, promiscuously, but in the development of a differentiated concept-formation in dynamic fields. Physical analogies may often be drawn without damage to clarification. On the other hand, it is always necessary carefully to avoid certain very easy errors, for example, in the adequate comprehension of the psychical field forces; and it must always be kept in mind that we have to do with forces in a *psychical* field and not in the physical environment.

On the question of the psychical sources of energy, the following should be noted briefly.

The stimulus itself may perhaps be considered in many perceptual processes as being at the same time and to a certain degree the source of energy for the process in the sensory sector (*e.g.*, in the field of vision). In actual behavior and emotions, however, as when one undertakes a journey upon the receipt of a telegram or becomes furious at a question, the physical intensity of the stimulus obviously plays no essential role. Hence it has been customary to speak of a "release," of a process which has been represented by the analogy of the explosion of a keg of powder by the discharging spark.

This conclusion will nevertheless have to be fundamentally changed in two directions.

1. Since the conception of the perceptual world as a sum of sensory elements must be given up, perception presenting us rather with actual things and events, which have definite meaning, the stimulus to perception (*e.g.*, the disfigured countenance of a wounded soldier) must be assessed not according to its physical intensity but according to its psychological reality. This sort of perceptual experience may carry with it immediately certain purposes or create certain needs which were not before present. To discuss whether and if so to what extent such perceptual experiences are themselves to be regarded as sources of energy is probably not very fruitful in the present state of research. In any event, there may occur reorganizations [*Umschichtungen*, literally "restratifications"] through which available [*arbeitsfähige*] energy becomes free; in other words tense psychical systems may arise which were not present before, at least in this form. Nevertheless, there is much evidence that the essential amount of energy of a psychical process does not flow out of the momentary perceptions themselves.

2. This is, to be sure, not equivalent to saying that we have here to do with a "release" in the sense of the function of the spark in the cartridge or the driving rod in the steam engine.

a. When, for example, a child wants to get to a certain object, perhaps a piece of chocolate, the direction of the process will change if a sharp edge or a cross dog threatens the path or if some other barrier is present. In the simplest case the child will make a detour and then strive toward the object in a new direction. In brief, the totality of the forces present in the psychical field, including the attractive object, will control the direction of the process, according, indeed, to laws which may be established in detail. Thus far then we have to do only with the well-known and fundamental fact that *forces control the course of a process.*

It holds no less for psychology than for physics that no unequivocal (definite) relation obtains between the magnitude of the forces and the amount of energy of the process. On the contrary, relatively slight forces may, when the whole field is appropriately formed, control relatively large amounts of energy. Conversely, large forces and tensions may go hand in hand with slight energies. Thus a relatively slight change in the kind or direction of these forces may direct a process permanently into other paths. (This plays a very large part in, for example, the technique of social dominance.)

In every process *the forces in the inner and outer environment are changed by the process itself.* This change of the forces controlling the processes may, however, be of very different degree in different processes, so that in many processes this change is not essential to the course of the process itself, while in others the course of the process itself is fundamentally influenced thereby.

The latter case, with which psychology frequently has to deal, is a process of the following type. Every movement starting upon the perception of certain objects changes at the same time the position, relative to the individual, of the field forces controlling the behavior. It can thus prescribe new directions for the process, for example, the child is driven out of his original direction by obstacles. Thus there occurs a *steering* of the process by the perceptual field.[1]

---

[1] W. Köhler, Gestaltprobleme und Anfänge einer Gestalttheorie, *Jahresbericht d. ges. Physiol.*, 1922–1924, 537 ff. Compare also as a concrete example from the oculomotor system: K. Lewin and K. Sakuma, Die Sehrichtung monokularer und binokularer Objekte bei Bewegung und das Zustandekommen des Tiefeneffektes, *Psychol. Forsch.*, 1925, **6,** 339.

A continuous control of the process by the forces of the outer psychological environment occurs when the activities are not (or are in only slight degree) autochthonous, or when the forces inherent in the course of the process as such are small relative to the field forces.   For example, a child is faced by a disagreeable situation in which he is threatened from different sides. If, instead of thrusting through with a single impulse and without succeeding on the other hand in inwardly insulating himself against his impressions, he moves slowly through this field of positive and negative valences,[1] then the steering of the process by the field forces comes to full expression even in every little phase of the movement.

As a rule, however, the action process is not to be regarded as such a continuous flow.   Rather, it proceeds typically in successive action steps which themselves form largely autochthonous wholes: for example, the running toward the chocolate as far as the first obstacle, the pause for reflection, the angry reaching with the arm, another pause, a detour around the barrier.   In such an action process with a marked whole character (when, that is, the forces which inhere in it as an autochthonous process are large as against the forces of the field) no continuous control of each individual phase of the autochthonous action unity by the forces of the field occurs.   But the steering by the field forces still holds in the large, especially for the succession of the action wholes, a circumstance of fundamental significance in, for example, the theory of detour behavior.

Whether the control of the process by the field of force occurs in this latter manner or in the sense of a continuous steering depends, on the one hand, upon the integral firmness and the forces of the action process itself and, on the other hand, upon the strength of the forces in the field.   Hence, changes in either of these circumstances lead to essential changes in the course of the process.   At all events, the steering processes are of fundamental significance for the whole field of impulsive and controlled behavior.

[1] For the meaning of this term, see p. 77 (with note).

(The concept of steering is, to be sure, used in a still narrower sense: for cases in which a relatively independent steering process changes the forces of the field continuously in such a way that a second simultaneously occurring process is thereby steered in its course. A physical example of this is the amplifying tube.)

b. Objects which, like the chocolate in the above example, form the goal of the process are also to be regarded primarily as objects from which a force, steering the process, goes out in the same way as from a sharp edge, from a breakable object, or from the symmetrical or asymmetrical disposition of objects on both sides of the path taken by the child.[1] But they may in addition have been the occasion for the evocation of those needs out of which, as a reservoir of energy, the process in this case ultimately flows (which does not need to hold in the case of, for example, the sharp edge). If the child had been supersatiated with sweets, the whole process would not have occurred. To this extent, then, the chocolate has here also a second function.

The presence or absence of this sort of reservoir of energy, that is, of certain needs or need-like tensions, makes itself noticeable again and again in various forms in the whole field of the psychology of will and impulse. It plays a part when the interest in or effort toward a goal ceases with *satiation* of the psychical need involved; when an intended act, after its completion (or the completion of a substitute act), is not repeated upon the occurrence of a second similar occasion; when a well-established act fails to occur even upon the occurrence of the habitual stimulus, if certain energies do not impel the individual to the act. Finally, this fact has basic significance for the problems of the *affective* process. The close connection described above (Sec. *a*) between the perceptual field and the course of the process must not let us forget that *the forces which*

---

[1] Cf. A. HERMANN-CZINER, Zur Entwicklungspsychologie des Umgehens mit Gegenständen, *Zeitschr. f. angew. Psychol.*, 1923 **22**, 337, BARTELT and LAU, Beobachtungen an Ziegen, *Psychol. Forsch.*, 1924, **5**, 340. DEXLER, Das Gestaltprinzip und die moderne Tierpsychologie, *Lotos*, 1921, **69**, 143.

control the course of the process remain without effect or simply do not arise when no psychical energies are present, when there exists no connection with tense psychical systems which keep the process in motion.

The occasions which set need energies free may, as in the above examples, be decisive forces for the special course of the process. Precisely this double function is frequently realized in psychology. It is closely related to a group of especially marked re-formations of the field by the process of the activity itself.

c. The attainment and eating of the chocolate are especially significant for the change of the field forces because the coming into possession of the chocolate and the beginning of the satiation process imply not only a change in the position of the field forces but at the same time a profound change of the psychical tensions which produce the behavior.

The perception of an object or event can thus:

1. Cause the formation of a definite tense psychical system which did not previously exist, at least in that form. Such an experience immediately produces an intention, or awakens a desire, which was not previously present.

2. An already existing state of tension, which may go back to a purpose, a need, or a half-finished activity, is interested in [*spricht an*] a certain object or event, which is experienced as an attraction (or repulsion), in such a way that this particular tense system now obtains control of the motorium. We shall say of such objects that they possess a *"valence."*

3. Valences of this sort operate at the same time (as do certain other experiences) as field forces in the sense that they steer the psychical processes, above all the motorium.

4. Certain activities, caused in part by valences, lead to satiation processes or to the carrying out of intentions and hence to the reduction of the tensions in the basic system involved to an equilibrium at a lower level of tension.

The particular processes by which the sight of the chocolate (Sec. *a*) causes the behavior cannot here be discussed in detail. It might be that the available energy already present in a psychical system momentarily in a state of tension is simply helped to break through to the motorium. Or it might be that, upon the presence of the valence, a system which until then has not been capable of work undergoes a radical transposition [*Umlagerung*] of such kind that now energy becomes free. One might even think at times of resonance phenomena and so on. It is nevertheless improbable that discharges in the special sense of the pure machine-like discharge play a considerable role. The fact that impulses show, as a rule, an inner, real [*sachliche*] relation to the special psychical energy sources on which they draw speaks against this assumption.

There are, naturally, all transitional degrees between valences which set free available energy and the field forces which control the remainder of the process. This does not affect the necessity of inquiring always as to the energy sources of the process involved.

This holds also for cases of steering in the narrower sense of the word. Here also one may not neglect the fact that the slight forces and energies necessary for steering are not identical with the energies of the steered system and that the effect fails to occur if the flow of energy to the primary process fails. (Analogy: failure of the plate circuit in an amplifying tube.)

We cannot here discuss the possible sources of psychical energy as to content. At all events, the needs and the central goals of the will are important in this connection. Nevertheless some general questions, which are appropriate here, as to the structure of psychical energetic systems must be considered.

Psychical Energies and the Structure of the Mind

It is customary, at present, again to emphasize somewhat more strongly the unity of the mind. This occurs doubtless as a protest against the atomistic dissection of the mind into piecemeal discrete sensations, feelings, and other experiences. The question of unity of the mind is, however, still very ambiguous, and in order to avoid misunderstandings we shall later (see page 61) have to mention a number of questions which might be raised in this connection. Suffice it here to note that we propose to discuss not the whole problem complex indicated by the ambiguous term "unity of the mind," but rather a definite problem concerning the psychical energies.

First, the following general considerations should be noted: Exactly when problems of wholeness are central, one must beware of the tendency to make the wholes outwardly as extensive as possible. Above all, it must be clear that concrete research must always go beyond vague generalities to inquire about the structure [*Strukturiertheit*] of the wholes concerned into subwholes, and about the special boundaries of the superordinate systems determining the particular case.

There is an inclination, probably correct, to regard the unity of the whole region of the psychical which makes up an individual as relatively greater than the unity of physical nature. But the proposition "Everything is related to everything else," which by no means adequately portrays the conditions in physical nature,[1] is also not wholly valid for the unity of the mind, although in both cases it contains an element of truth.

Twenty-five years ago I awoke, happy that I did not have to go to school that day, I flew a kite, came home late to lunch, ate a great deal of dessert, and played in the garden; these and all the other experiences that filled the following days and weeks may be reproduced under certain circumstances (perhaps in hypnosis) and are hence in that sense not dead. Doubtless, indeed, the whole of childhood experience may have a decisive significance for all development and consequently also for present behavior; moreover, certain special experiences may still have a very acute significance for present psychical processes. Thus each single everyday experience of the past may somehow influence the present psychic life. But this influence is in most cases to be evaluated in just the same way as the influence of some specific changes in a fixed star upon the physical processes in my study: *it is not that an influence exists but that the influence is extremely small, approximately zero.*

This lack of influence is by no means peculiar to experiences widely separated in time. I look out the window and notice the

[1] W. Köhler, *Die physischen Gestalten*, Weltkreisverlag, Erlangen, 1920.

movements of a column of smoke from a chimney.   To be sure, such an experience may in a special case profoundly influence the rest of the psychic life; but in general every psychical event is by no means related to each of the thousands of other daily little experiences.   Behavior would not be changed or would be changed imperceptibly if a great many of our experiences did not occur or occurred in other ways.

The proposition "In the psychical, everything is related to everything else" is inadequate, however, for other reasons than that it is necessary to separate the significant from the insignificant.   It does not suffice to say instead: "To be sure, not every experience, but certainly every profound or significant one, is related to all other psychical events."   Even such a quantitatively improved proposition, so to speak, remains inadequate.

The relations of psychical events to each other and the breadth of influence of each single experience upon the other psychical processes depend not simply upon their strength, indeed not even upon their real importance.   The individual psychical experiences, the actions and emotions, purposes, wishes and hopes, are rather *imbedded in quite definite psychical structures, spheres of the personality, and whole processes*.   One may, for example, be interrupted in the midst of a conversation by a telephone call about some relatively indifferent matter which is settled in a few words.   In this case the total situation may lead to a more rapid completion of the telephone conversation.   But the individual experiences, wishes, and purposes which dominated the preceding conversation and which dominate it again upon its resumption are as a rule practically insignificant for the telephone conversation, unless unusually strong tensions are involved.

Whether, and if so how, two psychological events influence each other depends to a large extent upon whether they are imbedded in the same or in different total processes or upon the *relation which these different psychical complexes have to each other*.   Thus an experience, weak in itself, may be of essential significance to a perhaps temporally relatively distant psychical event, while much stronger experiences which belong to another system may be practically without effect even upon temporally nearer processes.

The context which is built up in memory is also not dependent upon relations of intensity and time but is dominated by its actual belongingness to the same total process.[1]

This belonging to quite definite psychical systems is also in high degree characteristic of the dynamically basic psychical tensions and energies.

The individual psychical needs or the tensions which result from certain processes and experiences often have, of course, a certain connection with each other. Thus it may happen, for example, that affective energies out of one system may go over into another (perhaps those resulting from events in vocational life into processes in family life) and come to expression in the latter. Thus it may happen, also, that the satiation of a need produces consatiation of functionally adjacent needs. The intimacy of this communication varies greatly, however, among different tense psychical systems. The general tendency to communication seems also to vary in strength in certain psychical conditions and in different individuals. Nevertheless it must not be forgotten that each dynamic psychical system does not have clear communication with every other, but that the communication in many cases is extremely weak, indeed practically nonexistent.

If there were not this sometimes astoundingly complete segregation of different psychical systems from each other, if there were instead a permanently real unity of the mind of such kind that all the psychical tensions present at a given time had to be regarded as tensions in a uniform, unitary, closed system, no ordered action would be possible. Only the really extreme exclusion of the majority of all the simultaneously present psychical tensions, some of which are frequently much stronger, and the practically exclusive connection of the motor sphere with one special region of inner tensions make an ordered action possible. This exclusion for the purpose of a definite action

---

[1] W. POPPELREUTER, Über die Ordnung des Vorstellungslaufes, *Arch. f. d. ges. Psychol.*, 1912, **25**, 208–349.

does not always occur by means of temporary elimination of all the other tensions present in the mind; the psychical tensions arise of themselves in definite psychical structures or regions which have already been formed, or are then formed, by means of certain dynamic processes which we shall not here discuss.

Let us summarize the considerations of this section: The mind is often considered to be the very prototype of unity. The unity of consciousness, the unity of the person, are often used as the basis and self-evident presupposition of far-reaching speculations; and the integration of the individual, especially in its psychical aspects, seems closely connected with the special nature, the absolute uniqueness, which it is customary to ascribe to an individual.

Upon closer examination, however, we find here a whole range of problems of unity. The question of the unity of consciousness is not identical with the question of the unity of the whole region of psychical forms and processes, of tense and not-tense psychical systems, the totality of which may be designated as the mind. Further, it is at least questionable whether that which may be called the ego or self,[1] the unity of which is important for many problems, is not merely one system or complex of systems, a functional part region within this psychical totality (see page 61).

We are speaking here not of this problem of the unity of the self but only of the problem of the dynamic homogeneity of the mind.

Further, the psychical totality which is Mr. X is at least different from that of Mr. R. and from that of the child Q. This difference, which constitutes the individuality (*Eigenart*) of the person involved, his individuality in the sense of that which sets his nature apart from the individuality of other individuals, is probably evident in some way as always the same special, characteristic individuality, in each of its processes, parts, and expressions. Questions of individuality in this sense, that is, such questions as whether such identical charac-

[1] Cf. W. JAMES, *Principles of Psychology*, Holt, New York, 1890.

teristics of all the processes in the given mind are demonstrable and in what they consist (a basic question for individual psychology), are also here excluded. Such individuality or uniqueness of all that belongs to the same psychical totality (mind) might also be present even if the latter presented no firm unity, for example, if each of these totalities were comparable to a whole physical world and did not possess the unity of a physical organism or even of a single homogeneous closed system. We are not here discussing the question of the identical characteristics of processes which belong to the same psychical totality but solely the question of the causal-dynamic homogeneity of the mind, the question of the presence of relatively segregated energetic systems.

Finally, it should be noted that the existence of relatively segregated psychical energetic systems has nothing to do with the distinction of various psychical abilities such as memory, will, or understanding. On the contrary, the repudiation of sharp boundaries between these fields of inquiry is actually a presupposition of the present line of thought.

The next result of these considerations is as follows. Doubtless there exists in certain spheres, for example, within the motorium, a relatively high degree of unity. But however high one may estimate the degree of unity in a psychical totality, the recognition that within the mind there are regions of extremely various degrees of coherence remains an exceedingly important condition of more penetrating psychological research. We have to do not with a single unitary system but with a great number of such strong configurations (*starken Gestalten*), some of which stand in communication with others and thus form component parts of a more inclusive weak configuration [*schwache Gestalt*]. Other psychical structures, again, may show no real connection worth mentioning. The difference between the conception of the mind as a single whole, uniform in all its parts, and the conception of the mind as a sum of experiences is only formal and not in any way relevant to research. It is necessary, however, to recognize the natural structure of the mind, its psychical systems, strata, and spheres.

It is necessary always to determine where we have to deal with wholes and where not.

The formation of definite psychical systems is related in part to the ontogenetic development of the mind. It therefore also shows, as does that development, a specifically historical component.

The Tendency to Equilibrium: The Dynamic Firmness of Boundaries and Relative Segregation of Psychical Systems

The following considerations lead to similar conclusions as to the structure of the psychical in dynamic respects.

The psychical processes may often, by the use of certain points of view, be deduced from the tendency to equilibrium (as may biological processes in general, as well as physical, economic, or other processes). The transition from a state of rest to a process, as well as change in a stationary process, may be derived from the fact that the equilibrium at certain points has been disturbed and that then a process in the direction of a new state of equilibrium sets in.

In carrying through this line of thought, however, one must pay special attention to certain points.

1. The process moves in the direction of a state of equilibrium only for the *system as a whole*. Part processes may at the same time go on in opposed directions,[1] a circumstance which is of the greatest significance for, for example, the theory of detour behavior. It is hence important to take the system whole which is dominant at the moment as basis. Indeed, the concrete task of research will often consist precisely in the search for this determinative system, its boundaries and its internal structure. From these the particular events may then be directly deduced by means of the above-mentioned general proposition.

2. A state of equilibrium in a system does not mean, further, that the system is without tension. Systems can, on the contrary, also come to equilibrium in a state of tension (*e.g.*, a spring under tension or a container with gas under pressure).

---

[1] KÖHLER, *Die physischen Gestalten.*

The occurrence of this sort of system, however, presupposes a certain firmness of boundaries and actual segregation of the system from its environment (both of these in a functional, not a spatial, sense). If the different parts of the system are insufficiently cohesive to withstand the forces working toward displacement (*i.e.*, if the system shows insufficient internal firmness, if it is fluid), or if the system is not segregated from its environment by sufficiently firm walls but is open to its neighboring systems, stationary tensions cannot occur. Instead, there occurs a process in the direction of the forces, which encroaches upon the neighboring regions with diffusion of energy and which goes in the direction of an equilibrium at a lower level of tension in the total region. The presupposition for the existence of a stationary state of tension is thus a certain firmness of the system in question, whether this be its own inner firmness or the firmness of its walls.

We are here using the concept of the firmness of a system solely in a functional-dynamic sense without thereby making any special assertions about the material of the system concerned. Naturally, the firm walls of a system may be composed of a surrounding system in a state of tension. In this case the above-described presuppositions hold again for both systems as a whole.

The occurrence of such tense systems is very characteristic of psychical processes, at least after infancy. A tendency may readily be observed toward immediate discharge of tension (to a state of equilibrium at the lowest possible state of tension). Such an equilibrium, perhaps through the fulfillment of a wish, is, however, often not immediately possible because of the character of the total situation. It may be that the equilibration can only gradually be established, for example, by means of long-continued effort, or it may be that it is for the time wholly unattainable. Then there arises, at first, a stationary tense system which may, when a very profound disturbance of equilibrium is involved, embrace broad psychical strata. The child to whom an important wish is denied may throw itself upon the ground and remain there in a state of tension, rigid as if transfixed by despair.   As a rule, however (or after some time), there results a special tense system.   The unfulfilled wish, for example, or the half-finished activity does not cripple the whole motorium or charge the entire mind with tension, but there remains a special tense system which may not appear in experience for a long time and which may influence the course of the other psychical processes only slightly.   On appropriate occasion, however, it may assert itself most strongly (*e.g.*, by the resumption of the half-finished activity).

In many such tense systems, even when a direct equilibration of tension (*e.g.*, by fulfillment of the wish or completion of the activity at a later time) does not occur, a discharge may yet eventually result.   It may be that the equilibration of tension results from a substitute completion (compensation); or it may be that the segregation of the system is not so complete as to exclude equilibration with the adjacent systems (somewhat in the nature of diffusion).   Very frequently, however, the tensions of such special systems persist over long periods or may be, at most, only reduced.   Hence *there are systems of very considerable functional firmness and isolation in the psychical.*

In the adult, at least, there exists as a rule a great number of relatively separate tense systems which are influenced, to be sure, by a general discharge of the whole person but which can only rarely be actually discharged thereby, and then usually incompletely.   They form reservoirs of energy for action, and without their very considerable independence ordered action would be impossible.

The experimental investigations of half-finished activities[1] also show impressively that the mind is dynamically by no means a perfectly closed unity.   If, for example, in a series of experimental tasks several are interrupted by the experimenter before completion, there only seldom results a general state of tension which increases with each new unfinished task, and in these few cases only a slight general tension occurs.   Instead of a single total state of tension, which pushes toward discharge in any random way (*e.g.*, by further work on already finished

[1] Cf. Ovsiankina and Zeigarnik, below, Chap. VIII, p. 242.

tasks), there results a number of relatively independent tense systems which demonstrate their separateness in various directions. Only in the case of very strong tensions does the state of tension usually extend itself far over the neighboring regions.

The problem of whether the psychical is a single homogeneous system in which practically everything is related to everything else or whether relatively separate dynamic systems are present, is, incidentally, not identical with the problem of the unity of the self, which becomes acute in the phenomenon of split personality, although the two problems have certain relations to each other.

The question thereby raised is extremely difficult and far reaching. Its concrete discussion necessarily presupposes a much more advanced state of the experimental investigation of psychical structure. The following remarks, which are to be regarded merely as a groping beginning, grow out of the effort to avoid certain easy misinterpretations and at the same time to indicate some theoretical possibilities to the discussion of which we are repeatedly brought by the concrete experimental work on our problems.

It would be natural from Gestalt theoretical considerations to understand the self in terms of the psychical totality perhaps as its structural individuality. As a matter of fact, some such notion is basic to the concept of character, for the adequate conception of which one must start, not from the presence of certain isolated properties (traits), but from the whole of the person. If from this beginning one comes to the problem of the psychical dynamic systems, the attempt will in all probability be made to identify the self with the whole of the psychical totality.

A number of facts, however, drive one in the opposite direction to the view that a special region, within the psychical totality, must be defined as the self in the narrower sense. Not every psychically existent system would belong to this central self. Not every one to whom I say "*Du*," not all the things, men, and environmental regions which I know and which may perhaps be very important to me, belong to my self. This self-system would also have in functional respects—this is most important—a certain unique position. Not every tense psychical system would stand in communication with this self. Tensions which have to do with the self would also have functionally a special significance in the total psychical organism (see the next section), and it is possible that within this region differently directed tensions would tend to equilibrium considerably more strongly and that relatively isolated dynamic systems within it could much less readily occur.

One would have recourse to such a hypothesis or to similar ones only when weighty facts of dynamics, for example, in the field of emotion, drive him to it. It is necessary here only to note that the distinction of relatively separate psychical systems leaves open various possibilities for the question of the unity and homogeneity of the self.

In summary, the following should at all events be remarked. We have seen above that it is necessary for the investigation of causal relations and dynamic relations to pay especial attention to the psychical tensions and sources of energy. *These psychical tensions and energies belong to systems which are in themselves dynamic unities and which show a greater or less degree of abscission.* The structure of the dynamic system involved and the presence (in greater or less degree) or the absence of communication with various other psychical systems, as well as every change in boundary conditions, are hence of the greatest significance for the psychical process, for the equilibration of psychical tensions, and for the flow of psychical energy.

In the treatment of problems of the psychical energies and tensions one must therefore never forget that they have a position in definite psychical systems and hence must be treated from those points of view (Gestalt theoretical) which are valid for such systems.

Psychical Processes as Life Processes

In the treatment of the psychical sources of energy as dynamic systems which are in variously close communication with each other, one must not forget that in dealing with psychical processes one is dealing with life processes. This circumstance had naturally to be left in the background of the preceding discussion since in the present status of the problem of the psychical forces and energies we must at first be concerned with settling some general primitive questions. Hence in order to avoid misunderstandings it should be emphasized at least briefly.

The mere distinction of different degrees of communication between the dynamic systems will probably not suffice for the adequate description of the psychical structure. One will probably have to distinguish also layers or strata [*Schichten*] of different functional significance.

For example, the special significance which the motor process possesses for the equilibration of psychical tensions, the way in which the motorium may come into communication with certain psychical systems, and the circumstances under which this communication changes give to the motor sphere a relatively unique functional position. Similarly one may inquire as to the functional significance of conscious thought or of clear imagery. (Even within the perceptual process one will probably have to go beyond the inadequate distinction between central and peripheral processes to the distinction of special functional strata.)

Further, changes clearly of the types of development, of maturation, of growth, and of regulation play a great role.

This holds hardly less of the psychical energy sources also, for example, of the psychical needs. The needs show a marked ontogenesis. This is true not only specifically, of such needs as the sexual, but also generally. The typical small child enjoys throwing things down; later he pushes the things under the carpet; as a somewhat older child, he likes to hide and to play "hide and seek"; even certain lies of children are often largely "hiding." Or the young child likes at first to open and shut a certain little box; later still, sitting on the arm of his mother, he prefers to open and shut a door; still later, when he can walk, this door game is frequently extended indefinitely and he likes in addition to open and close all drawers.   In these cases and in similar ones it is necessary always to follow not only the development of ability in certain performances but also the development of the inclinations, the needs, the interests.[1]   In following the concrete need and the individual child it is important to note the development in the content of the need, where an increase occurs and where a decrease, where an originally broad need is narrowed down to a certain small sphere of valences, and where, on the other hand, a quite special inclination extends to neighboring regions.   In this connection one cannot depend upon the identity of the performance as the sole criterion of belonging to the same need. Outwardly quite different acts may belong close together in respect to their sources of energy, while outwardly quite similar acts, perhaps playing with dolls (or with building blocks, etc.), may be differently based in the two-year-old child and the four-year-old child.

Such developments frequently show a rhythm like, for example, the biological development of the egg: they occur in steps which are within themselves largely autonomous.   The concepts of maturation and of crisis become essential.

Superimposed upon the ontogenetic development is the quicker rhythm of the waxing and waning of the inclinations and needs (psychical satiation and return to an unsatiated condition).

Physiology, among the fundamental problems of which the energetic economy of the organism belongs, has been treated up to the very recent past as a "physics of life."   Energy exchange has been studied most exactly, but it was forgotten that these processes are here imbedded in the organism, and so the really biological problems of energy processes were neglected.   With the peculiar position which energy exchange, as a moment of the life process, acquires in biology, certain specific problems are presented; the attempt has been made to designate these by the term "*Mittel organischen Geschehen.*"

[1] E. G. Lau, *Beiträge zur Psychologie der Jugend in der Pubertätszeit,* 2d ed., Beltz Langensalza, 1924.

An analogous danger and an analogous difficulty, which become clear in carrying through the problems on concrete material, exist for the psychological problems of energy as well. For example, it is shown that certain systems with certain tensions and velocities of equilibration may be deduced from the degree of communication with adjacent regions of the system concerned and from the relation of their tensions; and in the treatment of these one can in principle succeed with the above-mentioned or related basic concepts of energy processes. But there also occur, occasionally, rather abrupt regulation phenomena (*e.g.*, the sort of thing usually spoken of as the intervention of self-control or a willing), which cannot be deduced from the principles originally taken as basis, principles which have proved adequate up to this point. In such cases the transition to more comprehensive regions (which, when treated as total systems, may clear up what was at first puzzling) is sometimes useful. It cannot here be discussed whether the explanation may always be attained in this way, by recourse to wholes of varying extent and varying strength, or whether the processes of psychical growth and maturation require the use of essentially other conceptual structures than those above described. For here we are faced with questions which embrace the whole field of life.[1] In any case the same concept of the dynamic whole in the pregnant sense of the dynamic Gestalt will play a decisive role, and a broad field is indicated to psychological experimental research which promises to yield important clarification toward the solution of the general problems of life.

[1] Cf. K. Lewin, *Der Begriff der Genese*, Springer, Berlin, 1922.

CHAPTER III

ENVIRONMENTAL FORCES IN CHILD BEHAVIOR AND DEVELOPMENT[1]

We have here to deal only with the psychological influence of the environment. This does not mean that the somatic effects of environment, for example, of nutrition or climate, do not have great psychological significance. On the contrary, the somatic as well as the psychological influence of the environment is constantly operating on the entire child.

INTRODUCTION

It has long been recognized that the psychological influence of environment on the behavior and development of the child is extremely important.[2] Actually, all aspects of the child's behavior, hence instinctive and voluntary behavior, play, emotion, speech, expression, are codetermined by the existing environment. Some recent theories, notably those of Watson and Adler, assign to environment so predominant an influence upon development that hereditary factors are usually neglected.[3] Stern's theory of convergence emphasizes, on the contrary, that a predisposition and an environmental influence

---

[1] Reprinted from CARL MURCHISON, *Handbook of Child Psychology*, Clark Univ. Press, Worcester, Mass., 2d ed. rev., Chap. 14, 1933, by permission.

[2] H. TAINE, *De l'Intelligence* (2 vols.) Paris, 1870 (3d ed., 1878). On Intelligence (trans. by T. D. Haye and rev. with additions by the author, 2 vols.), Holt & Williams, New York, 1889.

[3] J. B. WATSON, *Behaviorism*, People's Instit. Publ. Co., New York, 1924–1925 (rev. ed., Norton, New York, 1930); A. ADLER, *Über den nervösen Charakter. Grundzüge einer vergleichenden Individualpsychologie und Psychotherapie*, Bergmann, Munich and Wiesbaden, 1912 (4th ed., 1928). *The Neurotic Constitution: Outlines of a Comparative Individualistic Psychology and Psychotherapy* (trans. by B. Glueck and J. E. Lind), Moffat, Yard, New York, 1917.

must operate in the same direction in order to effect a particular mode of behavior.[1]

Average and Individual Milieu.

The fact of environmental influence has been thoroughly established in various ways in recent years by the psychological study of various environments. For example, the intelligence of country children has been compared with that of city children,[2] and the significance of size of family and position among siblings has been investigated.[3] Research upon foster children[4] and twins[5] has also played an important part. In the case of identical twins one can be sure of equivalent hereditary capacities and dispositions. Similarities in conduct in the face of differences in environment may thus yield important information as to the kind and strength of the effects of environment, on the one hand, or of heredity, on the other.

Present-day investigation of the environment uses primarily statistical methods. The average of as many school records as were obtainable for only children is compared, for example, with that of eldest, middle, and youngest children in families of three. Particular environmental factors may be excluded to a certain degree, for example, in the investigation of the effect of size of family or of position in the series of siblings, by

[1] W. Stern, *Psychologie der frühen Kindheit, bis zum sechsten Lebensjahre,* Quelle & Meyer, Leipzig, 1914 (6th ed., rev., 1930). *Psychology of Early Childhood, up to the Sixth Year of Age* (trans. from the 3d German ed. by A. Barwell), Holt, New York, Allen, London, 1924 (2d ed., rev., 1930).

[2] E. Hauck, Zur differentiellen Psychologie des Industrie- und Landkindes, *Jenaer Beitr. z. Jugend- und Erziehungspsychol.,* Beltz, Langensalza, 1929; H. E. Jones, H. S. Conrad, and M. B. Blanchard, Environmental Handicap in Mental Test Performance, *Univ. Calif. Publ. Psychol.,* 1932, **5,** 63–99.

[3] A. Busemann, Die Familie als Erlebnismilieu des Kindes, *Zsch. f. Kinderforsch.,* 1929, **36,** 17–32.

[4] B. S. Burks, The Relative Influence of Nature and Nurture upon Mental Development: A comparative study of foster parent—foster child resemblance, *27th Yearbook,* N.S.S.E., 1928, Pt. 1, 219–316; F. N. Freeman, *et al.,* The Influence on the Intelligence, School Achievement and Conduct of Foster Children, *27th Yearbook,* N.S.S.E., 1928, Pt. 1, pp. 103–218.

[5] A. Gesell, The Developmental Psychology of Twins, in *A Handbook of Child Psychology,* ed. by C. Murchison, Worcester, 1st ed., 1931.

including only children of approximately the same economic status. These investigations have brought to light a wealth of interesting facts; for example, that in certain social levels in Germany the number of children optimal for school achievement is three or four, but that in proletarian families, on the contrary, only children display, on the average, the best records.[1]

Valuable and indispensable as these facts are, they can rarely offer more than hints toward the problem of the forces of the environment. For, in the investigation of the fundamental dynamic relations between the individual and the environment, it is essential to keep constantly in mind the actual total situation in its concrete individuality. The statistical method is usually compelled to define its groups on the basis not of purely psychological characteristics but of more or less extrinsic ones (such as the number of siblings), so that particular cases having quite different or even opposed psychological structure may be included in the same group. Especially to be emphasized, however, is the following consideration: the calculation of an average (e.g., of "the one-year-old child") is designed to eliminate the "accidents" of the environment; the determination of the "average situation" (e.g., of the average effect of the situation of being an only child) is to exclude individual variations. But the very relation that is decisive for the investigation of dynamics—namely, that of the position of the actual individual child in the actual, concrete, total situation—is thereby abstracted.[2] An inference from the average to the concrete particular case is hence impossible. The concepts of the average child and of the average situation are abstractions that have no utility whatever for the investigation of dynamics.[3] The use of the average and the curve of

---

[1] A. BUSEMANN, op. cit.

[2] LEWIN, Conflict between Aristotelian and Galilean Modes of Thought in Psychology, Jour. Gen. Psychol., 1931, 5, 141–177 (Chap. I of this volume).

[3] Thus the environment researches become, in general, the more fruitful the more attention is paid to a comprehension of the concrete total situation instead of to the number of cases.

distribution is unexceptionable where the object is to obtain a numerical value to characterize the position of a given individual in a group. For the discovery of dynamic laws, however, it does not suffice to segregate a single property or a phenotypically defined event, without regard to the structure of the total situation, and then to treat statistically as many as possible of the situations that display this characteristic.

The laws of falling bodies in physics cannot be discovered by taking the average of actual falling movements, say of leaves, stones, and other objects, but only by proceeding from so-called pure cases. Likewise in psychology the forces of the environment and the laws of their operation on child behavior can be discovered only by proceeding from certain total situations that are simple but well defined in their concrete individuality. Only in this way, which usually implies experiment and systematic variation of conditions, can general propositions be made which will hold good even for the actual individual child and the concrete particular case.

It may, of course, be questioned whether it is possible to speak scientifically (*i.e.*, with conceptual rigor) of dynamic properties, especially of forces of the psychological environment.[1] Saying, for example, that bad treatment oppresses the child, or that praise exalts it, may obviously have a merely figurative significance.

In biology the tropism theory of Loeb attempted to establish in a scientifically precise way dynamic relations between environmental stimulation and the behavior of certain animals. It has, however, been shown that the circumstance of the animals' learning implies essential modification,[2] and, moreover, that their behavior depends upon their momentary "mood."[3]

---

[1] The speculative philosophical grounds which might be urged against such an attempt are not considered here. In America they are usually of a physical nature, in Germany partly physical and partly *geisteswissenschaftlich*.

[2] H. S. JENNINGS, *Behavior of the Lower Organisms*, Columbia Univ. Press, New York, 1906.

[3] F. ALVERDES, *Neue Bahnen in der Lehre vom Verhalten der niederen Tiere*, Springer, Berlin, 1922.

The biologists at present have in part gone back to an indeterministic or at least a nondynamic point of view according to which it is impossible to talk of a strictly lawful operation of environmental forces upon the individual. The influence of the environment is reduced essentially to the principle of trial and error. That is, the occurrence of the elementary actions is, so far as their relations to the environment are concerned, essentially accidental. The theory thus displays marked Darwinistic traits: it excludes the problem of a direct dynamic relation between environment and individual and limits the effect of the environment to the evocation of agreeable or disagreeable experiences. This theory may be regarded as an attempt to avoid the uncomfortable concept of environmental forces in a psychological sense and to derive an explanation of all behavior so far as this may be possible from the organism itself.

In child psychology also the principle of trial and error is regarded as fundamental for the development of child behavior.[1] On the other hand, it has recently been emphasized, first, that besides "experience" intrinsic maturation has fundamental significance for child development[2] and, secondly, that besides blind trial and error there is insightful behavior.[3] In the case of insightful behavior the conduct of the individual is again brought into immediate relation to the special structure of the situation.

Individual, Environment, and Law.

Before we consider in detail the question of the psychological forces of the environment, we must discuss briefly the relation of the concepts environment, individual, and law. Environ-

---

[1] K. Bühler, Die geistige Entwicklung des Kindes, Fischer, Jena, 1918 (new ed., 1929).
The Mental Development of the Child, Harcourt, Brace, New York, Kegan Paul, London, 1930.
[2] W. Stern, Psychologie der frühen Kindheit, bis zum sechsten Lebensjahre; K. Koffka, The Growth of the Mind; K. Bühler, op. cit.
[3] K. Koffka, op. cit.

ment is understood psychologically sometimes to mean the *momentary situation* of the child, at other times to mean the *milieu*, in the sense of the chief characteristics of the permanent situation. The following considerations apply to both concepts.

The actual behavior of the child depends in every case both upon his individual characteristics and upon the momentary structure of the existing situation. It is not possible, however, as is increasingly obvious, simply to single out one part to be attributed to the environment and another to be ascribed to the individual. But even when the primitive question, "Which is (in this case) more important, heredity or environment?" is given up, and the thesis is advanced that heredity and environment must work in the same direction in order to effect a certain mode of behavior, it is still assumed that hereditary dispositions may be defined as tendencies toward certain real modes of behavior without reference to a particular environment. Actually, reference to a specific environment, indeed, to an aggregate of specific environments, is indispensable to the concept of predisposition: a predisposition or individual characteristic of the person (P_a) (see page 72) cannot be defined by one specific mode of behavior, but only by an aggregate of modes of behavior of such kind that different environmental situations $(E_1, E_2, \ldots)$ are correlated with the modes of behavior $(B_\alpha, B_\beta, \ldots)$ they elicit. The individual characteristics of a person as regards both predisposition and momentary state are thus to be defined not phenotypically but genotypically in dealing with dynamic problems.

The variations in behavior $(B_\alpha, B_\beta, \ldots)$ with the same individual characteristics may be extremely large. A child that is negative in one situation may be shy in another and at ease in a third. Thus Kramer found in 100 per cent of his cases that bestial children lost their bestial behavior so completely when brought into an appropriate environment that they might better be characterized as dainty.

Sensitivity to environment varies considerably in different individuals. In general it is greater in psychopathic than in normal children.[1]

In order for one individual characteristic[2] (P_a) to be differentiated from another (P_b) it must be associated with *different* modes of behavior (B) in the *same* situations (E_1, E_2, E_n).

$$P_a = \begin{cases} E_1 \rightarrow B_\alpha \\ E_2 \rightarrow B_\beta \\ E_3 \rightarrow B_\gamma \\ \quad . \qquad . \\ \quad . \qquad . \\ \quad . \qquad . \\ E_n \rightarrow B_\nu \end{cases} \qquad P_b = \begin{cases} E_1 \rightarrow B_\xi \\ E_2 \rightarrow B_o \\ E_3 \rightarrow B_\alpha \\ \quad . \qquad . \\ \quad . \qquad . \\ \quad . \qquad . \\ E_n \rightarrow B_\mu \end{cases}$$

Thus, on the whole, different individuals may often display the same (or very similar) modes of behavior (B). Watson and Adler emphasize this similarity, and probably the ultimately possible modes of behavior of very many people might indeed show a considerable, if not a complete, measure of agreement. But this similarity of possible behavior does not imply similarity of the individuals, because it requires different situations to bring out (approximately) similar behavior.[3] Neither similarity nor difference in behavior (B) permits of direct unequivocal inference of similarity or difference of individual characteristics or of situation factors. Inference of an individual characteristic (P) is possible only when the environmental situations (E) agree, inference of the situation only when the individuals agree.[4]

---

[1] A. Homburger, *Vorlesungen über Psychopathologie des Kindesalters*, Springer, Berlin, 1926.

[2] These considerations apply equally to a single characteristic or personality trait and to the whole personality.

[3] These situations must, in general, be the more different the more different the individuals.

[4] Even if the Watson-Adler thesis that the overwhelming majority of mankind is capable of most tasks were right, it would imply neither similarity of endowment nor the decisive importance of environmental factors.

In such cases, to be sure, the inference is unequivocal. Indeed, psychological laws really say the same thing in another way: from a certain total constellation—comprising a situation and an individual—there results a certain behavior, *i.e.*, $(E_1, P_a) \rightarrow B_\alpha$, or in general: $B = f(PE)$.

In reality, *the dynamics of environmental influences* can be investigated *only simultaneously with the determination of individual differences* and with *general psychological laws*. The discovery of psychological laws, on the other hand, yields important insights into the significance of environmental factors and individual characteristics. It will be plain from these considerations what vital importance the systematic—especially the experimental—investigation of environmental changes with the same individual[1] has for the study of the environmental forces.

Environmental Structure and Needs.

An analysis of environmental factors must start from a consideration of the total situation. Such an analysis hence presupposes an adequate comprehension and presentation in dynamic terms of the total psychological situation as its most important task.

Loeb's theory, by and large, identifies the biological environment with the physical environment: the dynamic factors of the environment consist of light of specific wave length and intensity, gravity, and others of similar nature.[2] Others, notably von Uexküll, have shown, on the contrary, that the biological environment is to be characterized quite differently, namely, as a complex of foods, enemies, means of protection, etc. The same physical situation must thus be described for different species of animals as a specifically different phenomenal and functional world [*"Merk- und Wirkwelt"*].

---

[1] Only in the same individual or in identical twins can one be sure of dealing with the same individual characteristics.

[2] W. J. Crozier, The Study of Living Organisms, Chap. II, *The Foundations of Experimental Psychology* (ed. by C. Murchison), Clark Univ. Press, Worcester. Mass., 1929, pp. 45–127.

In child psychology, also, the same physical environment must be quite differently characterized according to the age, the individual character, and the momentary condition of the child. The life-space of the infant is extremely small and undifferentiated. This is just as true of its perceptual as of its effective space.[1] With the gradual extension and differentiation of the child's life-space, a larger environment and essentially different facts acquire psychological existence, and this is true also with respect to dynamic factors. The child learns in increasing degree to control the environment. At the same time—and no less important—it becomes psychologically dependent upon a growing circle of environmental events.

When, for example, one breaks a doll a few feet away from a baby, the latter is unaffected, while the same procedure with a three-year-old usually calls forth energetic intervention.

The later extension of the child's space-time beyond the room and the family circle also means not only an intellectual survey of wider relations but, above all, an extension of the environmental objects and events upon which the child is psychologically immediately dependent.

The mere *knowledge* of something (*e.g.*, of the geography of a foreign country, of the economic and political situation, or even of immediate family affairs) does not necessarily change the child's life-space more than superficially. On the other hand, psychologically critical facts of the environment, such as the friendliness or unfriendliness of a certain adult, may have fundamental significance for the child's life-space without the child's having a clear intellectual appreciation of the fact.

For the investigation of dynamic problems we are forced to start from the psychologically real environment of the child.

[1] E. Lau, Beiträge zur Psychologie der frühen Kindheit II. *Zeitschr. f. Kinderforsch.*, 1931, **31**, 481–501; C. Bühler, Kindheit und Jugend: Genese des Bewusstseins, *Psychol. Monographien*, **3**, Hirzel, Leipzig, 1928. *From Birth to Maturity.* (In preparation.) S. Fajans, Die Bedeutung der Entfernung für die Stärke eines Aufforderungscharakters beim Säugling und Kleinkind, *Psychol. Forsch.*, 1933, **17**, 213–267.

In the "objective" sense, the existence of a social bond is a necessary condition of the viability of an infant not yet able itself to satisfy its biologically important needs. This is usually a social bond with the mother in which, functionally, the needs of the baby have primacy.

But social facts, as essential constituents of the *psycho-biological* environment, very early acquire dominant significance. This does not mean, of course, that when the child of three months reacts specifically to the human voice and to a friendly smile[1] the relation to certain individuals has already become a stable constituent of the child's psychological environment. The age at which this will occur depends essentially upon the individual endowment and the experiences of the child.

The fact that certain activities (*e.g.*, playing with certain toys) are allowed and others forbidden[2] (*e.g.*, throwing things or touching certain objects belonging to grown-ups) begins very early—certainly before the age of two—to play an important dynamic part in the structure of the child's environment. With the growth of the child social facts usually acquire more and more significance for the structure of the psychological environment.

Social facts such as friendship with another child, dependence upon an adult, etc., must also be regarded, from the dynamic point of view, as no less real than physical facts. Of course, in the description of the child's psychological environment one may not take as a basis the immediately objective social forces and relations as the sociologist or jurist, for example, would list them. One must, rather, describe the social facts as they affect the particular individual concerned.[3] For the objective social factors have no more an unambiguous relation

[1] C. BÜHLER and H. HETZER, Das erste Verständnis von Ausdruck im ersten Lebensjahr, *Zeitschr. f. Psychol.*, 1928, **107,** 50–61; H. HETZER and K. WOLF, Babytests, *Zeitschr. f. Psychol.*, 1928, **107,** 62–104.

[2] G. WEISS, Aufgabegebundenes und aufgabefreies Verhalten von Fürsorgezöglingen, *Zeitschr. f. Kinderforsch.*, 1930, **36,** 195*ff.*

[3] LEWIN, Vectors, Cognitive Processes and Mr. Tolman's Criticism, *Jour. Gen. Psychol.*, 1933, **8,** 318–345.

to the psychological individual than objective physical factors have.   Exactly the same physical object may have quite different sorts of psychological existence for different children and for the same child in different situations.   A wooden cube may be one time a missile, again a building block, and a third time a locomotive.   What a thing is at any time depends upon the total situation and the momentary condition of the child involved.   Similar considerations hold also for the social factors.

In this dependence there becomes clear a matter of fundamental psychological importance, namely, *the direct relationship between the momentary state of the individual and the structure of his psychological environment.*[1]   That the psychological environment, even when objectively the same, depends not only upon the individual character and developmental stage of the child concerned but also upon its momentary condition becomes clear when we consider the relation between environment and needs.

Beside the quasi-physical and quasi-social environment, a mental task or a phantasy must sometimes be characterized from the dynamic point of view as environment.   Activities (*e.g.*, a game) may have the character of a region into or out of which the child may go.   In the same sense a mathematical problem may have this character.   The description of the child's environment would be incomplete without including the whole world of phantasy which is so important for the child's behavior and so closely connected with its ideals and with its ideal goals.

In the environment there are, as we have seen, many objects and events of quasi-physical and quasi-social nature, such as rooms, halls, tables, chairs, a bed, a cap, knife and fork, things that fall down, turn over, can start and go of themselves; there are dogs, friends, grown-ups, neighbors, someone who rarely gets cross, and someone who is always strict and disagreeable.   There are places where one is safe from rain,

[1] *Ibid.;* LEWIN, *Vorsatz, Wille und Bedürfnis mit Vorbemerkungen über die psychischen Kräfte und Energien und die Struktur der Seele.*

others where one is safe from adults, and still others where one may not go under any circumstances. All these things and events are defined for the child partly by their appearance but above all by their *functional possibilities* (the *Wirkwelt* in von Uexküll's sense). The stairs are something that one can (or cannot yet) go up and down, or something that one climbed yesterday for the first time. Thus history, as the child has experienced it, is also a psychologically essential constituent of the things of the environment.

With all these, however, there remain certain critical properties of the psychobiological environment still undescribed. Objects are not neutral to the child, but have an immediate psychological effect on its behavior. Many things attract the child to eating, others to climbing, to grasping, to manipulation, to sucking, to raging at them, etc. These imperative environmental facts—we shall call them valences[1] [*Aufforderungscharaktere*]—determine the direction of the behavior. Particularly from the standpoint of dynamics, the valences, their kind (sign), strength, and distribution, must be regarded as among the most important properties of the environment.

---

[1] These valences are not to be confused with what is generally understood by "stimulus," as the term is used in speaking of a stimulus-reaction process. The effect of the valence corresponds dynamically much more nearly to a command, a summons, or a request.

A fairly precise translation of *Aufforderungscharakter* is the term "demand value," which Tolman [E. C. TOLMAN, *Purposive Behavior*, Appleton-Century, New York, 1932] uses for the same concept. In order to avoid unnecessary misunderstandings, Professor Tolman and Lewin have agreed to use the same term and at Tolman's suggestion have chosen "valence."

[There is no good English equivalent for *Aufforderungscharakter* as the author uses it. "Positive *Aufforderungscharaktere*" and "negative *Aufforderungscharaktere*" might be accurately rendered by "attractive characters" and "repulsive characters," were it not desirable, for various reasons, to have a neutral term. Perhaps the most nearly accurate translation for the expression would be "compulsive character," but that is cumbrous and a shade too strong. In consultation with the author it has been decided to do a very little violence to an old use of the word "valence" (see the New English Dictionary). It should be noted that, in contrast to chemical valence, which is only positive, psychological valence or a psychological valence may be either positive (attracting) or negative (repelling), and that an object or activity loses or acquires valence (of either kind) in accordance with the needs of the organism.—Translators' note.]

The valence of an object usually derives from the fact that the object is a means to the satisfaction of a need, or has indirectly something to do with the satisfaction of a need. The kind (sign) and strength of the valence of an object or event thus depends directly upon the momentary condition of the needs of the individual concerned; the valence of environmental objects and the needs of the individual are correlative.[1] (Concerning induced valence, see page 97.) Even with objective identity of environment, the strength and the appearance of the valences are quite other for a hungry child than for a satisfied one, for a healthy child than for a sickly one.

The correlation between valence and environment leads to a fundamental change in the latter with the changing needs of increasing age. The objects bearing valences are different for the baby, the toddler, the kindergartener, and the pubescent.[2]

The valences change also with the *momentary state* of the needs. When the need for nourishment, for playing with a doll, or for reading history is in a hungry or unsatisfied condition, a bit of food, a doll, or the history book attracts the child, that is, has a positive valence; whereas, when this need is in a stage or state of satisfaction, the object is indifferent to the child; and, in the stage of oversatiation of the need, it becomes disagreeable to the child, that is, it acquires a negative valence.[3]

Since the psychological environment, especially for the child, is not identical with the physical or social environment, one cannot, in investigating environmental forces, proceed from the physical forces as Loeb, for example, does in biology. If we start primarily from the psychobiological environment

---

[1] LEWIN, *Vorsatz, Wille und Bedürfnis mit Vorbemerkungen über die psychischen Kräfte und Energien und die Struktur der Seele.*

[2] LEWIN, Vectors, Cognitive Processes and Mr. Tolman's Criticism, *Jour. Gen. Psychol.*, 1933, **8**, 318–345.

[3] A. KARSTEN, Psychische Sättigung, *Psychol. Forsch.*, 1928, **10**, 142–254; D. KATZ, Psychologische Probleme des Hungers und Appetits, insbesondere beim Kinde, *Zeitschr. f. Kinderforsch.*, 1928, **34**, 158–197; LEWIN, Die Bedeutung der "psychischen Sättigung" für einige Probleme der Psychotechnik, *Psychotechn. Zeitschr.*, 1928, **3**, 182.

and pay due attention to its dependence upon the actual momentary condition of the individual involved, it is quite possible to discover universally valid principles of the dynamic effects of the environment. To be sure, it will always be necessary to keep in mind the total structure of the existing situation.[1]

Psychological environmental forces [*Umweltkräfte*] may be defined empirically and functionally, excluding all metaphysical problems, by their effect upon the behavior of the child.[2] They are equally applicable to the momentary situation and to the permanent environment of the child.

In summary: to understand or predict the psychological behavior (B) one has to determine for every kind of psychological event (actions, emotions, expressions, etc.) the momentary whole situation, that is, the momentary structure and the state of the person (P) and of the psychological environment (E). $B = f(PE)$. Every fact that exists psychobiologically must have a position in this field and only facts that have such position have dynamic effects (are causes of events). The environment is for all of its properties (directions, distances, etc.) to be defined not physically but *psychobiologically*, that is, according to its quasi-physical, quasi-social, and quasi-mental structure.

It is possible to represent the dynamic structure of the person and of the environment by means of mathematical concepts. The coordination between the mathematical representation and its psychodynamic meaning has to be strict and without exception.

We shall first describe the psychological field forces and their mode of operation, without consideration of the question whether the object in any particular case has acquired its valence through some previous experience or in some other way.

---

[1] By situation is meant the psychological situation, with particular reference to its dynamic properties.

[2] The fundamental concepts of psychological dynamics are thus for the present to be defined purely from the point of view of psychology and biology. Whether they agree in their formal logical structure with the fundamental dynamic concepts of physics need not here be discussed.

The Region of Freedom of Movement. Forces and Fields of Force

The first presupposition for the understanding of the child is the determination of the psychological place at which the child concerned is and of his region of freedom of movement, that is, of the regions that are accessible to him and of those regions that psychologically exist for the child but are inaccessible to him by reason of the social situation (prohibition by the adult, limitation by other children, etc.) or because of the limitations of his own social, physical, and intellectual abilities.   Whether his region of freedom of movement is large or small is of decisive significance for the whole behavior of the child.[1]

One can characterize these possible and not possible psychodynamic locomotions (quasi-bodily, quasi-social, and quasimental locomotions) at every point of the environment with the help of the concept of topology, which is a nonquantitative discipline about the possible kinds of connections between "spaces" and their parts.

The basis for the coordination between mathematical and psychodynamic concepts so far as environmental questions are concerned is the coordination of topological path and psychodynamic locomotion.   The topological description determines which points the different paths lead to and which regions these paths cross.   The region which a child cannot reach one can characterize by means of barriers between these regions and their neighboring regions.   The barrier corresponds as a dynamic concept to the mathematical concept of boundary. One must distinguish between different strengths of barriers.[2]

Fundamental Properties of Field Forces.

To determine not only which locomotions (paths) are possible but which of the possible locomotions will occur at a given moment one has to use the concept of *force*.

[1] F. Wiehe, *Die Grenzen des Ichs*. (In preparation.) Lewin, *Die psychologische Situation bei Lohn und Strafe*, Hirzel, Leipzig, 1931 (Chap. IV of this volume).

[2] S. Fajans, *ibid.*

A force is defined through three properties: (1) direction, (2) strength, and (3) point of application. The first and second properties are to be represented through the mathematical concept *vector*. The point of application is indicated in the figures (as is the custom in physics) by the point of the arrow.

Dynamically the force is correlated with psychobiological locomotions in a one-to-one correspondence. "The real locomotion must occur in every case according to the direction and the strength of the resultant of the momentary forces" and "In any case of locomotion there exists a resultant of forces in its direction."

The direction which the valence imparts to the child's behavior varies extremely, according to the content of the wants and needs. Nevertheless, one may distinguish two large groups of valences according to the sort of initial behavior they elicit: the positive valences (+), those effecting approach; and the negative (−), or those producing withdrawal or retreat.

The *actions* in the direction of the valence may have the form of uncontrolled impulsive behavior or of directed voluntary activity; they may be "appropriate" or "inappropriate."

Those processes which make an especially goal-striving impression are usually characterized dynamically by a reference to a positive valence.[1]

One has to distinguish between *driving* forces, which correspond to positive or negative valences, and *restraining* forces, which correspond to barriers.

Direction of the Field Force. That the valence is not associated merely with a subjective experience of direction, but that a directed force, determinative of the behavior, must be ascribed to it, may be seen in the fact that a change in the position of the attractive object brings about (other things being equal) a change in the direction of the child's movements.

An especially simple example of an action in the direction of a positive valence is illustrated in Figs. 1 and 2. A six-

[1] See below, p. 120.

months-old infant stretches arms, legs, and head toward a rattle or a spoonful of porridge in accordance with the direction of the vector (V).

The direction of the field forces plays an important part in such intelligent behavior as has to do with detour [*Umweg*] problems. The child perhaps wants to get a piece of chocolate on the other side of a bench (see Fig. 3). The difficulty of such a problem consists primarily not in the length of the detour (D) but in the fact that the initial direction of the appropriate route does not agree with that of the vector from the valence. The detour is the more difficult, other things being equal, the more the barrier makes it necessary for the child in making the detour to start off in a direction opposed to the direction of the valence (Fig. 4).

FIG. 1.

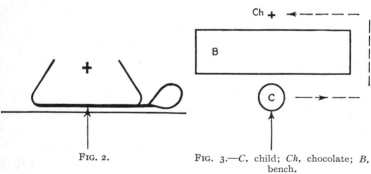

FIG. 2.

FIG. 3.—*C*, child; *Ch*, chocolate; *B*, bench.

The situation is similar when the child wants to take a ring off a stick, while the stick stands so that the ring cannot be pulled directly toward the child, but must first be moved upward or away from himself. Similar factors are operative when a child at a certain age may have difficulties in sitting down on a chair or a stone. The child approaches with his face toward the stone (*S*). In order to sit down he must turn around, that is, execute a movement opposed to the direction of the field force (Fig. 5).[1]

When the child finds the solution of such a detour problem, it happens by reason of a restructuring of the field.[2] There occurs a perception of the total situation of such a kind that the path to the goal becomes a unitary whole. The initial part of the route, which objectively is still a moment away from the goal (see Fig. 4), thereby loses psychologically that character and becomes the first phase of a general movement toward the goal.[3]

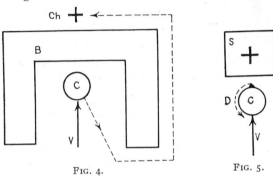

FIG. 4.   FIG. 5.

How critically important the question of *direction* is in this case is indicated by the fact that one cannot force a solution of the detour by increasing the *strength* of the valence. If the attraction is much too weak, it is, to be sure, unfavorable, because the child does not concern himself sufficiently with the affair.[4] But if we continue to strengthen the valence, the

[1] LEWIN, Die Auswirkung von Umweltkräften, *Proc. 9th Int. Cong. Psychol.*, 1929, 286–288.

[2] W. KÖHLER, *The Mentality of Apes* (trans. by E. Winter), Harcourt, Brace, New York, 1925.

[3] Frequently this transformation is not immediately complete, and the first part of the route retains a sort of double character.

[4] Bogen found, even among school children who were working on such tasks voluntarily, that solutions were found more frequently if the valence of the goal was strengthened by the addition of a piece of chocolate (see H. BOGEN and O. LIPMANN, *Naïve Physik*. Arbeiten aus dem Institut für angewandte Psychologie in Berlin. Theoretische und experimentelle Untersuchungen über die Fähigkeit zu intelligentem Handeln, Barth, Leipzig, 1923).

solution of the task ceases to be facilitated and instead becomes more difficult. The strength of the attraction then makes it doubly difficult for the child to start in a direction opposed to the field force. Instead, the child will execute, with all its energy, affective meaningless actions in the direction of the valence (see page 96).[1] Above all, that relative detachment and inward retirement from the valence which are so favorable to perception of the whole situation and hence to the transformation [*Umstrukturierung*] of the total field, which occurs in the act of insight, are made much more difficult (see page 152). For the same reason, the prospect of an especially intense reward or punishment may impede the solution of intellectual tasks.

To older children of normal intelligence the preceding examples of detour problems offer no difficulty, because they already have a sufficient survey of such situations or corresponding experiences. For them, it no longer requires a special act of intelligence in order that, instead of the spatial directions, the *functional* directions become decisive for the movement.

We may at this point remark a circumstance of general importance: direction in the psychobiological field is not necessarily to be identified with physical direction, but must be defined primarily in psychological terms. The difference between psychological and physical direction appears more prominently in older children. When the child fetches a tool or applies to the experimenter for help, the action does not mean, even when it involves a physical movement in a direction opposite to the goal, a turning away from the goal but an approach to it. Such indirect approaches are more rare among babies. This is due to the slighter functional differentiation of their environment and to the fact that *social* structure has not yet the overwhelming significance for them that it has for older children.

---

[1] The impulsive struggles of Thorndike's cats may have been due in part to such a situation (see E. L. THORNDIKE, *Animal Intelligence*, Macmillan, New York, 1911).

Fajans[1] found, for example, that in a certain situation in which three- and four-year-old children usually applied to the experimenter for help (indirect approach), the corresponding turning of the baby to its mother was more a withdrawal from failure than a seeking for help.

In the cases mentioned, the direction of the field forces is determined by objects which, by reason of visual or auditory distance perceptions, have a definite place in the environment. In the case of newborn children, it is possible to speak of such precisely directed field forces only in so far as the psychological environment has sufficient structure and solidity.

Directed action in response to certain forms of tactile stimulation may be observed very early. Touching the child's cheek with the nipple may elicit a turning of the head in the corresponding direction.

Also among older children the (psychological) *separation of the self from the valence* remains in many respects a necessary condition for the directedness of the action upon the valence. Fairly often the action does not proceed immediately to the use of the object, but the field force disappears (or is at least very much weakened) as soon as the object comes into the "possession" of the individual involved. An example from our films: a nine-month-old child before which two rattles are laid does not begin to play after getting one of them, but is interested only in the rattle that he does not have. The close relation between directed field forces and the separation of the self from the goal object can also be demonstrated in various ways with older children.

Strength of the Field Forces. For the strength of the valences, internal factors, especially the actual momentary state of the child's needs, are of crucial significance.[2] In addition, the strength of the field force going out from a valence depends also upon the position of the valence relative to the individual and upon the presence or absence of other valences.

[1] S. Fajans, Erfolg, Ausdauer und Aktivität beim Säugling und Kleinkind, *Psychol. Forsch.*, 1933, **17**, 268–305.

[2] A. Karsten, *op. cit.*

Fajans[1] has shown that, other things being equal, the strength of a valence increases with its apparent proximity, at least in certain cases. This is expressed by both the duration and the intensity of the efforts toward the goal. (In these experiments actual attainment of the goal was impossible.)

In a group of babies approximately ten months old, for example, the average total duration of approaches in the first three minutes at distances of 9, 40, and 100 cm. was respectively 75, 39, and 27 sec. In a group of three-year-olds the average total duration of approaches in the "near" experiment was 58 sec., in the "far" experiment 28 sec.

The activity, as well as the duration of approaches, increases with the degree of proximity of the valence. The reason for this is different for younger and for older children.

Again one may not, to be sure, simply assume that psychological distance corresponds to physical distance. In the first place, a difference in apparent distance is significant only within a rather narrowly limited range, in accordance with the smallness of the child's life-space; and this range, as the work of Fajans shows, is considerably smaller for the one-year-old than for the three-year-old child. Just as visual extent in perceptual space (e.g., with reference to the law of apparent size) increases with age,[2] so the life-space of the child increases and differentiates in dynamic respects. Difference in distance cannot be purely physically defined also because the range in which the child almost gets the desired object has qualitatively a special character. This "almost" situation has an especially marked significance, for example, with reference to experiences of success and failure, and cannot be reckoned simply as a smaller distance (see page 88).

An obvious discrepancy between spatial and psychological distance was observed in a group of four-year-old children who experienced the situation less as an objective task than as a social relationship with the experimenter. They were

[1] S. FAJANS, Die Bedeutung der Entfernung für die Stärke eines Aufforderungscharakters beim Säugling und Kleinkind, *Psychol. Forsch.*, 1933, **17**, 213–267.
[2] E. LAU, *op. cit.*

simply faced by an adult who would not give them a doll. For these children the kind and duration of approach remained independent of the distance of the valence. Indeed, for the social route to the valence (by way of the experimenter), the psychological distance is the same in any case.

With older children the intellectual appreciation of the functional and particularly the sociological relations (perhaps of their dependence upon the might of other children and of adults) is so far developed that physical distance usually plays a much smaller part in such situations.[1]

Weiss found in her Fraenkel experiments (see page 75) with rather uninhibited five-year-old children that the distance of the toys on the table was no longer important to the choice made; the child fetches what he wants. To be sure, when inhibitions are present, the distance again plays a considerable role, even with older children.

With increasing age temporally distant events also acquire increasing significance. To the psychological situation belong not only those facts that are actually perceptible and objectively present, but also a range of past and future events. A censure or a commendation may long remain a present psychological fact for the child, and an expected event may have psychological reality in advance of its occurrence.

As an example of the increase in the strength of the valence with temporal proximity, it may be pointed out that, among the inmates of homes for delinquent children, reform schools, and similar institutions, it is not infrequently observed that they become especially difficult just before their discharge. We noted this paradoxical behavior, so sharply opposed to their own interests,[2] especially in previously well-behaved individuals. The essential reason was found to be the following: Even for the youth who is at first well behaved in the home (H) the wish for freedom (F) is an important motive of his

[1] Of course, where very strong valences are concerned or very fundamental needs, primitive physical distance usually plays a considerable role, even with adults.

[2] It not infrequently happens that the prospective discharge is thereupon revoked.

behavior. At first this freedom is a distant half-imaginary goal, and, most important, good conduct in the home is the way that shall ultimately lead him there. Now that his discharge is approaching, the longed-for, but until now uncertain, world of freedom is just ahead (Fig. 6). The boundary of the home thereby acquires in much greater degree the character of a marked barrier (B) which separates the youth from his almost-

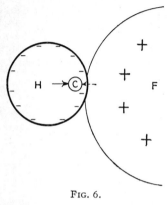

FIG. 6.

attained goal. Hence the home acquires a pronounced negative valence. Emotional and rebellious actions are further facilitated by the very high *state of tension* (see page 95) and by the fact that the youth already feels half free.[1] In a topologically similar experimental situation with infants an increase of affectivity occurred in 85 per cent of the cases when the field forces in the direction of the goal behind the barrier were strengthened and the general state of tension thereby raised.[2] In many cases the impatience of children can be explained by a similar structure of the environment.

The experiments of Fajans show that the restraining forces corresponding to the barrier increase when the strength of the valence behind the barrier is increased (see page 90).

Constellations of Forces. Conflict.

The ways in which different valences may interact in a situation are naturally very numerous. I select for discussion the case of conflict because of its special significance.

Conflict is defined psychologically as the opposition of approximately equally strong field forces. There are three basic cases of conflict, so far as driving forces are concerned.

---

[1] It has happened that a prisoner sentenced to three years tried to escape within a week of his discharge.

[2] S. FAJANS, Erfolg, Ausdauer und Aktivität, beim Säugling und Kleinkind.

1. The child stands between two positive valences (Fig. 7). He has to choose perhaps between going on a picnic (*P*) and playing (*Pl*) with his comrades. In this type of conflict situation decision is usually relatively easy. As a result of the fact that after the choice is made the goal chosen often seems inferior (for reasons to be described later), oscillation does sometimes occur.

2. The child faces something that has simultaneously both a positive and a negative valence (Fig. 8). He wants, for

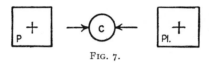

FIG. 7.

example, to climb a tree (*Tr*), but is afraid. This constellation of forces plays an important part in cases in which a reward is offered for an activity (*e.g.*, a school task) which the child does not want to execute.[1]

Conflict situations of this type usually develop rather quickly also in the detour experiments mentioned above, in the experiments of Fajans, or in other situations in which the attainment of the goal is impeded by some barrier. At first

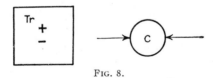

FIG. 8.

the child sees a difficult barrier (*B*) between himself and his goal (*G*), which hinders the completion of actions in the direction of the field forces (Fig. 9). But after the child has run against the barrier several times and perhaps hurt himself, or had the wounding experience of failure, the barrier itself acquires a negative valence (Fig. 10). Beside the positive, there comes into existence a negative vector, and we have the Type 2

[1] For these and the following remarks, see Chap. IV, below.

conflict situation. The negative vector usually increases gradually in strength and finally becomes stronger than the positive. Accordingly, the child *goes out of the field*.

This withdrawal [*Aus-dem-Felde-Gehen*] either may be physical, as when the child retreats, turns away, or possibly leaves the room or place, or may be an *inward* going out of the field, as when the child begins to play or to occupy himself with something else.

It not infrequently occurs, for example in embarrassment, that the child makes certain bodily movements toward the goal but at the same time is mentally occupied with something else. In such cases the bodily act has the character of a more or less set gesture.[1]

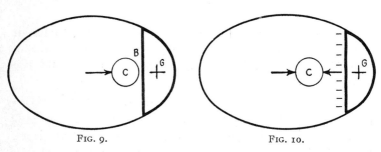

FIG. 9.   FIG. 10.

In such situations the withdrawal is at first almost always merely temporary. The child turns away, only to return after a while for another try at the barrier.[2] A final and permanent withdrawal usually occurs only after several temporary withdrawals, the duration of which increases until finally the child does not return.

Unusual persistence in such a situation is not necessarily an indication of activity. On the contrary, active children usually go out of the field earlier than passive children. It is not the duration but the kind of approach that is significant for activity.[3]

[1] LEWIN, Kindlicher Ausdruck, *Zeitschr. f. päd. Psychol.*, 1927, **28**, 510–526; S. FAJANS, Erfolg, Ausdauer und Aktivität beim Säugling und Kleinkind.

[2] S. FAJANS, *ibid.*

[3] *Ibid.*

Related to this is the fact that under certain circumstances the single actions in such a conflict situation are longer with the infant than with the young child,[1] although in general the duration of action unities increases with the age of the child.[2]

3. The third type of conflict situation occurs when the child stands between two negative valences, for example, when it is sought by threat of punishment (*P*) to move a child to do à task (*T*) he does not want to do (Fig. 11).

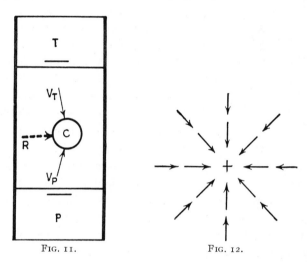

FIG. 11.   FIG. 12.

There is an essential difference between this and the conflict situation described under 1. This becomes clear when one proceeds to represent the total distribution of forces in the field of force.

Field of Force. The field of force indicates which force would exist at each point in the field if the individual involved were at that point. To a positive valence there corresponds a convergent field (Fig. 12).

As a simple example of the structure of the field of force in a conflict situation of Type 2, a case from one of my films

[1] A. HOMBURGER, *op. cit.*
[2] C. BÜHLER, *op. cit.*

may be adduced: a three-year-old boy wants to fetch a rubber swan out of the water to the beach, but is afraid of the water. To the swan (S) as positive valence there corresponds a convergent field (Fig. 13). This field is overlaid by a second field which corresponds to the negative valence of the waves. It is important that here, as frequently in such cases, the

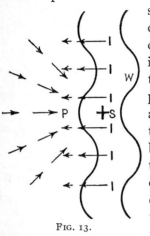

FIG. 13.

strength of the field forces which correspond to the negative valence diminishes much more rapidly with increasing spatial distance than do the field forces corresponding to the positive valence. From the direction and strength of the field forces at the various points of the field it can be deduced that the child must move to the point P where equilibrium occurs. (At all other points there exists a resultant which finally leads to P.) Corresponding to the momentary oscillations of the situation, above all to the more or less threatening aspect of the waves, this point of equilibrium approaches and retreats from the water. Indeed, this oscillation is reflected in the child's approaches to and retreats from the water.

If we return now to Type 3 of the conflict situation and compare it with Type 1, the chief difference is shown in Figs. 14 and 15: in both cases two central fields overlap. But while in Type 1 a stable equilibrium exists at the point P (Fig. 14) so far as sidewise movements (on line S) are concerned, in Type 3 this equilibrium is labile (Fig. 15). That is, there exists in the case of threat of punishment (Fig. 11) a situation which evokes a tendency to break out toward the side, in accordance with the strong sidewise resultant (R) of the two vectors (V_p and V_t). Consequently the child always goes out of the field unless other circumstances prevent it. Hence, if the threat of punishment is to be effective, the child must be so inclosed by a barrier (B) that escape is possible only by way of the punishment or by way of doing the disagreeable task.[1] That is, in addition to requiring the execution of the task, it is necessary to limit the child's freedom of movement,

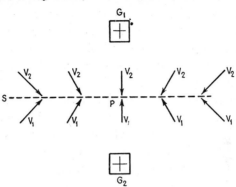

Fig. 14.—(*From K. Lewin, Vectors, Cognitive Processes, and Mr. Tolman's Criticism, Jour. General Psychol.*, 1933, **8**, 323.)
→Driving force corresponding to goal (*G*).
....line of equilibrium.

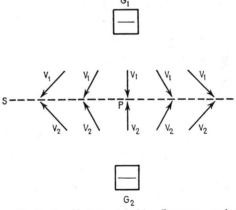

Fig. 15.—(*From K. Lewin, Vectors, Cognitive Processes, and Mr. Tolman's Criticism, Jour. General Psychol.*, 1933, **8**, 323.)
→Driving force corresponding to goal (*G*).
....line of equilibrium.

thus creating (by physical or social means) a more cr less constrained situation.

[1] The barrier may derive its firmness psychologically from the power of the adult, from the child's sense of honor, or from some other such factor (see Chap. IV, below).

With the young child, the opposition of two approximately equal field forces in the conflict situation leads typically (so far as it is not an unstable equilibrium) to a relatively rapid alternation of actions in the direction of each of the two field forces in turn. It is a characteristic indication of greater self-control when, instead of this oscillation of action, the child displays a relatively calm type of behavior while the conflict remains unresolved.[1]

Ability to endure such unresolved conflict situations is an important aim of the education of the will. Of course, the occurrence of such conflict situations presupposes that the two opposed field forces are of approximately equal strength. If threats of punishment, pressure from the adult, or other restrictions leave the child little enough freedom, no real conflict situation can develop.

If a situation becomes *hopeless*, that is, if it becomes as a whole inescapably disagreeable, the child, despairing, *contracts*, physically and psychically, under the vectors coming from all sides and usually attempts to build a wall between himself and the situation. This is expressed both in the typical bodily gestures of despair (crumpling up, covering the eyes with the arms,[2] etc.; see Fig. 16) and by a sort of encysting (Fig. 17) of the self: the child becomes obdurate.

State of Tension.

The opposition of the two field forces in a conflict situation leads indirectly, as may be deduced in detail, to an increase in the total state of tension[3] of the child, especially when there is an outer barrier. (See the constrained situation with threat of punishment in Fig. 11.)

---

[1] The principle that self-control is not a consequence but a condition of obedience finds a theoretical justification in these considerations: see M. MONTESSORI, *Selbsttätige Erziehung im frühen Kindesalter* (trans. by O. Knapp), Hoffman, Stuttgart, 1913.

[2] See Lewin: appendix to W. STERN, *op. cit.* The experiments of Fajans also show how in cases of great embarrassment the field forces drive the child, on the one hand, to turn away, to forget, to go (bodily or psychically) out of the field, or, on the other hand, to increased passivity.

[3] Tension is defined as the opposition of field forces in every direction.

Especially with children, in whom the psychological delimitation between self and environment is still slight (see page 106), any increase in environmental tension is usually immediately reflected. This sensitivity may be seen in the fact that a tearful or a cheerful mood in the environment, travel preparations, the mother's bad humor, or any other excitement usually transfers to the child even when every effort is made to conceal the circumstances from him.

In the simplest case, an increase in the general state of tension is expressed by restless behavior [*Unruhehandlungen*]. Restless behavior is a diffuse, undirected discharge of tension which, in conjunction with the directed forces of the particular

Fig. 16.

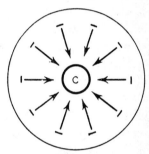

Fig. 17.

situation, may culminate in affective outbursts, such as fits of rage.[1]

The basic case of restless behavior is unambiguously clear in the infant and has very similar forms in pleasant and in unpleasant expectancy. If one holds out a rattle or nursing bottle near the baby (the psychological situation corresponds to that shown in Fig. 2), he stretches with arms, legs, and mouth in the direction of the valence. He does not remain calmly in this position, however, but begins to wave his arms and legs about.

With somewhat older children the least intense form of restless behavior, corresponding to an increase in the general state of tension, is a rapid change of occupation. An example:

[1] T. DEMBO, Der Ärger als dynamisches Problem, *Psychol. Forsch.*, 1931, **15,** 1-144.

a three-year-old child in a Montessori kindergarten was very fond of drawing, but one day the director was unable to supply the requisite paper.   Thereupon there occurred a number of varieties of *substitute behavior;* the child caressed the pencils, watched the drawing of older children, etc.   Finally the child took up other occupations, but the average time he stayed with them was only 3.5 min. as against 14.6 min. on the preceding and 12.3 min. on the following day.   The increased tension resulting from the impassable barrier between the child and his goal had thus produced a fourfold increase in the frequency of his changes of occupation.

Ucko has demonstrated an analogous increase in frequency of change with older children in an experimental investigation of similar situations.[1]   In addition, the increase in tension made the occupation more superficial.

Although marked restless behavior is essentially a diffuse discharge, its *form* depends upon the topology of the particular situation.   For example, if the restless behavior is produced by the fact that there is a barrier between the child and the positive valence, the restless movements occur so that so far as possible there is no increase in the child's distance from the positive valence.   In other words, the restless movements occur in the line of equilibrium; that is, when approach is prevented by a barrier, they take a direction perpendicular to that of the field vector.

In the case of the child who has difficulty in sitting down on a stone (Fig. 5) this may lead to circling the stone.   If a sufficiently strong positive valence is enclosed by a circular fence (F, Fig. 18), the restless behavior (R) (apart from actions in the direction of the valence) may take the form of circling the barrier.[2]   If, on the other hand, the child is inside and the valence outside the circular barrier, the typical behavior is a very slight oscillation along the side toward the valence (Fig. 19).

---

[1] In these experiments the tension was produced by interrupting the child in his favorite occupation.

[2] K. LEWIN, Die Auswirkung von Umweltkräften, *Proc. 9th Int. Cong. Psychol.*, 1929, 286–288.

Induced Valences

As already mentioned, the valences correspond in part directly to the momentary needs of the child. A positive or negative valence may, however, be induced in an object or event by other environmental factors. This fact is of special importance in children.

Social Fields.

It is a fundamental fact of childhood that the child's environment is not subject to his own control. The child faces a

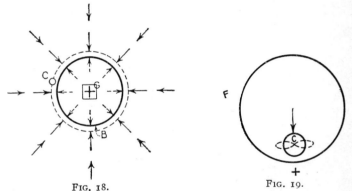

FIG. 18.   FIG. 19.

FIG. 18.—(*From K. Lewin, Vectors, Cognitive Processes, and Mr. Tolman's Criticism, Jour. General Psychol., 1933, 8, 323.*)
    →Driving force corresponding to goal (*G*).
    ⇢Restraining force corresponding to barrier (*B*).
    ....line of equilibrium.

host of demands and difficulties. Difficulties arise from physical facts of the environment and the limitations of the child's own abilities: an object that he wants to lift proves to be too heavy, a staircase down which he wants to crawl too steep, or the pencil does not go over the paper as it should. Still more important are social factors, especially the authority or power of adults and of other children.

In the life of the neonate these social powers are first effective as sheer physical mastery (the child is bathed, dried, made to drink, etc.). But very soon their influence upon the child's psychological environment acquires increasing significance.

The adult forbids or permits the handling of certain objects, characterizes behavior as good or bad, praises and blames.

For the infant of a few weeks or months the valences depend essentially upon his own needs and their momentary condition. If he does not want a food he cannot be moved by psychological means to eat it.[1] He simply spits it out. With the older child the possibility of influencing him by psychological means is disproportionately greater. The disagreeable act may be imbedded in a game or in another action unity, and its meaning (and hence its valence) thereby radically changed.

The possibility of direct influence is correlated with the increasing psychological reality for the child of social facts,

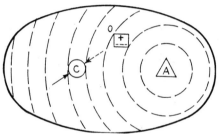

Fig. 20.— → Induced force.

especially of the powers of others.[2] Many objects in the environment, many modes of conduct, and many goals acquire a positive or a negative valence or the properties of a barrier, not directly from the needs of the child himself, but through another person. This induction may be brought about by an expressed prohibition or command. More important, however, is the effect of example, that is, of that which the child sees characterized by the behavior of adults as positive or negative for them. Even the very young child usually has a very fine sensitivity to social evaluations and forces.

The negative valence of a forbidden object (*O*, Fig. 20) which in itself attracts the child thus usually derives from an

---

[1] Apart from simple distraction.

[2] Dynamically considered, these spheres of influence constitute fields of force for the child.

inducing field of force of an adult (A). If this field of force loses its psychological existence for the child (*e.g.*, if the adult goes away or loses his authority) the negative valence also disappears.

In addition to the sphere of power of the adult, the behavior and spheres of power of other children or of a group of children are of critical importance for the kind and strength of induced valences.

The strength and extent of the fields of force of other people in the child's environment vary greatly, depending especially upon the economic situation, the character of the parents, the number, sex, and kind of children in the family and among friends.

As a rule, the domain in which the child's environment is "free" (*i.e.*, essentially, dependent only on his *own* sphere of power) is relatively small. Too strong or too extensive alien spheres of power may lead to a real oppression of the child or to a particularly violent revolt. This is equally true in cases of too great strictness and of too great fondness. In either case the child has not enough life-space in which the valences and other dynamic properties of his psychological environment may be determined by his own needs. Wiehe,[1] in an experimental investigation of the effect of a strange room or a strange person, distinguishes various degrees of strength of such a field, which degrees can be correlated quantitatively with distinct kinds of behavior, among others with the different kinds and degrees of approaches to and withdrawals from a strange person. The degree of strength of such a social field of force is, excluding the individuality of the child and of the stranger, a function of the spatial distance of the strange person, the duration of his presence, and his behavior. The strongest degree of pressure is expressed by the child's becoming motionless; a somewhat weaker, in his crying and showing a tendency to run away, where possible, to the neighborhood of the mother or to another field in which he feels at home. In the other actions of the child also a very strong pressure of strangeness [*Fremdheitsdruck*]

[1] F. WIEHE, *op. cit.*

evokes inhibited, a somewhat weaker pressure overexcited or overemphasized, behavior. Only a further reduction of the pressure leads to a natural free behavior (see Chap. VIII, Fig. 9, page 261).

As an example of the effect of alien fields of force upon the child, let us consider the significance of the level of the external demands made upon him. Experiences of success and failure have, as Adler correctly emphasizes, an extremely marked effect upon the child's encouragement and discouragement, and hence upon his later performance. In experiments on success and failure with three- to four-year-old children Fajans found the following: if one distinguishes four grades of activity (from very active to very passive), the child's activity on the same act may be reduced three grades by failure.[1] On the other hand, the activity of passive children could be increased by about the same amount. The effect upon the general self-consciousness is also considerable.

Hoppe[2] has shown that the occurrence of success and failure experiences depends upon the momentary "level of aspiration" [*Anspruchsniveau*], and that this level of aspiration is in turn related to the ability of the individual: with "quite too hard" and "quite too easy" tasks no experience of success or failure occurs. The child, for example, has no essential experience of failure when it cannot do something that only adults or much older children can do. Nevertheless, the level of aspiration is by no means determined *solely* by the ability of the individual. On the contrary, a level of aspiration decidedly above (or below) the child's real ability may be produced by the demands of adults or by the performances of comrades. For this reason there may develop a feeling of inferiority (or of superiority) which may be severely prejudicial to the child's general conduct and actual achievements.

---

[1] This holds chiefly for repetition of the same act within a certain interval of time. Adams (D. K. Adams, Experimental Studies of Adaptive Behavior in Cats, *Comp. Psychol. Monog.*, 1929, **6**, No. 26, pp. 41, 47, 92, etc.) has reported marked reduction in the duration of activity with failure of cats in puzzle boxes.

[2] F. Hoppe, Erfolg und Misserfolg, *Psychol. Forsch.*, 1930, **14**, 1–62.

Fajans found that the effects of failure could be materially reduced by a verbal consolation of the child (Fig. 21). Here again the significance of the social field for the consciousness of self is evident. The offer of a substitute satisfaction [*Ersatz-befriedigung*] is even more effective than such consolation.

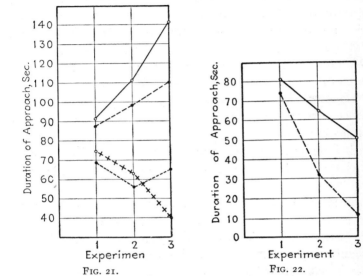

FIG. 21. FIG. 22.

FIG. 21.—Comparison of the effects of success, encouragement, substitution, and failure upon the duration of approach [*Zuwendungsdauer*].
———— Success with concomitant encouragement. Increase in duration of approach from first to third experiment [*Versuch*] = 48 per cent
.... Success. Increase in duration of approach = 25 per cent
. . . . . Substitute success. Diminution in duration of approach = 6 per cent
.... Failure. Diminution in duration of approach = 48 per cent
FIG. 22.—Effect of success (————) and failure (...................) upon the infant.

Even for children of from six to nine months, success or failure changes the degree of activity and the duration of action toward the goal. But at this age the repetition itself, after a success, leads to a diminution in the duration of actions toward the goal (Fig. 22).

Jucknat,[1] in an experimental investigation of some hundreds of school children, found that success and failure in one region may, under certain circumstances, change the level of aspiration

[1] JUCKNAT, Leistung und Anspruchsniveau. (In preparation.)

in other regions: namely, when the two regions have sufficient dynamic connection and when the child's goal level in the region concerned is not too firmly fixed.

Means and Substitutes.

An object or event possessing special emphasis may also, like a social field, induce an effect upon the environment.

A strongly accented goal so transforms the situation that practically all objects acquire a reference to this goal.[1] A building block that has just been a locomotive for the child becomes a hammer when he desires to drive a stick into a hole. An object that becomes a *tool* may thus possess a derived valence. In the same way a bench may have the properties of a *barrier* in front of one goal or of a *means* to another, perhaps to climbing on the table.[2] Other environmental facts acquire the character of either a means to the goal or a barrier from it.

Another effect of the general directedness of the environment upon a chief goal is the occurrence in certain cases of substitute goals [*Erastzziele*].[3] Substitution plays a large role in children, probably larger than in adults. A child that would like to stroke a dog, but is afraid to, may stroke instead the child holding the dog.[4] The adult usually employs the possibility of satisfying the child with a substitute, of diverting his wishes to a substitute goal, in the most various ways. As a rule, such a procedure creates less friction than a prohibition of the desired act. A different consequence of a prohibition (by reason of certain total structures which cannot here be discussed) is an implicit or overt counterreaction, the so-called negative behavior of the child, which is the more fundamental in that the

---

[1] This is not merely an extension of an agreeable character to a larger field. On the contrary, quite different, both positive and negative valences and other kinds of shifts may be induced in surrounding objects by a positive valence.

[2] T. DEMBO, *op. cit.*; W. KÖHLER, *The Mentality of Apes*.

[3] We are not here concerned with the theory of substitution which plays an especially important part in Freudian theory, except as it touches the question of *environmental* forces. See T. Dembo, *op. cit.*

[4] LEWIN, K., *Die Entwicklung der experimentellen Willenpsychologie und die Psychotherapie*, Hirzel, Leipzig, 1929.

whole psychological emphasis of the desired act is considerably enhanced by the adult's prohibition.[1]

Such processes are very often significant in pretending or play-acting behavior. A child would like to strike another child but contents himself with a threat; he would like to throw a ball very high and makes an exaggerated gesture.

With certain children, those Lazar has called "gesture children," the tendency to substitute a mere gesture for a real performance or a serious action is so strong as to constitute an essential character trait.

For children in general, the serious and the playful, reality and make-believe are much more fluid, less sharply distinct than for adults. This fact is related to a property of the psychological environment which we must discuss briefly.

STRATA OF REALITY IN THE ENVIRONMENT

The psychological environment of the adult shows a rather marked differentiation into strata of various degrees of reality. The plane of reality may be characterized briefly as the plane of "facts" to which an *existence independent of the individual's own wishes* is ascribed. It is the realm of realistic behavior, of insuperable difficulties, etc.

The more unreal planes are those of hopes and dreams, often of ideology. A stratum of greater unreality is dynamically characterized as a more fluid medium.[2] Limits and barriers in such a stratum are less firm. The boundary between the self and the environment is also more fluid. In a plane of unreality "one can do what he pleases."[3]

A complete description of the psychological environment must always set forth the structure not only of the level of reality but also of the levels of unreality. If conditions on the plane of reality become too disagreeable for any reason, for example, as a result of too high tension, there arises a strong

---

[1] It is possible that the proposition that "action and reaction are equal" holds also for psychological dynamics.

[2] J. F. BROWN, Über die dynamischen Eigenschaften der Realitäts- und Irrealitätsschichten, *Psychol. Forsch.*, 1933, **18**, 1–26.

[3] T. DEMBO, *op. cit.*

tendency to go out of the level of reality into one of unreality (flight into dream, into phantasy,[1] or even into illness).

These facts hold in principle equally for the adult and for the child. Nevertheless, it is characteristic of the child's psychological environment (a) that the differentiation of various degrees of reality is much less marked and (b) that transitions between the levels of reality and unreality occur much more easily than in adults.

The psychological environment of the small child can be characterized neither as a real nor as an unreal world, but the two strata are still relatively undifferentiated. Jaensch[2] and his students have shown for sensory psychology that the eidetic images [Anschauungsbilder] of children have the properties still undifferentiated of both the perceptions and the imaginings of adults. Piaget[3] has shown that the child's conception of the world, especially his ideas of causation, is still essentially "magical" and "animistic," that name and thing, act and magic word, are not yet clearly separated.[4]

These properties of the child's perceptions and intellectual view of the world are only an expression of the general fact that in the child's psychological environment the differentiation between the levels of reality and unreality is still slight. This fact is further displayed in the peculiar seriousness of the child's play. From it derives the relative lack of distinction between wish and reality that is expressed, for example, in the very tenuous distinction between "falsehood" and "truth."[5] The great "suggestibility" of children is related to the same fact. For not only are the child's psychical processes closely depend-

---

[1] See below, pp. 145ff.

[2] E. JAENSCH, Über den Aufbau der Wahrnehmungswelt und die Grundlagen der menschlichen Erkenntnis, Barth, Leipzig, 1927.

[3] J. PIAGET, La causalité physique chez l'enfant, Paris, Alcan, 1927. The Child's Conception of Physical Causality (trans. by M. Gabain), Harcourt, Brace, New York, Kegan Paul, London, 1930.

[4] See also D. KATZ and R. KATZ. Gespräche mit Kindern. Untersuchungen zur Sozialpsychologie und Pädagogik, Springer, Berlin, 1928.

[5] C. STERN and W. STERN, Errinnerung, Aussage und Lüge in der ersten Kindheit. (Monog. ü. d. seel. Entwick. d. Kindes, Vol. 2), Barth, Leipzig, 1910.

ent upon his present physical condition (*e.g.*, illness), but, which is more often overlooked, the reverse also holds. Bodily condition may be very greatly influenced—especially in children—by the psychological. Thus it is that a small child's pain ceases when one blows on the spot and that the horse may be "gone" when someone "throws him out the window."

The relatively slight differentiation between strata of reality and of unreality may still be noted in puberty: sometimes beside the real life a second life of phantasy is led for years, the events of which have the greatest significance for the child. Even for adolescents ideologies still in general possess much more real forces than for adults.

It would, of course, be false to believe that a differentiation between real and unreal strata is completely lacking in the child.[1] This is primarily true in the field of his real needs, both somatic and psychological. Even though the child may, under certain circumstances, be satisfied with an imaginary sweet instead of a real one or treat a piece of wood better than a real doll, there are still very early indications of differentiation, at least in many respects, between reality and unreality.

Sliosberg[2] found that such an unreal object is accepted as a substitute only when the child is in a play situation.

Play.

The following circumstances constitute in my opinion the foundation for a dynamic theory of play: whether a given behavior (*e.g.*, game *X* in the sand box) is to be characterized as playful or nonplayful cannot be determined from the standpoint of the adult but solely in terms of the child's own lifespace. The fundamental dynamic property of play is that it has to do with events which belong in one respect to the level of reality, namely, in so far as they are activities visible also to other persons (*e.g.*, as against daydreams). But at the same

---

[1] Piaget's thesis may have to be limited even for the child's intellectual concept-world (see I. HUANG, Children's Explanations of Strange Phenomena, *Psychol. Forsch.*, 1930, **14,** 63–182; K. BÜHLER, *op. cit.*)

[2] S. SLIOSBERG, Zur Dynamik des Ersatzes in Spiel- und Ernstsituationen. *Psychol. Forsch.*, 1934, **19,** 122–181.

time play behavior is much less bound by the laws of reality than is nonplay behavior: both the goal setting and the execution are in much greater degree subject to the pleasure of the person.   This dynamic fluidity, in respect of which the play field approximates the dynamics of unreality, is evident, among other ways, in the changeableness of the meaning of things and of the child's own person (playing roles), which goes far beyond what is possible in the level of reality.   The play field is hence a region more or less limited as regards reality which shows even in its content a most immediate relation to the unreality of air castles and wish ideals.[1]

The various games may be differentiated according to their dynamic fluidity.   They vary rather considerably in the degree of their dynamic fluidity, and the "rules of the game" may be so strict that the game may, dynamically, approach the rigidity of reality.

A strong tendency to go out of reality into unreality occurs, especially when an overstrong pressure dominates the former.

The course of differentiation depends not only upon the individual characteristics of the child, but also in essential ways upon the situation and lot of the particular child.   Among proletarian children this stratification usually develops earlier.[2] An early and sharp separation of reality and unreality seems to be unfavorable to the child's development.   Important as a sufficiently clear separation of these planes is, the kind of relation obtaining between them remains decisive of, among other things, all creative behavior and determines whether the ideal goals, which belong dynamically to the level of unreality, more or less directly condition behavior in the plane of reality.

Boundaries of the Self

Closely related to the slighter differentiation of the child's psychological environment into real and less real or unreal planes is a second factor: for the child, the boundary between the

---

[1] See below, Chap. IV.

[2] H. HETZER, Kindheit und Armut, *Psychol. d. Fürsorge*, **1**, Hirzel, Leipzig, 1929.

self and the environment is less defined than for the adult. This circumstance is of critical significance to the operation of the environment upon the child.

The individual is dynamically a relatively closed system. How strongly the environment operates upon the individual will therefore be determined (apart from the structure and forces of the situation) by the functional *firmness of the boundaries* between individual and environment. The internal structure of the *child* individual is characterized dynamically by a relatively slight differentiation among the psychological regions [*Bereiche*] and by slight functional firmness in the boundaries of the various psychological systems.[1]

In other words, the child, to a greater extent than the adult, is a dynamic unity.[2] The infant, for example, acts first with its whole body and only gradually acquires the ability to execute part actions.[3] The child learns only gradually to separate voluntarily certain parts of its environment, to concentrate.

Analogously to this relatively slight delimitation among the various inner psychological systems, the functional firmness of the boundary between his own person and the psychological environment is also in general less with the child than with the adult. This is expressed, for example, by the fact that the "I" or self is only gradually formed, perhaps in the second or third year. Not until then does the concept of property appear, of the belonging of a thing to his own person.[4] The same relative indistinctness of the limits of the self is apparent in the fact that external impressions touch the central nucleus of the child's personality decidedly more readily than is the case with adults. Conversely, needs or other tensions of the inner

[1] This is not the place for a more comprehensive discussion of the internal structure of the personality.

[2] A "strong Gestalt" in Köhler's sense (see W. Köhler, *Gestalt Psychology*.)

[3] Coghill's (*Anatomy and the Problem of Behavior*, Macmillan, New York, Cambridge Univ. Press, Cambridge, 1929; Individuation versus Integration in the Development of Behavior, *Jour. Gen. Psychol.*, 1930, **3**, 431–435) important researches have shown that in embryological development even the reflexes are formed by a gradual differentiation of reactions which originally involved the whole organism. See also Lewin, Kindlicher Ausdruck.

[4] W. Stern, *op. cit.*

psychological systems burst through very easily in the form of impulsive behavior and uncontrolled affective demonstrations (see the examples on pages 94 and 95).

The slighter firmness of the boundary between self and environment has a direct bearing upon the slighter separation of real from unreal strata (see page 103). For it (the former) implies that the psychological environment of the child is more intimately connected with and responsive to his momentary needs and wishes.

The functional firmness of the limiting layer between the child and the environment varies greatly, even in the same child, in different situations and toward different persons. This is equally true of the child's receptivity or inaccessibility toward external impressions, and of the ease with which internal states, especially tensions, come to expression.

It has been found in the course of psychopathological investigations that in certain circumstances children are more readily induced to talk openly of personal matters when they are naked.[1] Children also are usually inclined to talk more freely about experiences otherwise kept back when they are going to bed in the evening.[2]

The functional firmness of the wall between the self and the environment depends not only upon the age but also upon the individual characteristics of the person. It is especially slight among certain psychopathic children.[3] The cause of this may be a greater fluidity and at the same time a slight (relative to chronological age) degree of differentiation of the

---

[1] James has emphasized the close relation between clothing and the psychological person as a social being. It is hence (and on other grounds) understandable that under certain circumstances nakedness diminishes the firmness of the psychological wall between child and environment.

[2] Cf. D. KATZ and R. KATZ, *op. cit.* The greater frankness of children shortly before going to sleep may be related to a beginning of the partial dissolution of the boundary between reality and unreality that is characteristic of sleep and dreaming. (See also G. H. GREEN, *The Daydream. A study of development*, Univ. London Press, London, 1923.)

[3] LEWIN, Filmaufnahmen über Trieb- und Affektäusserungen psychopathischer Kinder (verglichen mit Normalen und Schwachsinnigen), *Zeitschr. f. Kinderforsch.*, 1926, **32**, 414–447.

person. This fluidity is also apparent in the dynamics of the environment, so far as the latter is psychologically determined. Feeble-minded children are also characterized by a relatively slight degree of differentiation of the person (see Chap. VII, page 194).

As distinguished from the above described psychopathic children, certain types at least of the feeble-minded are characterized by a slight fluidity of the psychical systems. This inflexibility leads to an "either-or" behavior that is evident in a sphere of the psychology of the will in an especially strong fixation of certain valences and modes of behavior (stubborness, pedantry). The immobility of the psychological systems and of the psychological structure of the environment is at the same time a decisive dynamic cause for the difficulties of these children in intellectual fields.

Even when a marked separation of the self from the environment has already occurred there may exist a particular dynamic union between the self and other persons, for example, the mother of some friend. This union may be expressed in various ways, among others by the child's behaving worse with the mother than with other people, by outspoken protest against even a temporary absence of the mother, by turning to the mother—"hiding behind her skirts"—in any disagreeable situation. In such cases the presence or absence of the mother changes the total structure of the psychological environment essentially, especially the child's feeling of security or insecurity. As a consequence of the close psychological relationship between the mother and the child's own person, the real abilities of the mother, her effectiveness as against the things and persons of the environment, have for the child the functional significance of an extension of his own security and power against the environment. A departure of the mother thus means to the child a weakening of his strength against the environment.[1]

The animistic character of the child's view of the world may also be related to the fact that his psychological environ-

[1] The tendency of children to take a doll or some favorite toy along to bed is another expression of the close union of these objects with the self.

ment generally has *personal* fields of force as prominent dynamic features of its structure.

Not only other persons but other objects may have a close psychological relation with the self of the child. To the "I" in this sense there belong not only the child's own body but certain toys, a particular chair, etc. Such objects are dynamically somewhat like his own body in that they represent points of special sensitivity to invasions by environmental forces. Whether an object belongs to the self or to the outside world depends, according to Wiehe,[1] among other things upon the present needs and internal tension systems of the child and changes with them. It happens, for example, that the destruction of an incomplete production of the child, in consequence of its belonging to the self, is felt by him as a violent invasion; while destruction some time after completion of the task leaves him quite unaffected. An internal discharge of tension is usually accompanied by a loosening of the appurtenances of the self, and this is especially marked in children.

The Influence of Environmental Forces on Development

The same factors that are critical for the momentary situation are also characteristic of the *total milieu* of the child over longer periods of his life. Their effects upon the development of the child's personality and his whole behavior are similar to the effects of the forces described in the momentary situation upon his momentary behavior. Particular features of the environment are usually less important than its total character in determining its effect upon development and, more particularly, upon the rate and mode of differentiation of the child's personality. Overly harsh or severe surroundings may lead to the child's encapsulating or insulating himself from the environment. The child becomes stubborn and negativistic (see pages 94 and 95). Optimal environmental conditions, for example, optimal tension level, vary considerably with different individuals. It is a well-known fact that infants and

[1] F. Wiehe, *op. cit.*

young children who grow up in an institution generally show a slower development in many respects than children who grow up in a family.

It is already clear from the circumstances just discussed what great significance a change of environment may have for the child's development. The so-called difficulties of training are not infrequently related to the particular requirements of the parents, to their characters, and to the way they get along together. These difficulties disappear as soon as the child has been for some time in a suitable environment. To be sure, the difficulties usually begin all over again after a return to the old environment.

Enuresis is not infrequently treated successfully by changing environment.[1] Of course, the improvement is often only temporary. Grisch describes the disappearance of a voluntary dumbness with change of environment.

Up to now we have been describing the effects of the present situation upon development. These effects cease with a change in the situation. Nevertheless, the operation of the environment always produces, as a consequence, a more or less marked change in the individual himself, and thus changes his basis of reaction to all later situations. This influence of the present situation upon future possibilities of conduct, which is particularly significant to development as a process considerably extended in time, is due not only to the child's acquisition of certain intellectual experiences but, above all, to the fact that his whole person is changed in certain specific ways.

This indirect operation of present upon future situations may be expressed in favorable as well as in unfavorable ways. Its importance is especially great in view of a condition which might be termed the *circular causal relation* [*zirkuläre Rück-koppelung*] *between self and environment*. A feeble-minded child, for example, is at a disadvantage among his comrades in two ways. In the first place, he cannot do a task (*e.g.*, corking a bottle, writing with a pencil) even when the con-

[1] J. ZAPPERT, Kritisches über Enuresis nocturnis, *Arch. f. Kinderhk.*, 1926, **79**, 44–69.

ditions are so arranged as to be actually the same for the feeble-minded child and his normal playmate (*e.g.*, when both are gotten to grasp the pencil or cork and bottle in the same way). In practically all cases in practical life, however, there is a second difficulty: when the more intelligent child is given a task, he knows that he must look for the mode of manipulation that involves the least difficulties under the conditions given. The less intelligent child has a narrower field and sees less into the internal relations of the environment. He does not find out, perhaps, that it is most convenient to hold the bottle as near the mouth as possible. More generally, he is less likely to discover the easiest way of solving the problem.

The less intelligent child is thus not only less able, but the actual demands made upon him by apparently the same problem are usually really greater than those made upon the intelligent child. The poorer solution of the weaker child thus usually has the double character of an *inferior performance* of a *more difficult task*.

If, now, the less gifted child experiences a failure, he will, as we have seen, attack subsequent problems less intensely. The increased fear of failure creates, wholly apart from the child's inferior ability, a situation psychologically still more unfavorable. In the new situation the already weaker child will thus fail or give up all the more readily. He stands usually before a (psychologically considered) harder task, and his total situation is, owing to his earlier experiences, more unfavorable.

Quite analogous cumulative series due to this vicious circle may be seen in psychopathic children or in other children that have difficulties in social groups. The overexcitable or socially disagreeable child is not only less competent in his social situation, and thus makes his task harder, but also the other children reject him, drive him to a defensive attitude, etc. The child soon gets himself into a social situation, originating perhaps in some quite trivial conflicts, that would tax the capacities of a child of high social endowment. Similar developments of a circular causal relationship between capacity and environment are basic, for example, to stammering.[1] Conversely, not the least advantage of the gifted child consists in the especially favorable environmental conditions that he usually creates for the future.

I consider it one of the fundamental tasks of pedagogy so to constitute the situation of children in difficulties that the severe injuries usually occasioned by the circular causal relation may be avoided or undone. For here at least lie genuine pedagogical possibilities which do not require changing the child's "abilities."

[1] A. HOMBURGER, *op. cit.*

CHAPTER IV

THE PSYCHOLOGICAL SITUATIONS OF REWARD AND PUNISHMENT

In the following presentation, the problem of reward and punishment will not be discussed in its entire scope. To raise the pedagogical question of the possibility of entirely avoiding reward and punishment is to pass over into the fundamental dialectical problem of authority in education. Consequently, a positive or negative attitude toward a system of pedagogy based on reward and punishment as essential educational principles is less a problem of psychology than of *Weltanschauung*.

In this discussion I intend to limit myself chiefly to a psychological problem, or, from the pedagogical point of view, a technical one: namely, that of *utilizing the prospect of reward or punishment as a means* of bringing about or suppressing certain definite behavior in the child.

Reward and punishment are not to be regarded here as sociological or juridical but as psychological categories. Hence an identical action may be in one case a punishment, in another a reward, according to the total situation in which the child is placed.

The prospect of reward or punishment only arises when the child is required to perform an action, to behave in a certain way, other than that which at the moment he prefers. The child must solve a problem, do a piece of work, or otherwise engage in some activity toward which he is antagonistic, indifferent, or too slightly interested to make the necessary sacrifices. He must solve a problem in arithmetic but does not like to calculate. He is to eat a certain food distasteful to him.

If the activity desired by the educator possesses in itself a sufficient attraction for the child reward and punishment are unnecessary. The child will be prompted by his own needs to move in the desired direction.

Reward or punishment must, therefore, lead the child either to carry out a given command or to respect a given prohibition: to refrain, that is, from carrying out some natural or desired activity.

The situation involving either reward or punishment is then to be contrasted with that in which the behavior of the child is dominated by an original or derived interest in the thing itself.[1]

From a purely psychological point of view the question may be raised as to which is more favorable for the performance of a definite task: interest in the thing itself, or the prospect of reward or punishment. At first sight natural interest might be judged the more favorable on the ground that the need of the child directly provides sufficient psychical energy, which might be lacking in the other situation. It would, however, be hasty to maintain the thesis that greater psychical energy is available in the case of natural interest. Sufficiently strong punishment or a longed-for reward may under certain circumstances bring into play much greater and more persistent forces than would interest in the thing itself.

The attempt to prove the psychological superiority of the "naturalness" of interest in the one situation as against its "artificiality" in the other involves the use of concepts which, to say the least, need much more precise formulation if they are

[1] I restrict myself in discussing the general situation of reward and punishment to those cases in which the child actually experiences the reward as reward, the punishment as punishment. I thus refrain from considering here those cases in which punishment is for any reason desired by the child, as, for instance, where it relieves an unendurable situation, or offers the child the possibility of associating with a particular person, or the like. Again, under reward, I do not consider cases where a child, to his surprise, is rewarded for something that he actually wanted very much to do. The discussion is based, in part, upon our experimental investigations. Cf. F. Hoppe, Erfolg und Misserfolg, *Psychol. Forsch.*, 1930, **14**, 1–62; S. Fajans, Die Wirkung von Erfolg und Misserfolg auf Ausdauer und Aktivität beim Säugling und Kleinkind, *Psychol. Forsch.*, 1933, **17**, 213–267; T. Dembo, Der Ärger als dynamisches Problem, *Psychol. Forsch.*, 1931, **15**, 1–144; and an investigation by Ucko upon the effect of prohibition (in preparation).

to be psychologically unambiguous. Even in those cases in which the child is interested in the thing itself, the interest is probably derived: a natural interest of the child in figures or letters may, for instance, derive in a particular case from an interest in various street-car lines, in house numbers, or in store signs.

And, even though the child is of himself interested in numbers or letters, this interest may be designated as "natural" only with reservations. It has developed from living in a definite metropolitan milieu and is in any case somehow mediate and derived from more original needs. This holds for most instances even though the interest involved is quite lively.

From the above point of view reward and punishment might appear solely an attempt of the pedagogue to bring about intentionally an indirect accentuation of interest when it had not occurred in the child's past. Actually, one frequently finds the opinion held in child and developmental psychology (and not only in reflexology) that with small children the important function of reward and punishment is to bring about associatively the desired emphasis. Such a view would obscure the deep psychological difference between an interest pedagogy and one based on the application of reward and punishment. This confusion, though quite convenient for many educators, would be considered psychologically fatal by others.

To understand the nature and scope of the processes in question, it is necessary to achieve a penetrating insight into the *structure of the concrete psychological situation*. The behavior of a child in response to reward and punishment can be as little derived from isolated stimuli or separate psychological processes as can any other type of behavior—as little, for that matter, as the psychological meaning of any environmental influence. The child's behavior is not sufficiently characterized by being ascribed to a "natural" or derived need. Rather, an understanding of the effect of an environmental interference or of an actual act is possible only when the process concerned is considered in its relation to the whole present concrete situation. Indeed, conceptual derivation of the actual occurrence is possible only through consideration of the relations existing between a specific individual and the particular structure of the present situation.[1]

In work and play, in expression, action, emotion—everywhere the actual occurrence is conditioned by the present structure of the environment. By environment is here meant not only the momentary situation in the narrower sense of the word but also the inclusive psychological life-space ordinarily referred to as milieu. The task of scientifically representing the psychological environment is thus of fundamental significance. It is especially so for the most important problem of psychology, namely, the explanation of psychological dynamics. Nevertheless, there has existed up to the present a great lack of proper tools for the purpose. This discussion, aside from its special theme, may be taken as an elementary example of the application of a method which I regard as an essential step in the fulfillment of this task.

In the following analysis of the situation I shall attempt to develop a precise topological *representation* of its total structure and of those factors most generally important for dynamics. The results will be presented directly, and, trusting in the immediate intelligibility of the terms, I shall not attempt here to justify the designation of certain psychological characteristics of the situation as "barriers," others as "vectors" (forces), or others as "areas."

Herein exists the proper task of research, and here lie great difficulties of representation, however simply they may appear in result. In such topological representation one need not consider separate particulars of the situation in relative isolation, as one is too tempted to do in purely verbal description. Rather the procedure used forces one to start out primarily from the present *total situation* as a unity. For this reason, and on account of the conceptual precision of such

[1] LEWIN, The Conflict between Aristotelian and Galileian Modes of Thought in Contemporary Psychology, Chap. I above; Zwei Grundtypen von Lebensprozessen, *Zeitschr. f. Psychol.*, 1929, **113**, 209 ff.

a means of representation, one must always, in using it, consider a whole range of implicit codetermined consequences.

On the other hand, and for the same reasons, such a repre-sentation permits one in a peculiarly high degree to unify a mass of apparently unrelated or contradictory details and to clarify their mutual relationships. I shall limit myself in the following to a discussion of the main features of the momentary total situation. These provide also the basis for an understanding of the differentiated stratification of many particular cases.

I shall first briefly discuss a few properties of the situation determined by interest in the thing itself, 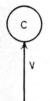and then consider the psychological situation in reward and punishment. There, situations involving a command will be considered first.

This is not the place to consider whether psychology is justified in using the concepts of mathematical topology, a nonmetrical qualitative science of relationships of a very general nature. I should like to emphasize, however, that the problem is not that of representing the physical-geographical, nor yet the objective sociological situation, but rather the structure of the psychological situation, that is, the situation as it exists for the child. I scarcely need to remark that the vectors used in the following representations do not stand for physical forces.

FIG. 1.

THE INTEREST SITUATION

Dynamically considered, the structure of the situation in which a child turns toward an occupation (*e.g.*, playing with a doll) because of interest in the occupation or task itself is relatively simple. The situation is dominated by an attraction, or in our terms, by a positive valence (Fig. 1).[1] The child (*C*) sees a doll. Playing with the doll (*D*) momentarily possesses for the child positive valence. There exists a psychical field force, a vector, proceeding from the child in the direction of the activity of playing with the doll. If this attraction is

---

[1] We shall indicate a positive valence by +, a negative by —. It is important to note that valence may be possessed by any psychological object—a concrete physical object, a social ideal, an activity, a way of acting, a state (sleeping), or any kind of goal.

strong enough relative to the other psychical forces existing in the situation, an action of the child in this direction will occur.

How does the child behave when such action in the direction of the attraction encounters difficulties? How does he act, for instance, when a bench blocks his progress toward the doll, or when an adult's prohibition or the sphere of power of another child hinders his attainment of this goal? Psychologically such a difficulty, be it physical or social, constitutes a barrier

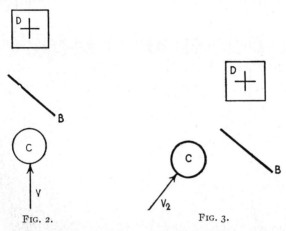

FIG. 2.   FIG. 3.

(*B*, Fig. 2) between the child and the doll. Such a barrier will hinder the activity of the child in the direction of the goal; usually it does not completely stop the child, but acts in such a way as to force him out of the original direction.[1] The child will, perhaps, try to go around the bench, to "get around" the adult, or to borrow the doll from his playmates "at least for a while."

To summarize, occurrences conditioned by interest in the goal itself exhibit the following characteristic dynamic properties. If the child is forced out of its original direction by difficulties (Fig. 3), the direction of the field force also changes

[1] What occurs in a concrete instance depends upon the firmness and form of the barrier, and upon its direction relative to the direction of the field vectors. Above all, it depends upon whether the barrier completely encloses the goal, or leaves open possible avenues of approach.

in accordance with the changed local relations between individual and goal. Further, the change of direction is of such a character that a *vector in the direction of the goal* constantly arises and initiates the corresponding behavior. The behavior thus makes a pronounced goal-seeking impression. A natural teleology reigns.

What is ordinarily designated as teleology and taken as the criterion of the behavior of living beings is in large part nothing other than an expression of the following fact: a positive valence controls the situation in such a way that with changes in the position of the person the direction of the field forces changes in the manner just described.

COMMAND WITH THREAT OF PUNISHMENT

Nature and Disposition of Valences.

In the reward or punishment situation the occupation, or more generally, the behavior required of the child possesses, as mentioned above, not a positive but a negative valence. The child, for example, has no desire to fill a page with the letter "i," or he does not wish to calculate. Thus a vector (V_T) in the sense of a thrust away from the task operates upon the child (Fig. 4).

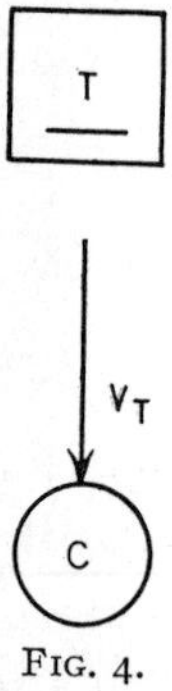

From this circumstance follow several simple but pedagogically important facts. The child shows a tendency, corresponding to the negative valence, to hold himself as aloof as possible from the task. Thus his behavior contrasts with that shown in the interest situation, in which there is a tendency for the child to approach the task as closely as possible. Instead, as in the latter situation, of welcoming and utilizing every possibility of approach, the child actively seeks to prevent approach and endeavors to postpone as long as possible the execution of his task. When no escape is open, such tasks are generally performed at the last moment. There exists also the tendency to abandon the task as soon as possible.

If despite his disinclination we wish to get the child to calculate, it is necessary to turn him from his present occupation, perhaps some kind of play, toward the arithmetic task.

FIG. 4.

Dynamically this means that by some method a field force must be produced, oppositely directed to the previous force (V_T), and strong enough to overcome it.

One such method is threat of punishment. It is essentially indifferent whether the character of the punishment is apparent to the child as such or is concealed.

One may say: If you don't do your arithmetic you will be whipped; you will not be allowed to go on the picnic; you will get a bad mark; you must stay after school. In these cases one makes use of a second negative valence, a further unpleasantness. Further, in order to procure a field force opposed in direction to the vector proceeding from the first negative valence, the second negative valence must be placed behind the child.

The fundamental situation in threat of punishment is represented topologically in Fig. 5. The child finds himself between two negative valences, the arithmetic task (T) and the punishment (P). If the threat of punishment is to be effective, the vector (V_P) proceeding from it must not only be strong enough to overcome vector V_T even when the child comes into immediate contact with the unpleasant task, but also continue to hold the child within the field of this task.[1]

The following abstract consideration will help to clarify the difference between the foregoing and the interest situation. If in the latter the child is obstructed by a difficulty, the direction of the vector immediately changes, as we saw, in such a way that the child continues to act in the direction of the original goal. If in the punishment situation the child is similarly forced away by a difficulty, he will immediately tend to take a direction opposite to that of the task to be completed.

If one is to bring about a renewed movement in the direction of the undesired task, the second negative valence, the punishment, must acquire such a position that it is again opposed to the present direction of the vector $(V_T,$ Fig. 6). In this situation there is thus lacking the pedagogically important

[1] Once the child is in the field of the task, other factors also come into play (see pp. 136 f.).

property of the interest situation, according to which the child when thrust away by difficulties *resumes of himself the direction of the task* (see Fig. 3), providing the difficulties are not too unpleasant.

Even, however, without special difficulties in the performance of the task, in the threat-of-punishment situation there exists from the beginning and as a constant condition a dynamic

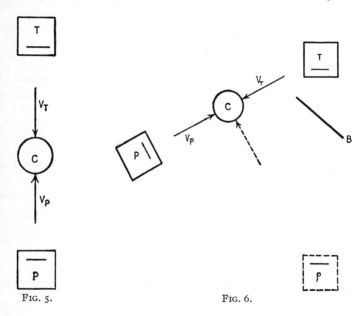

FIG. 5.   FIG. 6.

configuration in which the child is forced away from the task. The negative valence of the task itself works dynamically like a difficulty barrier. In many respects it hinders approach with even greater strength. The situation is further complicated by the presence of a second negative valence, creating a conflict situation for the child.

Types of Conflict.

A conflict is to be characterized psychologically as a situation in which oppositely directed, simultaneously acting forces of approximately equal strength work upon the individual.

Accordingly, three fundamental types of the conflict situation are possible.

1. The individual stands between two positive valences of approximately equal strength (Fig. 7). An instance of this sort is that of Buridan's ass starving between two stacks of hay.

In general this type of conflict situation is solved with relative ease. It is usually a condition of labile equilibrium. Approach to one attraction is in itself often sufficient to give it predominance. The choice between two pleasant things is generally easier than that between two unpleasant unless questions are involved which cut deeply into the life of the individual.

Such a conflict situation can upon occasion also lead to an *oscillation* between two attractions. It is of considerable importance that in these cases a decision for one goal alters its valence in such a way as to make it weaker than that of the renounced goal.

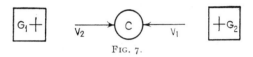

FIG. 7.

2. The second fundamental type of conflict situation occurs when the individual finds himself between two approximately equal negative valences. The punishment situation just discussed (Fig. 5) is a characteristic example which we shall examine more fully in a moment.

3. There exists finally the possibility that one of the two oppositely directed field vectors derives from a positive, the other from a negative valence. In this case conflict arises only when both positive and negative valences are in the same place. A child may wish, for instance, to stroke a dog which it fears, or to eat a forbidden cake. In these cases there exists the conflict situation represented in Fig. 8. We shall have occasion later to go into such a situation in more detail.

Escape Tendencies. The Outer Barrier.

Threat of punishment creates for the child a conflict situation of the type represented in Fig. 5. The child stands between two negative valences and the corresponding field forces. In response to such a pressure on both sides the child necessarily reacts with the tendency to avoid both unpleasant things. Thus there exists an unstable equilibrium. The situation is such that the slightest sidewise displacement of C must produce

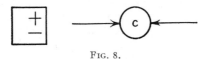

FIG. 8.

a very strong resultant (V_R) perpendicular to the direction punishment-task (Fig. 9). Thus the child in avoiding both the task and the punishment will try to get out of the field (in the direction of the dotted arrow in Fig. 9).

It may be added that the child does not always come into the threatened-punishment situation in such a way that it stands immediately between punishment and unpleasant task. Often the child may find himself at first entirely outside the whole affair. For instance, he may be required on pain of punishment to finish an unpleasant school task within a fortnight. In this case punishment and task constitute a relatively unitary, undifferentiated whole which is doubly unpleasant to the child (see page 169). The child will have nothing to do with the disagreeable affair. In this situation (Fig. 9a) there exists a strong tendency to flight, often resulting more from the threat of punishment than from the unpleasantness of the task itself. More precisely, it may result from an increased unpleasantness of the total complex due to the threat of punishment.

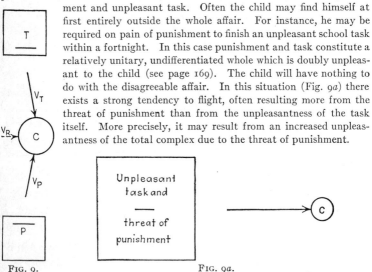

FIG. 9.   FIG. 9a.

The most primitive attempt to avoid simultaneously task and punishment is a bodily going-out-of-the-field, running away, hiding. Frequently going-out-of-the-field takes the form of postponing for several minutes or hours the performance of the task. In cases of repeated, severe punishment a new threat may result in an actual attempt by the child to run away from home.   Fear of punishment frequently plays a role in the early stages of childish vagabonding.[1]

Another form of going-out-of-the-field consists in engaging in some other task.   Often the child seeks to *conceal* his going-out-of-the-field by choosing an occupation against which as such the adult can find no objection.   Thus the child may take up another school task more pleasing to him, execute some previously given commission, or the like.

Finally, the child occasionally escapes both punishment and unpleasant task by *deceiving* the adult more or less crassly. In cases where the adult has difficulty in checking up, the child may claim to have carried out the task even when he has not, or he may say (a somewhat more refined form of deceit) that a third person relieved him of the unpleasant task or that for some other reason its execution became unnecessary.

The conflict situation resulting from threat of punishment thus creates a very strong tendency to go out of the field (see Figs. 5 and 9).   With the child, such a *going-out-of-the-field*, varying according to the topology and field forces of the situation, *necessarily occurs unless especial measures are taken to prevent it*.   If the adult wishes the child to undertake the task despite its negative valence, mere threat of punishment is not sufficient.   The adult must see to it that the child cannot leave the field.   The adult, that is, must erect some sort of *barrier* which will effectively prevent such escape.   He must so erect the barrier (B) that the child can gain freedom only by carrying out the task or by incurring the punishment (Fig. 10).

Actually, threats of punishment intended to get the child to carry out some definite task are always so framed that they, together with the field of the task and that of the punishment, completely enclose the child.   The adult is forced so to construct the barriers that no "hole" remains through which the child may slip out.   Should the adult be too unskilled, or should

[1] G. HOMBURGER, *Psychopathologie des Kindesalters*, Berlin, 1926, p. 508.

his power in this respect be insufficient, the child will slip through if aware of the slightest hole in the barrier.

The most primitive type of such barriers is the physical-corporeal: the child may be shut up in a room until he has finished the task.[2]

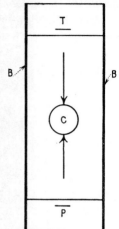

FIG. 10.[1]

In general, however, the barriers are *sociological*.[3] The barriers surrounding the child are the instruments of power possessed by the adult in virtue of his social position and the inner relationship existing between him and the child. Such a social barrier is no less real than a physical one.

Barriers resulting from social factors may restrict the child's freedom of movement to a narrow spatial area. The child, for instance, is not locked in but is forbidden to leave the room before completing the task.[4] In other cases the external freedom of movement is practically unrestricted but the adult keeps the child under constant surveillance. He is not allowed out of sight. Since, ordinarily, the child cannot be followed about constantly, the adult often

---

[1] In this and later diagrams barriers will be represented by thick lines. Thin lines will be used to bound qualitatively definite areas, for example, the area of the task where the boundaries do not possess psychologically very great dynamic firmness. It is both possible and necessary to distinguish different degrees of firmness of boundary (cf. G. Birenbaum, Das Vergessen einer Vornahme, *Psychol. Forsch.*, 1930, **13**, 218–284). We may, however, limit ourselves here to a schematic differentiation of two degrees.

[2] It should also be mentioned that with a child definite, narrow limits must be set for the completion of the task (see p. 128). In diagramming the situation one is limited to the psychological present (for reasons that cannot here be discussed in detail, cf. Chap. II). The sequence of occurrences must thus be represented diagrammatically as a succession of situations. Time restrictions are therefore to be shown in the single representation only in so far as they are sensed by the child in the present situation as limitations of its freedom of movement.

[3] For the most part the concepts and occurrences that constitute the psychological field are determined by social rather than by physical facts.

[4] Restriction of one's freedom of movement is itself frequently used as a punishment. Even then the confinement is often effected by nonphysical, social, or quasi-magical means. The child, for instance, may be placed in a corner, or bound to the leg of a chair by a thread of twine. (Cf. W. von Kügelgen, *Jugenderinnerungen eines alten Mannes*, Stuttgart o. J.)

makes use of the child's world of magic. The capacity for constant control of the child is assigned to the policeman or to the bogey man. A God that knows everything the child does, from whom no escape is possible, is not infrequently used to the same effect. Secret eating of sweets may, for instance, be controlled in this way.

Often the barriers are directly constituted by life in a given social milieu, by the customs of the family in which one lives, or by the organization of the school.

For effectiveness it is essential that the social barrier possess a sufficiently real firmness. If at a particular point it is not resistant enough the child will break through. For instance, if the child knows that a threatened punishment is only verbal or if he can rely with some certainty upon the probability of being able to wheedle the adult out of executing the punishment, he will instead of completing the task trust to the possibility of breaking through the barrier. A similar weakness of barrier exists when a mother delegates the responsibility of watching over the child's completion of a task to a nurse, teacher, or elder child, who, unlike herself, does not possess sufficient resistance to prevent the child from going out of the field.

Along with physical and social barriers there exists a third type, closely dependent upon social facts but differing in important respects from the last-mentioned examples. One may appeal, for instance, to the child's pride ("Remember you are not a street urchin!" "You're not a bad boy!"); or to the social standards of a group ("Remember you are a girl!" " . . . a boy!"). One turns in such cases to a definite system of ideology, to goals and values recognized by the child himself. Such an appeal to the ideology contains a threat: danger of exclusion from the group. At the same time, and most importantly, this ideology constitutes an outer barrier. It defines for the individual the boundaries of freedom of action recognized by the ideology. Many threats of punishment are effective only so long as the individual feels bound to these limits. If he no longer recognizes the ideology, that is, the moral limitations of the group, threats of punishment frequently become ineffective. The individual refuses to allow his freedom of action to be confined within these limits.

The strength of barrier necessary in a specific case depends upon the nature of the child and upon the strength of the negative valences of task and punishment. *The more intense the negative valence, the firmer must be the barrier.* For the stronger the barrier, the stronger is the sidewise directed resultant force. Thus the greater the pressure the adult must exert upon the child to bring about the desired behavior, the firmer, the less penetrable must be the barrier erected.

The Constrained Character of the Situation.

The barrier surrounding the punishment situation constitutes not only an enclosure against the surrounding environment, but also a more or less decided restriction of free movement on the part of the child. This restriction not only means that the child must carry out the specified task but constitutes at the same time a *general* limitation of freedom of movement.

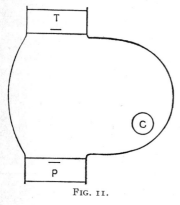

FIG. 11.

This fact is perhaps most clear in those instances in which the child is locked in his room. Even, however, in cases where apparently only the performance of a definite action is required and the child is given freedom in its other movements, the actual barrier effects a general restriction of freedom of movement. If this were not so, but the play area—topologically the space enclosed by the barrier (Fig. 11)—were allowed to become as large as desired, the child would have the opportunity of engaging for as long as he cared in as many occupations as he wished before accomplishing the task. In reality the child would of course take advantage of this possibility. Thus while remaining within the field he would be able, as regards reward and punishment, to go out of the field. Expressed in other terms, the barrier would recede psychologically to a great distance, becoming thereby unreal.

The extent of freedom of movement left the child by physical or social barriers is certainly of importance psychologically and pedagogically; but it must be strongly emphasized that *threat of punishment always and necessarily gives rise to the structure of a constrained situation.* The constrained aspect of the situation is prominent in proportion to the sharpness of pressure the adult must exert in order to get the child to carry out the task. Constraint depends not only on the fact that in these cases the barrier must be particularly firm and lacking in holes, but also on the tendency of the adult to restrict the barrier in order to avoid weak places and to reduce to a minimum the play space left the child. The sharper the threatened punishment the greater, ordinarily, is the *general* restriction on the life of the child and the stronger is the tendency of the adult to revert to primitive physical barriers. The more the child's milieu is founded on threats of punishment and the severer these punishments are the more the milieu as a whole assumes the constrained character of a prison or reformatory marked by bars, locked rooms, and constant surveillance.

The barrier surrounding the punishment situation need not always be erected for the special instance. The area within which the child can move, his sphere of freedom, is itself limited corresponding to his restricted sphere of power. The sphere of power of the single adult and above all of the organization of adults who control the communal life is all powerful and ordinarily completely surrounds the sphere of freedom of the child. Only definite areas exist in the child's life within which it can find respite from the threat of immediate adult interference. The life of the child in a secret gang, friendship and conversation with other children, or certain play zones may constitute such areas. But even these afford the child freedom and inaccessibility for only a definite time. Indeed, the fact that the child's physiological conditions of life, its nourishment and shelter, are controlled by the adult causes the sphere of movement of the child to lie as a rule in the sphere of power of the adult.

Whether a threat of punishment necessitates in addition *special* barriers is a question of the particular instance. Very often a slight threatened punishment makes such an increased limitation necessary. Frequently the adult's mode of living or the conditions and habits required by living in a house, which previously had not been sensed as restrictions, acquire for the child as a result of threatened punishment the meaning of a barrier limiting his freedom of movement.

Punishment Situations without Barriers.

In certain cases despite a threat of punishment special barriers are not demonstrable. The child, though standing before an unpleasant task, even one of decidedly negative valence, may yet complete it without any apparent barrier to prevent his going out of the field. There may even appear to be no threat of punishment. The admonition of the adult to perform the task seems sufficient to cause the child obediently to complete it.

We are not considering here cases in which the child performs the task out of love of the adult. These would fall under the problem of reward. Rather, we are concerned with situations in which behind the admonition there stands an unexpressed threat of punishment. Precisely in a milieu in which the child's attitude toward the adult is foreign and hostile he may behave as though undertaking the unpleasant task of his own free will. The erection of particularly narrow barriers may thus be unnecessary. Indeed in just such milieux it is not infrequently pointed out with pride that the child is left much freedom, that it is not narrowly restricted.

A representation of this type of situation by the topology shown in Fig. 10 would not be exactly correct. The enclosure of the field through a barrier expresses topologically the fact that the psychical field is completely surrounded. But in addition it indicates that a special region, the barrier, acts as a *bounding zone* of an inner sphere, the area which it encloses. This *inner sphere* within which the child is free to move may as we mentioned before be large or small. The freedom within this area is certainly not to be considered as equal to the freedom in a sphere without an outer barrier. Rather, because of the barrier the character of the entire field and its dynamic peculiarities are changed qualitatively in important respects. In a moment we shall consider these in more detail. In the punishment situations mentioned above, however, there exists a relatively free sphere of activity, an inner sphere, which is to be distinguished from the barrier felt as such. Even when the child is confined within a room he can, if recalcitrant and innerly unbroken, do essentially what he pleases.

In the situation just sketched, however, such a particular barrier and inner sphere are actually lacking. The power of

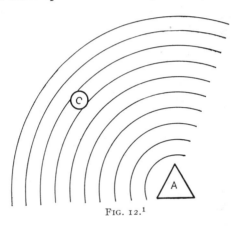

FIG. 12.[1]

the adult and his threats of punishment have so penetrated the whole life-sphere of the child that areas in which he can move freely and independently are as good as nonexistent. It is unnecessary to hinder the child's going-out-of-the-field by the erection of an outer barrier because the function of this barrier has spread out over the whole field. The child finds himself in a field completely controlled at every point by the power of the adult (Fig. 12).

---

[1] The psychological field corresponding dynamically to the sphere of power of the adult (A) will be schematically represented in this and later figures by concentric circles. Actually, of course, the field of force of the adult will not pervade the sphere of action of the child in such a homogeneous fashion but will be of different density in different places. For our present purposes, however, we need not consider this inequality.

Naturally such a condition is never completely attained. If the child is to live at all he must retain the possibility of a minimal independence of movement. The condition which we have in mind does not correspond simply to the situation in which the free sphere of action within the outer barrier is made as small as possible. Nor can it be created simply by such a restriction of the sphere of action. It is more apt to occur when the adult either by particularly severe punishments or through a definite ideology so dominates the child that he dare not resist. The child may thus carry out unpleasant tasks unhesitatingly because *at every point within his sphere of action he is internally controlled* by the wishes of the adult. This dependence may go so far that special threats of punishment are unnecessary. In extreme cases it is scarcely necessary for the adult even to mention his wishes.

How far such penetration of the entire field by a regime of punishment is possible depends, of course, not only upon the milieu but also upon the nature of the individual child. But even in cases where there is no extreme restriction of the child's freedom of movement it is important to keep in mind whether the structure of the total situation corresponds to the topology represented by Fig. 9 or to that shown in Fig. 12.[1] The latter case must be especially emphasized since it is in precisely the most severely constrained situations that this characteristic is particularly noticeable. Since in these instances inner domination of the child plays a decisive role the actual force exercised by the adult is difficult to recognize. Yet the less apparent its action from without in, the stronger it is. In many cases which are to be regarded throughout as forced actions there may in a superficial and even in a rather exacting examination appear to be exhibited exactly those characters so typical of the dynamically opposite situation. I refer to the apparent free will characteristic of the child when it acts from interest in the task itself, freely following its needs in a situation actually without barriers.

[1] Naturally there exist transitional and mixed cases. One may think of Fig. 12 as showing an extension of the barrier throughout the entire field. This is a possible notion since the barrier is conceived throughout as functionally defined.

Consideration of the situation outlined above is complicated by the fact that instances occur in which such a complete penetration of the child's life-sphere and its transformation into a constraint-situation is caused by the adult's over-weening love and constant protection. In this way as well the child may be placed in an overpowering field of force.

Leaving the above case in which erection of a special outer barrier is unnecessary, we shall return to a discussion of the typical punishment situation. Even this is to be characterized as a constrained situation, especially when, as previously mentioned, the inner sphere is very small. That such an outer barrier produces the characteristics of constraint becomes clearer when a situation of this kind is compared with one in which not threat of punishment but interest in the task itself is the dominant factor. In such cases (see Figs. 1 to 3) it is unnecessary to erect an outer barrier since the positive valence itself continually leads the child back to the task. Neither is it necessary to limit in any respect the freedom of movement of the child. In contrast to that of punishment, the total situation can remain free and unconstrained.

State of Tension.

The situation involving threat of punishment was in its general topology characterized by the opposition of two negative valences (the task on one hand, the punishment on the other) and by the outer barrier hindering sidewise escape. For a general characterization of the situation it is necessary in addition to determine the state of tension in the field.

We have seen above that a conflict is thus produced; in consequence of two negative, oppositely placed valences, two opposed vectors (V_T and V_P) work upon the child (Fig. 10). These vectors are not two isolated forces in an otherwise uninfluenced field, but lead to an increase in the state of tension within the total situation.

This means that the vectors operating on the child are not limited to those from task and punishment. Instead there exist opposed field forces of approximately equal strength affecting movements in every other direction. At *all positions* in the field the child is subject to an increased *general pressure.*

That this increased total tension in the field is a necessary consequence of the two negative valences in the punishment situation is readily deduced from our general principles.[1] We have already discussed the production by vectors V_T and V_P of a strong resultant (V_R) directed sidewise in the direction of the outer barrier (Fig. 9). Otherwise expressed, the conflict situation results in a tendency to go out of the field. If, however, the child attempts to move in the direction of this resultant he strikes the outer barrier. He may break through. If he does so the topology of the total situation is changed and the punishment becomes ineffective. This case will be discussed later. On the other hand the barrier may hold fast. The barrier itself then acquires a negative valence. This may result from a variety of causes: the child has hurt himself, perhaps bodily by running against the barrier; he has experienced his own impotence; or the like. Nonphysical barriers, furthermore, consist largely of prohibitions and act directly as barriers in virtue of their negative valence.

Thus in so far as the punishment situation is maintained there proceeds from the barrier a vector $(V_B$, Fig. 13) opposed in direction to the previous resultant (V_R). Movement in the direction of this resultant leads to conflict; that is, two oppositely directed field forces are acting along the same line.

The same dynamic situation is created when the child seeks to go through the barrier at any point. Opposed field forces exist for the child at every point in the field acting in every direction (Fig. 14); a state of tension exists in the field.[2]

The degree of tension in the field depends obviously upon the strength of the negative valences of punishment, task, and barrier. An important influence in determining the strength of the negative valence of the punishment is the child's previous experience in the present or earlier instances of collision with the barrier. For example, the negative valence of the punish-

---

[1] The following discussion of the relation between certain field forces and tension in the total field although based upon the punishment situation has a general psychological significance for a whole group of similar situations.

[2] As a dynamic concept, tension is defined as oppositely directed vectors.

ment is very strong when the child has previously been severely punished for attempting to go out of the field. The negative valence of the barrier in its acute effect upon the individual case is, however, largely dependent on the strengths of the negative valences of task and punishment. In the last analysis the minimum firmness of barrier and minimal threat of punishment necessary for making such a threat effective depend upon the strength of the negative valence of the task.

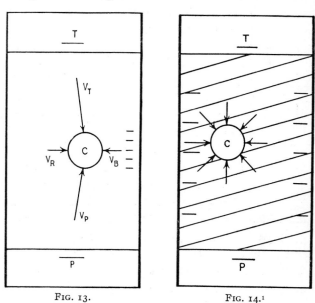

FIG. 13. FIG. 14.[1]

Modes of Behavior in the Punishment Situation.

In the previous section we have discussed the general characteristics of the topology and field forces existent when an attempt is made, by threatened punishment, to force the child to act in a certain way. We shall now briefly consider the possibilities of actual behavior that exist for the child in such a situation.

Execution of the Command. Through threat of punishment the child is induced to perform the task, that is, to show the

[1] The crosshatching represents the condition of tension.

desired behavior. The vector (V_P) proceeding from the punishment shows itself stronger than the opposed vector (V_T, Fig. 15). The outer barrier remains sufficiently firm. Thus the child enters the field of the task. Completion of the task signifies for the child the way to freedom, escape from the punishment.

Once the child has entered the field of the task the situation may be fundamentally altered. The circumstance that the

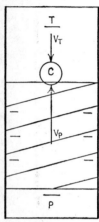

FIG. 15.

task no longer stands over against the child but is rather a field in which he finds himself may suffice to bring about this transformation. Sometimes the affair is not so bad as it had appeared in advance. A small child, for instance, may not want to eat a new food but notices at the first bite that it does not taste so bad as expected.

The fact that the child because of threatened punishment enters a field so unpleasant in appearance is in itself, however, not favorable to such a transformation toward pleasantness. On the contrary it may often result in the task's remaining unpleasant. Frequently, moreover, the child is already familiar with the actual unpleasantness of the task.

Standing-within-the-task is in any case psychologically quite a different situation from that of threat of punishment.[1]

Acceptance of the Punishment. The situation in which the vector proceeding from the task is stronger than the negative valence of the punishment (Fig. 16) is in a sense the opposite of the preceding. If in this case the outer barrier is sufficiently strong the child will take the punishment. He goes into the field of punishment because punishment constitutes a way to freedom, similar to that offered by the task in the previous case.

---

[1] In the World War it could be clearly observed that returning to the front constituted a much more unpleasant situation than being at the front.

The following is an example of this type of behavior.

A father says to his three-year-old son, "If you do not gather up your things you will be whipped." The child goes to his father, turns his back to receive the blow and says, "All right!" It is clear that the child had construed his father's remark to mean that he was presented with two possibilities of action.

It is to be noted that the youngster had never received a whipping. Some time before a switch had been procured and had been used as a threat. The pedagogical atmosphere in the home was, however, characteristically free and lively and the acquisition of the switch rather an isolated event.

It is possible, moveover, that curiosity may have played a role in the decision of the child since during the Christmas holidays a short time before there had been a good deal of reference to the switch, as well as to Santa Claus.

Again the situation underwent transformation for the child as he took the punishment. He noticed that the actual experience of the punishment was in reality not so bad as the ideology of the adult had made it appear in advance.

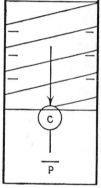

As punishment for too uproarious conduct, a girl of ten years was confined in a small dark room by her teacher, with whom she generally stood well. The child sat on a vacuum cleaner, pounded lustily with her feet, and sang. To the teacher's astonishment the girl, upon being released, was pleased and answered back jokingly without noticeable embarrassment.

The child had actually succeeded in transforming the punishment into a playful occasion. The real unpleasantness was not very great once she had decided not to take the punishment in a moral sense (see page 138).

Fig. 16.

The child in experiencing various punishments builds up a certain knowledge of the actual degree of unpleasantness of different punishments. He views a threatened punishment no longer from without but from within, weighing the unpleasantness of the task against that of the punishment. He becomes callous to the punishment and thus less sensitive to threats. An important step in this direction occurs when the child attempts at least retrospectively to minimize the degree of reality of the punishment and the moral degradation which accompanies it.

An intelligent, lively girl of six years who had been going to school for three months tilted back on her chair. As a punishment the teacher made her kneel.

When the child returned home she did not *appear* in the least sad and said to her mother, "I like to kneel."

This particular event stood in a larger context for both teacher and child. The teacher thought it advisable to proceed against the child with stricter disciplinary measures. The child, although at first very much delighted with school, began to withdraw into herself, and her attitude toward the punishment was at the same time an expression of an incipient struggle against the teacher's sphere of power. That this transformation in the school atmosphere really bore heavily upon the child and that her indifference toward it was quite superficial manifested itself clearly in her total behavior. She became afraid of the dark, had nightmares, and cried at night in her sleep, "Don't always look at me so, teacher!"

More important than experiencing the degree of unpleasantness of the task is the circumstance that in such cases the execution of the punishment is apt to lead to a revolution in the ideology of the child. His system of values may become transformed. The adult always represents the punishment as something bad, morally degrading. This moral disgrace is ordinarily a major source of the negative valence of the task.

Related to the above is the fact that public punishments are particularly shunned. That social standing is thus injured by punishment is not only of importance to adults but is one of the main grounds for children's fear of punishment.

A certain five-year-old boy was ill. Whenever he was naughty the little negro puppet which hung over his bed was turned with its face to the wall. Thus the fact of his naughtiness was apparent to everyone who came into the room. This exposure acted as a decided sharpening of the already painful circumstance that the beloved negro puppet must hang with its face to the wall. Incidentally, the youngster himself never attempted to turn back the puppet although it hung just above his bed.

Once a transformation of values occurs, however, once punishment loses for the child its aspect of disgrace the strength of its negative valence decreases considerably. There then stands behind the threat only the specific unpleasantness of the present punishment. Timidity before the entire sphere of punishment no longer exists. No longer does the child think anything of being punished. Eventually he may reach the point of view that failure to perform the task is more worthy of pride than is its completion.

The following circumstance is dynamically important in the origin of such a transformation. If the negative valence of the task is so strong that the child prefers punishment, the latter as the lesser evil becomes relatively positive. This shift of relative position is made more difficult by the fact that something belonging to a morally inferior sphere must now appear as being in some way superior to the morally unobjectionable action desired by the adult. When this occurs the unique moral position of the punishment sphere is at one point and thus, in principle, broken down.

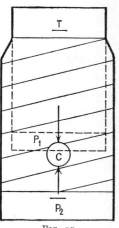

FIG. 17.

The child who attempts to gain freedom by going topologically through the punishment generally finds himself, however, *disillusioned*. Ordinarily the adult is not content merely to inflict the punishment but demands anew the completion of the hated task. At the same time he often threatens a more severe punishment (P_2).

Thus acceptance of the punishment does *not* actually mean for the child a way to freedom. He finds himself afterwards (Fig. 17) still in the same constrained situation facing the prospect of increasing punishments, which in general finally make him docile. This is probably significant in explanation of the fact that punishment is relatively seldom chosen by the child.

At times, however, punishment actually constitutes a way to freedom. It may be that the adult cannot bring himself to resort to more extreme measures, or perhaps the task in question cannot be executed later on.

The following is an instance in which acceptance of the punishment really constituted an escape from the constrained situation. W. von Kügelgen at the age of five years was sent to a girls' school. The femininity of the girls was so repulsive to him that on the second day he told his mother that he would not return to school. "Finally, amazed at such staunch resistance she played her trump card and asked me which I would choose, a 'crop of whippings,' as she expressed it, or returning to school. And with that she lost the battle. One thought of the faces of the girls and their gentle ways stopped any hesitation. I chose the 'crop.' The punishment was appropriately severe, yes, as I remember it, beyond expectation. Yet it was not to be compared with the detestable dungeon of girls. I was now free. And my mother never presented to me again a similar alternative."[1]

Action against the Barrier. The third behavioral possibility in the punishment situation, along with performance of task and acceptance of punishment, is action in the direction of the barrier.

In this case the vectors proceeding from task and punishment are too great and the child moves in the direction of the resultant (V_R). There may, then, ensue either a blind, uncontrolled charge against the barrier (the child locked in a room may knock his head and legs against the walls), or a considered attempt to break through. The exact procedure employed by the child in specific cases depends naturally upon the nature of the existing barrier. He may attempt to gain freedom through flattery, defiance, or deceit.

If the barrier is very firm, there is no way out for the child. Under these conditions and with sufficiently strong tension in the total field, there may develop tendencies toward suicide. Suicide then appears as the last remaining possibility of going-out-of-the-field.

As a result of her parents' strictness, Martha, ten years of age, lived in constant terror of poor grades at school.[2] "The fear of poor marks was especially evident shortly before Easter when the question of promotion was to be decided. It was so strong that the child often cried out in her sleep, ran to her mother's bed, and wanted to stay with her because she was afraid. Her parents treated Martha very sternly. Once the mother threatened, 'If you are not promoted you need not come back home!' After this utterance the child entertained thoughts of suicide." The tendency to better her position with her parents by particular neatness was also observable. She "helped about the house more than was required of her, in order to make her mother happy."

Most of these attempts to break through evince not only the escape tendency but also more or less open strife with the adult.

---

[1] W. VON KÜGELGEN, *op. cit.*

[2] A. DOHME, Beitrag zur Psychologie und Psychopathologie typischer Schulkonflikte auf den verschiedenen Altersstufen, *Zeitschr. f. Kinderforsch.*, 1930, **36,** 458.

These aspects are related to a condition which we shall proceed to discuss more in detail.

Struggle with the Adult. We have already mentioned that as a rule the outer barrier is essentially social in nature and rests upon the actual power of the adult over the life-sphere of the child. When, then, the child turns against the outer barrier he directs himself in the last analysis against the will and power of the adult to whom the erection of the barrier is due.

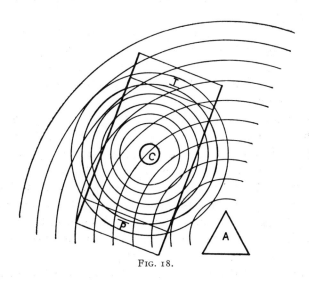

Fig. 18.

In addition, the threatened punishment and finally the task itself is set by the adult. All the vectors and barriers controlling the situation may in the end be traced to the adult who is responsible for maintaining them. Were only the power of the adult to collapse, the whole situation would fall to pieces; task, punishment, and barrier would cease to exist. All valences determining the situation thus derive dynamically from the circumstance that the field is controlled by the adult (Fig. 18). The field of force corresponding to the sphere of power of the child is not strong enough to maintain itself against the sphere of power of the adult. The struggle of the child is an attempt to make a stand against this superior force.

We have previously spoken (see page 131, Fig. 12) of the domination of the total field by the adult. We were concerned there with peculiarly crass types of constrained situation, in which threat of punishment was effective seemingly without especial barriers. We now see that quite generally the punishment situation is related to the situation there discussed.

Nevertheless, there exists a considerable difference between the former situation and the one here considered. It is possible that, although the outer surrounding barrier is extraordinarily firm due to the actual power of the adult, the child may yet possess within the enclosed area distinct freedom of movement. Threat of punishment, here, is directed specifically toward one task. Not every point in the total situation assumes the character of constraint, as in the examples sketched above.

The actual connection of the adult with task, punishment, and barrier may not be intellectually quite clear to the child, but owing to the very fine sensitivity of even small children to social relations within their sphere of life, this connection is clearly enough felt.

The punishment situation, therefore, tends to produce an action of combat against the center whence issue dynamically the negative valences and upon which the whole painful situation depends, namely, against the adult himself.

Thus the *threat of punishment creates* necessarily a *situation in which child and adult stand over against each other as enemies*. Herein lies one of the most important differences between this situation and that in which the child undertakes the task because of interest in the task itself.

The nature of the struggle, as well as the direction in which it takes place, may vary extraordinarily and depends upon the character of the child, of the adult, and upon the peculiarities of the momentary situation. In essence the strife of the child may be directed against the task, against the punishment, or against the barrier thwarting the attempt to go out of the field.

In a direct struggle against the task, the child, as previously mentioned, may advance difficulties which the adult must recognize. The notebook has disappeared, the pen is broken, other pressing assignments must be prepared, and so on. Not infrequently the struggle is carried on by means which Adler[1] would designate as "arrangements." That is to say, the

---

[1] *Cf.* ALFRED ADLER, *Über den nervösen Charakter*, Bergmann, Wiesbaden, 1912. (English trans., *The Neurotic Constitution*, Moffat, Yard, New York, 1917.)

difficulty which the adult must recognize consists in the fact that the child has developed a headache, a phenomenon that is frequently to be observed before school examinations.

The struggle may be directed more specifically against the punishment. Among children a favorite method of anticipating blows at school is to put on particularly thick clothes. A helpful illness is a good defense against punishment. Even flattery, standing in well with the adult, may have the character of such a struggle. The exercise of every form of cheating and deceit occurs more readily in proportion as the situation acquires for the child the character of strife. In such a strife the child may use without hesitation methods which it would probably not employ in any but a hostile atmosphere.

A simple example of an attempt to evade punishment by *deception* after the deed is described by Schurz.[1] Schurz received a poor mark on his report card. "Whether it was due to shame over my failure or to fear of my father's severity, the fact was that on Saturday when I came home I tried to make my father think that the chaplain had forgotten to write on my card, or something of the sort. My uncertain behavior convinced my father at once that something was wrong. A few questions brought me to confess the true state of affairs. The following conversation then occurred: 'You have neglected your duty and have tried to hide the truth from me. Don't you think you deserve to be whipped?'

" 'Yes. But please let us go into the cow-shed where no one can see or hear us.' The request was granted. I underwent my chastisement in the seclusion of the cow-shed. It was not severe, and no one knew anything of it. My father forgave me and treated me as before. But the bitter consciousness of having been humiliated deservedly remained with me some time as a heavy burden. For a long while I avoided the cow-shed, the scene of my shame, whenever possible."

The tendency discussed above to attempt to prevent one's punishment from becoming public is clearly shown in this illustration.

Finally, the struggle may center specifically against the outer barrier, which hinders going-out-of-the-field.

Whether they are directed especially against the task, the punishment, or the barrier, all of these fighting activities characteristically show a *double aspect*, conditioned by both the structure of the situation and the dynamic source of the field forces. They are at the same time a flight from and a

[1] KARL SCHURZ, *Lebenserinnerungen*, cited by BAÜMER and DROESCHES, *Von der Kinderseele*, Leipzig, 1908, p. 236.

struggle against the adult. Actually the child can go out of the field only by going through the barrier, task, or punishment, and in the last analysis all these are only different embodiments of the adult himself.

If the total milieu is such that the child must frequently count upon threatened punishments, he may carry on the strife against the adult beyond the specific punishment situation, attempting in this way to shake or undermine his power. Here belong the struggle between teacher and pupils, the so-called problem of discipline, and the endless variety of active and passive obstruction which children are accustomed to raise against those parents and teachers who lay especial emphasis on authority.

Encysting. Defiance. Going-out-of-the-field need not result in breaking through the boundaries of the punishment situation. It may also be achieved by a sort of *encysting* of the child within the field. Without actually leaving the field the child attempts to make himself unassailable, at least for a time; to erect a wall between both task and punishment, and himself. Functionally and in meaning, such an encysting is in many respects equivalent to going-out-of-the-field.

The encysting is usually the more marked the higher the tension and the less the prospect of escape. The child mentioned above (page 140) who entertained thoughts of suicide from fear of not being promoted showed this encysting. "Martha had no chum. Aside from playing with her girl classmates on the way home from school she remained alone. Neither did she have any friends among the children of the neighborhood. She played only occasionally with them, preferring to associate with smaller children."[1]

Closely related to encysting, indeed a special form of it, is the *defiance* reaction.

The child withdraws into himself. He does not, however, attempt to avoid the strong pressure of the environment, to evade every unpleasant contact. Rather, encysting here consists in taking up a defiant, fighting attitude toward the environment.[2] As it is displayed for instance in the case of a new punishment threatened immediately after previous punish-

[1] A. Dohme, *loc. cit.*
[2] Cf. Fajans, *loc. cit.*, and Winkler, *Der Trotz*, Munich, 1929.

ment (see example on page 140), the defiance reaction is both a convulsive summing up of one's forces and self-assertion in a tense hostile situation. It signifies an insensitivity toward the threat and at the same time a struggle against the field of power of the adult. The insensitivity results chiefly from the fact that the values and demands set up by the foreign field of force are no longer recognized as binding for the individual concerned. Along with encysting and strife, defiance involves also a certain revolution in the child's ideology.

In children defiance frequently occurs as a first sign of independence, of breaking through the social field that until then has been overpowering. With suppressed, passive children the first welcome sign of activity often consists in being impudent.

Flight into Unreality. Emotional Outburst. Among the various types of actual behavior which may occur in the punishment situation, there remain to be discussed certain processes which have a direct relation to the state of tension in the situation, namely, flight into unreality and emotional outburst.

In the psychological life-sphere in addition to the plane of reality there usually exist various *levels of unreality*. Unreality (the plane of dreams, of so-called imagination, of gesture) is roughly characterized by the fact that in it one can do as he pleases. Dynamically there is a lack of firm barriers and a large degree of mobility.[1] And the boundaries between the ego and the environment are also fluid.

The degree of reality of psychological processes and inventions is such a fundamental category that it is to be used as a special third dimension for all more exact representations of the psychical environment (see Fig. 18). A consideration of this dimension in a more detailed presentation of the problems of reward and punishment would undoubtedly be very important. It is closely related to questions of morality and to the general ideology of the child.

If the condition of tension in the situation of threatened punishment becomes too unpleasant without prospect of a way out, there arises a strong tendency to go out of the field by fleeing from the plane of reality into that of unreality. One

[1] J. F. BROWN, Über die dynamischen Eigenschaften der Realitäts—und Irrealitätsschichten," *Psychol. Forsch.*, 1933, **18**, 1–26.

succeeds, of course, in going out of the unpleasant field not bodily, but only psychologically.

The differentiation of the psychical environment into levels of reality and unreality is at first not clear in the child.   This condition expresses itself in the magical structure of his conception of the world,[1] in play, and in the lack of a firm boundary between truth and falsehood, dream and reality, gesture and action.   Furthermore, transition from reality to unreality occurs readily.

Fear of punishment may not only dominate dreams, but may lead eventually to enuresis and similar phenomena.[2]   It may also result in intensive daydreams.

Within the level of unreality those things upon which the unpleasantness of the plane of reality rests are removed.   The child is no longer in a constrained situation in the power of the adult, but is free.   The unpleasant task is finished or put aside.   The child himself is dominant, not the adult.   When definite needs and wishes are sharply blocked on the plane of reality, a sort of substitute satisfaction[3] of just these needs may occur in the level of unreality of play or daydream.

The following literary example, to be presented rather fully, illustrates not the conflict situation between unpleasant task and punishment but rather the fluctuating situation after the misdemeano₁, the fear of coming punishment.   The topology of the situation in the second part of the story corresponds closely to that of the punishment situation.   The child, locked in his bedroom, faces the threatened punishment in a situation of decided constraint.

Nikolaj[4] received a failing mark in his history lesson under Teacher Lebedew, because he had learned nothing.   He feared censure and punishment from his tutor, St. Jerome, whom his brother had at first deceived about the mark.   Furthermore, he had run out of the room for a while during the hour.   This was discovered by Mimi, his sister's governess, who would tell his grandmother about it.   Thirdly, Nikolaj had secretly opened a brief case containing letters

[1] J. PIAGET, La représentation du monde chez l'enfant, Alcan, Paris, 1926. (English trans., The Child's Conception of the World, Harcourt, Brace, New York, 1929.)

[2] Cf. HOMBURGER, op. cit., and DOHME, loc. cit.

[3] In psychoanalytic theory substitution, as is well known, plays a great role. Concerning the dynamics and types of substitution processes, see Dembo, op cit.

[4] L. N. TOLSTOY, Lebensstufen, Diederichs, Leipzig, 1903, pp. 255 ff.

of his father and in doing it had broken the small key. He therefore anticipated a punishment from his loved father.

" 'Mimi's complaint! The bad mark! And the key! Nothing worse could have happened. Grandmama—for Mimi's tale, St. Jerome—for the zero, Papa—for the key. . . . And all this will come down on my head not later than tonight!'

" 'What will happen to me?'

" 'A-ah! What have I gotten into?' I said to myself walking up and down on the white rug of the work room. 'Eh,' I said to myself, taking the candy and cigars, 'what must come, must come!' And so I ran back into the house.

"This fatalistic sentiment which I learned in my childhood from Nikolaj has exercised a soothing, momentarily quieting effect upon me in all the heavy hours of my life. As I entered the room I was in a somewhat excited and unnatural but completely gay frame of mind.

"After dinner the games began and I participated in them in the liveliest manner. We were playing 'cat and the mouse.' In my awkwardness I bumped the governess of the Family Kornakow who was playing with us, stepped accidentally upon her dress and tore it. I saw that all of the girls, especially Sonitschka, were prepared to enjoy with the greatest pleasure the way in which the governess with angry expression hurried into the girls' room to sew her dress, and I made up my mind to repeat for them the pleasurable incident.

"As a result of this amiable intention, I commenced as soon as the governess came back to our room to prance around her. Persisting in this game long enough I snatched a favorable moment to again entangle myself in her clothes and tear them. Sonitschka and the children of the countess could scarcely keep from laughing. My own pride was flattered to the last degree. But St. Jerome, who must have seen through my game, came up, wrinkled his forehead (which I could barely stand) and said that my playfulness did not become me, and if I did not behave better it would end badly in spite of the celebrations of the day.

"I found myself, however, in the excited condition of one who has already lost more in play than he has in his pocket, who fears to settle his accounts, and who in his despair keeps playing new cards without hope of regaining them in order to prevent himself from coming to consciousness. I laughed up at him impudently and left him standing."

Dynamically the situation described is to be characterized somewhat as follows (Fig. 18a). The *fields of force* dominating the life-space of the child (*C*) are, above all, those of the father (*F*), of the grandmother (*G*), and of the tutor, St. Jerome (*J*). The child experiences the field of power of St. Jerome as hostile. Now, however, because of his own guilt the fields of his father and grandmother possess vectors directed against him. These latter are the persons to whom the child feels most closely bound, who have control of the house, and from whom in the last analysis the sphere of power of the tutor, St. Jerome, derives. At present all these fields have acquired a threatening significance for the child.

As a result of these threats from all sides the inner tension of the child is extraordinarily great. His first reaction consists in going-out-of-the-field in the direction of unreality. The child comforts himself in attempting a fatalistic weakening of reality ("What is to come, will come!"). Naturally this is not sufficient to relieve the tension, which is intensified by the gaiety of the celebration occurring on the plane of reality. Pronounced restless activity and emotional outbreaks ensue.

This affectivity soon leads to a new severe clash with the tutor St. Jerome, who meantime has discovered the bad mark and has exposed the boy in public. The child hits the tutor and is thereupon locked in the attic.

In despair and full of fear of the coming punishment the boy sits in the room. The level of reality (*LR*) in his situation is to be represented approximately as follows (Fig. 18*b*).

Out of the whirl of the preceding scenes he is brought into an externally quiet environment. It is, however, at the same time a situation of pronounced bodily constraint, a physical prison. This prison is an expression of the hostility of

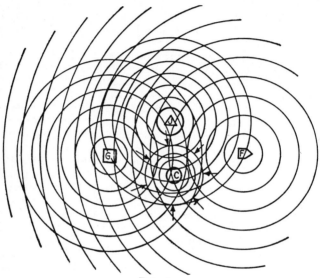

FIG. 18*a*.

St. Jerome and simultaneously an expression of the strength of this inimical sphere of power. In the social level of reality the child's own field of force is wholly inferior to this hostile power. St. Jerome himself had locked the child in the bedroom. The heaviness of the situation is the more oppressive since acutely hostile actions of the highest authorities, the father and grandmother, are to be anticipated in the near future.

In spite of the extraordinary state of tension there occur no true emotional outbreaks, as had happened shortly before. Outwardly the child appears rather quiet. This behavior may in part result from the fact that the child, now alone and left to himself, possesses within the prison a definite even though narrowly limited freedom. The following considerations are probably more important. If pressure from the environment becomes so great and so all sided that the situation appears without possibility of escape (such conditions are typical of despair) a certain bodily rigidity frequently results.[1]

[1] LEWIN, Kindliche Ausdrucksbewegungen, in W. STERN, *Psychologie der frühen Kindheit*, 6th ed., Quelle u. Meyer, Leipzig, 1930, p. 502 (English trans., *Psychology of Early Childhood*, Holt, New York, 1930).

In this prison situation in which a bodily going-out-of-the-field is impossible the tension within the plane of reality leads to an inner going-out-of-the-field, to a *transition* from the plane of reality into that of unreality. Lively imagining and daydreams occur. The affective tension expresses itself within the plane of unreality by restless thinking. The special structure of the level of unreality which thus shows itself, and the events occurring in it, are reproduced below rather extensively because of their typical characteristics.

"I did not weep but it was as though a stone lay on my breast. Thoughts and ideas flew with accelerated speed back and forth in my confused imagination.

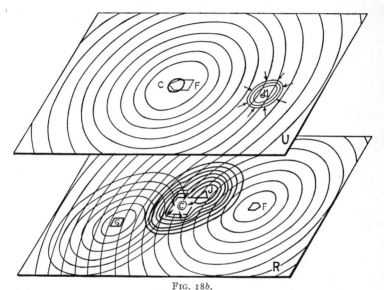

FIG. 18*b*.

But the memory of my misfortune constantly interrupted their strange chain, and I fell back again in an endless labyrinth of uncertainty over my fate.

"It soon came to me that there must surely be some unknown cause of the universal lack of love, yes, even hate, shown me. (I was at that moment firmly convinced that everyone from grandmother to the coachman Philip hated me and rejoiced in my present sorrow.) Perhaps, I said to myself, I am not, after all, the son of my Father and Mother, Volodja's brother, but an unfortunate waif, a foundling kept from pity. And indeed this foolish thought not only provided me a certain doleful comfort but seemed fully probable. It was an ecstasy to think that the cause of my unhappiness was not my guilt but my fate from birth, a destiny resembling that of the unfortunate Karl Iwanowitsch.

"And talking on to myself, I asked why this secret remain concealed now that I had seen through it. Tomorrow morning, I thought, I will go to papa and say, 'Papa, in vain you hide from me the secret of my birth: I know it.' He will reply, 'What is to be done, my dear child? Sooner or later you would surely have discovered it. You are not my son. I have, however, taken you as a son and if you prove yourself worthy of my love, I shall never desert you.' And I shall answer, 'Papa, although I have no right to give you this name, still I will use it this one time more. I have always loved you and will love you. I shall never forget that you have been my benefactor. Yet I can remain no longer in this house. Here no one loves me, and St. Jerome has sworn to destroy me. Either he or I must leave your house. I cannot answer for myself. I so hate this man that I am capable of anything. I shall kill him. Yes, I swear it, Papa, I will kill him.' Papa reasons with me but I put out my hand and say to him, 'No, my friend, my benefactor, we cannot live under one roof. Let me go.' I embrace him and say, I know not why in French, *'Oh, mon père, oh mon bienfaiteur, donne-moi pour la dernière fois la bénédiction et que la volonté de Dieu soit faite!'* And I sat on the chest in the dark room and wept, sobbing loudly at this thought. Suddenly I thought again of the shameful punishment awaiting me. Reality came back to me in its true light and the pictures of my imagination faded instantly."

The subjective oppression of the situation is not least dependent upon the fact that it is traceable to the child's own guilt. The first flight into unreality consists in a separation of these guilty occurrences from his own ego. As frequently occurs after failure[1] one's own responsibility for the unpleasant state of affairs is shifted by rationalization. Fate, for whom no one can answer, is to blame. The inner alienation of the grandmother and above all of the father, so feared by the child, is explained by the fact that he is not a real son of his father, but a foundling. The child (suddenly breaking into French) refuses pathetically all consolation and draws the tragic (and thus not guilty) consequence: he leaves the house; he thinks, "I shall soon die." The flight from the prison is completed, even though on the plane of unreality.

Gradually there occurs a general *structural reorganization of the plane of unreality*. This continues until the child possesses in this plane what he lacks in reality, especially until his social position is radically changed and indeed completely reversed.

"Soon I saw myself free, far from our house. I was a hussar entering battle. From all sides the enemy pressed down upon me. I drew my sabre, killing the first assailant with one stroke. Another stroke sufficed for the second, and another for the third. Finally exhausted from wounds and fatigue I sank to earth crying, 'Victory!' The general rode by, and asked, 'Where is he—our deliverer?' All pointed to me. He fell on my neck, crying through tears of joy, 'Victory!' Later, convalescing, I was walking along the Twer-Boulevard. I was a general! The Czar met me and asked, 'Who is this wounded youngster?' 'The famous hero, Nikolaj,' he was told. The Czar approached me, 'I thank you. Ask of me what you will. I will grant you anything.' Bowing respectfully and leaning on my sabre, I replied, 'I am fortunate, mighty Czar, to have been able to spill my blood for my country. I would gladly have offered my life. Since, however, you are so gracious as to grant me a request, permit me to destroy my enemy, the foreigner, St. Jerome.' I approached St. Jerome threateningly, 'You are to blame for my unhappiness. Kneel!' Suddenly, however, the thought came to me that the real St. Jerome might enter with a rod at any

---

[1] HOPPE, *op. cit.*

minute. Again I saw myself not as a general saving his country, but as a most deplorable, pitiable creature.

"Soon the thought of God came to me and I asked why he should be punishing me. I had not neglected to pray, morning and evening. Why then should I suffer? I can definitely say that the first step toward the religious doubts of my boyhood days occurred at this instant. It was not because unhappiness drove me to grumbling and disbelief but because the thought of the injustice of Providence came to me. And in that twenty-four hours of solitude and complete mental confusion the thought was like an evil seed that, falling after a rain in loose earth, quickly sprouted and took root. Soon I imagined that I should surely die, and pictured vividly St. Jerome's astonishment when he would find my lifeless body in the attic. I remembered the tale of Natalja Sawischa, that the soul of the expired lingers about the house for forty days. In thought I wandered after death unseen through the rooms of my grandmother's house, hearing Ljubotschka's whining, the complaints of grandmother, and Papa speaking with August Antonowitsch. 'He was a good boy,' Papa would say with tears in his eyes. 'Yes,' St. Jerome would counter, 'but a great rogue.' 'You should have respect for the dead' Papa censured. 'You were the cause of his death. You intimidated him. He could not stand the humiliation you caused. . . . Out of my house, miserable one!'

"St. Jerome sank to his knees, begging forgiveness. Then the forty days were over and my soul flew to heaven. I saw there something wonderfully beautiful, white, transparent, and felt that it was my Mother."

The situation in unreality is a complete reversal of that in reality. The child's own field of force that had just shown itself quite weak on the plane of reality (*LR*, Fig. 18*b*) becomes, on the plane of unreality, thanks to his heroic behavior, the socially dominant field. At the same time the particularly painful separation from his beloved father is overcome. Whereas in reality the socially most powerful field of force (that of the father, *F*) is turned against the child, in unreality because of this reunion it stands at his disposal; the father fulfills the punishment of St. Jerome.

The previous daydream had also created on the plane of unreality a very similar situation. There it was the Czar, the most powerful person in the world, whose field of force was placed at the disposition of the boy. Both imaginal situations led to the destruction of St. Jerome, whose power in reality was keeping the boy prisoner in the attic. On the plane of unreality the child is not weak and imprisoned, but powerful and free. The most powerful victorious enemy of the actual moment, on the contrary, is impotent and defeated.

The imaginal picture stretching into unearthly power and freedom climaxes in the reunion with the dead mother.

We shall not examine later occurrences on the plane of reality. The child refuses to make apology to the teacher. A final attempt at actual flight from the house is frustrated by the father.

If the opposed vectors controlling the conflict situation are very strong, the tension may result in diffuse discharge, that is, in an *emotional outburst*. This is illustrated in the above example. The child raves, cries out, weeps. When this happens in the punishment situation, it generally occurs when a momentary attempt at flight is frustrated.

Even if no marked emotional expression occurs, as in the story above, the increased state of tension may decidedly influence the quality of work. We shall consider a case of especial pedagogical interest, the solution of intellectual tasks.

Intellectual tasks undoubtedly require for their solution a certain tension, a vector in the direction of completion of the task. It is unnecessary to discuss again (see pages 120 f.) the fact that positive valence of the task itself provides a more favorable condition for the solution of intellectual tasks than aversion to the task. In the former case despite the occurrence of difficulties, that is, barriers, in the course of its solution a child continues to work in the direction of the task.

It is to be noted further that a conflict situation, especially when it leads to a strong total tension, is peculiarly unfavorable to the solution of intellectual tasks. In its general psychological structure the solution of an intellectual problem consists essentially in a transformation of the Gestalt relations within the sphere of the problem, in a mental "clicking," so to speak.[1] A necessary condition for the occurrence of such "clicking" is that the individual achieve a view of the field as a whole. The decisive transformation of the structure of the field also requires that the person be able to stand above the situation. He must have the possibility of gaining some distance from the task. Only thus is it possible to see the total system of relations instead of simply several isolated facts in the field.

If the child is in a conflict situation with a strong state of tension he feels himself to be standing under the situation, that is, without a view from above. This obviously constitutes an unfavorable condition for calm intellectual solution of the problem.

We have completed our discussion of the topology of the situation involving threat of punishment in the case of a com-

[1] W. KÖHLER, *Intelligenzprüfungen an Menschenaffen*, Springer, Berlin, 1924. (English trans., *The Mentality of Apes*, Harcourt, Brace, New York, 1925.)

mand. We shall not proceed immediately to threat of punishment in the case of a prohibition but shall first consider the situation arising when there is a prospect of reward.

Command with Prospect of Reward

Pedagogically, reward appears as the opposite of punishment. Nevertheless, the general situations in which reward and punishment occur are in certain respects similar. As in the case of punishment, the prospect of reward is only offered when the child is to be led to a type of behavior which the natural field forces of the moment will not produce. The child is to do something which he does not wish to do or to refrain from doing something he desires to do. We shall first consider the situation in which the child is to be gotten by reward to carry out an undesired task.

Nature and Disposition of Valences and Barriers.

The child (C) is again placed opposite a task (T) of negative valence. Whereas in threatened punishment the attempt is made to overcome the vector proceeding from the task by means of a second negative valence, in the present situation a positive valence is utilized. This may be a good mark, a toy, a piece of candy, a promotion, being praised as a good child, or the like. Since the attraction proceeding from the positive valence must overcome the repulsion of the task, the reward (R) must be in the same direction as the task (T). It must also be placed behind the task (Fig. 19).

Thus we are again confronted with a conflict situation. As we have seen, this means that two approximately equal oppositely directed field forces are working on the child. In this case the conflict situation is of the third type discussed above (page 123).

The vector (V_R) proceeding from the reward must again be stronger than that proceeding from the task (V_T), and its strength must vary with the unpleasantness of the task.

Such a situation would, however, by no means suffice to get the child to complete the task. To the child, attracted by the reward, the unpleasant task constitutes a barrier, lying between him and the goal (*G*). In this respect the topology corresponds to that of the situation in which a difficulty prevents the child from attaining his goal (Fig. 2). As a rule in such a situation, where the goal is blocked, the child attempts to get around the barrier. It is the situation in which the *Umweg* (detour) typically occurs. Or the child may attempt to find a weak spot in the barrier. Thus, as in the case of punishment, the child may attempt, when the prospect of a reward is offered, to reach the attractive goal (*e.g.*, candy) without fulfilling the task (Fig. 20). Unless measures are taken to insure that such an evasion of the task is not possible, he will, for example, attempt to obtain the reward from the adult by flattery or by an effort to conceal his failure to finish the task.

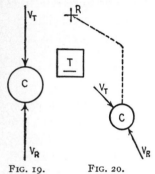

Thus it is also necessary in the reward situation so to erect barriers that access to the reward is possible only through carrying out the task (Fig. 21).

FIG. 19.   FIG. 20.

One may represent this situation without using particular barriers. The fact that the reward may be reached only through the task is also represented if the task is pictured as a zone surrounding the reward (Fig. 22). Topologically the two representations are in many respects equivalent. In both, the zone of the reward (*R*) is entirely enclosed. The representations differ in that in Fig. 22 the enclosing zone is relatively homogeneous, consisting only of the task, whereas in Fig. 21 it consists partly of the task, partly of the special barrier (*B*). In most cases Fig. 21 probably represents the situation more accurately. There are usually special barriers, firm conduct of the adult, for example. Generally a series of other precautions, physical and social, are also necessary to insure that the child will attain the reward only through completing the task.

Comparison of the Total Situations Underlying Reward and Punishment.

Important parallels appear in the comparison of the total situations of expected reward and expected punishment. Both

are conflict situations, and there occur in both general consequences of conflict: increase in tension and tendency to
deviate from the direction of the task. In both cases there is
lacking the natural teleology characteristic of the interest
situation (see page 120).

Certain differences, however, exist. In considering them,
we shall not be primarily concerned with the moral aspects of

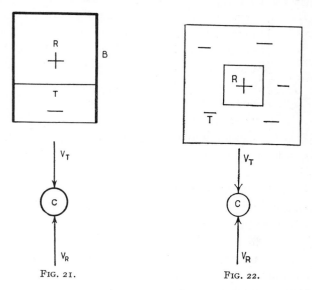

FIG. 21.   FIG. 22.

reward or punishment, nor with their effect upon self-consciousness, nor the encouragement or discouragement incidental
to their occurrence. One major difference lies in the fact that
with threat of punishment the child is surrounded by a barrier,
whereas in the reward situation he stands outside the ring
constituted by both barrier and task. Thus a prospect of
reward does not restrict the child's freedom of movement as a
whole. Rather, within the life-sphere of the child only one
specific object, the reward, is made unattainable (until, of
course, it is reached through completion of the task).

Further, when prospect of reward is presented merely in order
to bring about completion of a task (see page 130), the situation
lacks the constraint characteristic of the punishment situation.

Behavior in the Reward Situation.

1. If the reward possesses an attraction strong enough to counterbalance the unpleasantness and duration of the task and if the remaining barriers surrounding the reward are strong enough, the child will carry out the task.

Nevertheless, as with punishment, there is lacking here also, the natural teleology characteristic of the interest situation

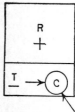

FIG. 23.

(where the child constantly orients himself toward the actual goal of the task). Frequently upon approach or actual entrance into the field of the task, the child's movement quickly reveals a discrepancy between the direction of the task's goal and of the reward (Fig. 23). The child veers in the direction of the reward during the completion of his task. He will break off the task as soon as possible, perhaps before completion, if only the reward can be attained.

2. If the unpleasantness of the task is stronger than the reward, the child will abandon the reward, analogously to taking the punishment.

Frequently there occurs a relative shift and reevaluation of worths (see page 138). Often the reward is given a moral tone. And not infrequently this moral tone signifies a social elevation of the good child above his comrades. Renunciation of the reward usually means that the child at least in the given instance stands outside the ideology in which the reward (a good mark, for example) is considered morally desirable.

There exist, however, important differences between the situation just sketched and that of punishment. In consequence of the lessened condition of constraint in the reward situation the processes are on the whole of an easier character. Further, the moral reevaluations that occur when the child accepts punishment as the lesser evil are in part of different type from those that occur when the child abandons a reward or gives up an ambition to achieve a good mark.

Only rarely does reward follow a definite action of the child as a factually necessary consequence, independent of the adult's will.[1] Such situations are psychologically related in important

[1] Punishment may also, under certain circumstances, possess the character of a natural sanction against transgression of a command or prohibition.

respects to those in which behavior is determined by interest in the thing itself.

3. With strong unpleasantness of task and strong attraction of reward the child may attempt to break through the barrier, to participate, for instance, in an excursion promised as reward even though his task be unfinished.

This situation resembles in certain respects that of punishment. To be sure, a break through the barrier leads in this case to reward rather than to freedom. But a parallel exists in that the barrier here also rests essentially upon the power of the adult. Breaking through has thus the character of a struggle with the adult. Corresponding to the lack of a pronounced condition of constraint, the strife is generally less bitter. In addition there exists a stronger tendency to conduct the struggle by flattery or some other accepted method, since the child is striving to induce the adult to allow it some pleasure.

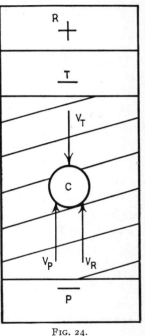

Fig. 24.

Combination of Reward and Punishment.

The reward situation just sketched seldom occurs in this pure form. Usually the adult relies upon a pedagogy neither of reward alone nor of simple punishment, but rather upon a combination of the two, "sugar and the switch." Generally with presentation of a reward there is at the same time a more or less hidden threat of punishment should the reward prove ineffective.

The school system of grading is perhaps the simplest and most characteristic example of this case. A good grade has the character of a reward, a bad one that of punishment, and the total situation is such that one or the other necessarily occurs.

When the child is faced with an unpleasant school task which will be graded, the tendency to solve the problem as well as possible derives both from the negative valence of a bad mark and from the positive valence of a good one (Fig. 24).

This simultaneous fear of punishment and hope of reward is characteristic of many situations of the type in question.

PROHIBITION WITH THREAT OF PUNISHMENT

So far we have discussed cases in which threat of punishment or prospect of reward has served the purpose of getting the child to perform a definite action, that, for instance, of completing a definite task. Let us now briefly consider the topology of those cases in which prohibition rather than commanded performance of a desired action is to be insured. We shall discuss first prohibition with threat of punishment.

There occur cases of threatened punishment in which one might as well speak of command as of prohibition. If a teacher threatens a child with punishment should he fail to behave, the child is faced in the first place with a prohibition of certain unmannerly actions (laughing, acting "fresh," and so on). In addition, he is expected to display a group of well-intentioned positive types of action, a minimum of which may not be evaded in fulfilling the prohibition. Thus a command also exists. Although the following cases may not always lend themselves to unequivocal classification in one or another definite group, it is preferable to proceed from such definite fundamental cases for the elucidation of psychological dynamics.

The child is faced by a desired goal, a positive valence. For a negative valence to be effective as an opposing force it must lie in the same direction as this goal. Thus arises a conflict situation of the third type (see page 123), similar to that existing when a command is presented with prospect of reward.

The most obvious representation of the situation, therefore, would be analogous to Fig. 21 or to Fig. 22: threat of punishment stands as an opposing force before the desired goal (*DG*, Fig. 25).[1]

[1] In Fig. 25 the representation of the topology is analogous to that of Fig. 22. A representation analogous to Fig. 21 would in this case be less adequate.

The behavior of the child testifies that to a certain extent this representation actually fits the situation. A two-year-old child has been forbidden to pick flowers in the garden. Consider his behavior as he hesitates before a flower, saying threateningly to himself, "No, no." Such conduct gives the impression that the threat of punishment really stands as a barrier in front of the desired goal.

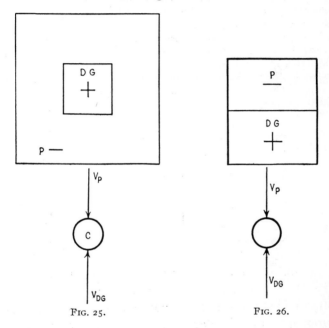

FIG. 25.   FIG. 26.

Nevertheless punishment does not stand before the wanted goal in the same way as the unpleasant task before the reward. Punishment is not something that temporally precedes the attainment of the goal. It is not a possible way to the goal, but stands rather temporally behind it.

In attempting to represent this temporal relation it is, nevertheless, not possible to place the punishment forthwith behind the desired goal, as in Fig. 26. For this would represent the goal as immediately attainable by the child, who would then be free to move away from the punishment. Actually should the child carry out the desired activity he would thereby incur

the punishment.   Once he enters the field of the desired goal
he finds himself surrounded by the punishment.   The situation
after entrance into the desired activity (the second phase) may
be represented topologically as in Fig. 27.   The child, as it were,
stands in a cage from which he strives
to escape by all available methods.

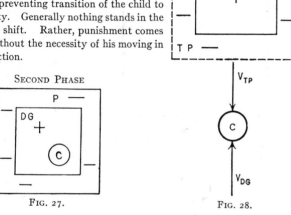

The further fact that the child cannot escape
punishment by lingering in the field of the goal
is not represented, although such attempts are
sometimes observed.   The punishment is here
not a barrier preventing transition of the child to
another activity.   Generally nothing stands in the
way of such a shift.   Rather, punishment comes
to the child without the necessity of his moving in
a definite direction.

FIG. 27.

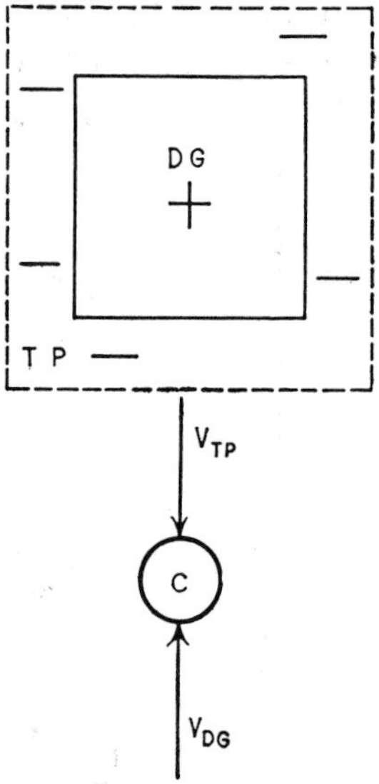

FIG. 28.

A certain *transformation* of its topology is thus characteristic
of the prohibition situation.   Before acting (first phase Fig.
28) the child sees the threat of punishment (*TP*) as an obstacle
between him and the desired goal.   This obstacle, however,
is essentially different from the barriers we have previously
discussed.   It can be passed without any present difficulty
or unpleasantness.   It does not thus represent the actual,
real punishment but only reflects the barrier that acquires
full reality after entrance into the desired activity.   Thus
in the first phase the barrier has more or less the unreality
of all future events, of everything whose advent is not yet
certain.[1]

[1] For the significance of degrees of reality in dynamics, see Hoppe, *op. cit.*, and
Dembo, *op. cit.*   The fact that the unreality of future events is not quite the
same as that of thought is left unconsidered here.

In the case of command with threat of punishment a definite time is set within which the command must be executed.[1] This furnishes as we have seen an element of constraint; the child is surrounded by a barrier (Fig. 10). In the case of prohibition with threat of punishment such a temporal limitation need not exist. The constrained character is in general less pronounced. The child remains free to move except in the definitely bounded area of the forbidden action. The constrained character of the situation, however, increases if the forbidden area is very large or if it touches a central life-sphere (as when association with a loved friend or indulgence in a favorite occupation is forbidden).

Digression on the Degree of Reality of Punishment.

The degree of reality of reward or punishment plays a large role in determining the actual behavior of the child. This degree of reality depends upon a whole group of factors. Above all it is a function of the certainty with which the child anticipates punishment or reward (thus indirectly of the actual power of the adult, his sympathy, and so on). It depends equally upon the character and upon the momentary condition of the child (*e.g.*, immersion in his own dreams and the degree of reality of his conception of the world). I remember quite exactly my childish attitude toward whips. Since I never experienced whippings at home the cane-handled switch at school always had for me something of the incomprehensible and unreal, although it was not infrequently used. This unreality was so strong that once when I was forced to face it the situation filled me with amazement. The teacher was astonished, as I observed with surprise and without crying the lively pain of the separate blows.

The importance of the degree of reality of punishment is shown above all in the fact that children who once have experienced a punishment are wont to behave quite differently in

---

[1] Or the command may be conditional. A definite action, for instance, is to be carried out upon occurrence of certain conditions. Thus, "If someone comes you are to say, 'Good day,' nicely."

the face of a threatened repetition from whose who have never experienced it. The reason that the burned child shuns the fire, that one who has been severely punished generally shows less resistance in the face of a new threat of punishment, is not to be sought merely in an associative coupling with pain. More essential is an increase in the degree of reality of the punishment, the transformation of the punishment from an imagined, possible occurrence in a level of unreality into part of the plane of reality. We have already mentioned that such transformation of the degree of reality does not always result in increased fear of punishment but may lead to devaluation of the punishment and eventually to release from the previous ideology. Descent from levels of unreality to the plane of reality makes things not only harder, but also more naked, simple, and more easily surveyed in their whole extent.

A certain *transformation* in time of the *degree of reality* is to be observed in all the reward and punishment situations we have discussed. With increasing nearness punishment and unpleasantness of task both become more real. Occurrences within this interval may lead to sudden shifts in the degree of reality of either. Punishment of another child by the adult, even mention of some other punishment—anything making the adult seem particularly dangerous or harmless are examples of such occurrences. Such shifts often play an essential role in determining the time and nature of the child's decision. Should the degree of reality of punishment and task differ too greatly a pronounced conflict situation does not generally arise.[1]

In the event of incompletion of the task in the situation of command with threat of punishment, the punishment continues to gain in reality as it approaches. In the last discussed instance of prohibition with threat of punishment, the punishment is typically an *ex post facto* affair, especially when the forbidden goal of desire (perhaps some attractive sweets) is present and therefore possesses a very much higher degree of reality. "Opportunity makes the thief." It is also naturally

---

[1] We may recall that one of the necessary conditions for the origin of a true conflict situation is the approximate equality of opposed vectors.

characteristic of these situations that there exists a relatively great difference between the degrees of reality of the positive and negative valences. Herein often lies the child's chief difficulty in making a stand against the attraction.

Related to the fact that punishment is psychologically farther off than satisfaction of the desire is the circumstance that a certain intellectual maturity is a necessary condition of the effectiveness of such threatened punishments. The world of a little child is of small extent temporally as well as spacially. Events which can be surveyed in direction of past or future and which as part of the momentary situation determine the behavior of the child develop in the first year of the child's life from initially very small temporal extents. Not until a sufficiently large temporal span becomes a psychologically real present for the child can a threat of punishment be effective by reason of such a topology.[1]

A general property of threat of punishment frequently becomes noticeable in the last-mentioned situation and is to be related to natural differences in the degrees of reality of punishment and desired goal. It is precisely because of threat of punishment that an originally neutral event first acquires *positive* attraction.[2] Corresponding opposed shifts in valences may also be observed in commands. These processes are closely related to phenomena of defiance. Here lies a realm of fundamental psychological significance. I shall go into it only in so far as it bears upon the topology of the situation in general.

Prohibition isolates a definite area from the life-sphere of the child in that it surrounds this area with a barrier. It delimits the zone of free movement of the child. Thus there occurs an interference in the sphere of power of the child. This naturally releases an opposed action, in which the child seeks to assert himself against the sphere of power of the adult. The perverting effect of a command and above all of a prohibition upon the valence of an object is from this point of view to be understood as a struggle for freedom of movement in the life-space of the child. Here lies also the explanation of why, at just the age of two to three years, these reactions of

---

[1] We shall discuss later (p. 169) still another possible effect of punishment.

[2] I do not here refer to cases in which the punishment as such possesses positive valence.

defiance are particularly frequent.[1]   An especially pronounced stabilization of the ego of the child takes place at this time, showing itself, for example, in the development of the concept of property.

With respect to degree of constraint the prohibition situation with threat of punishment is related to the command situation with prospect of reward. On the whole the child retains freedom of movement. Only one definite area, that of the desired goal, is enclosed. Nevertheless when the occurrence is viewed not by itself but as included in the total surrounding situation, the condition of constraint in the former case is somewhat more pronounced. The adult's domination of the field appears more clearly in the foreground.

PROHIBITION WITH PROSPECT OF REWARD

The situation involving prospect of reward for refraining from some action is rather special in nature. The reward promised is always contingent upon continued avoidance of the action *within definite time limits*. Either this action may attract directly (*e.g.*, the eating of sweets) or for some more indirect reason it may be difficult to avoid. Thus rewards are often resorted to in an attempt to combat enuresis; they may be promised to a pair of siblings for cessation from their frequent teasing.

The situation is thus characterized by a positive valence or an equivalent pressure toward a definite action. The reward, a second valence introduced by the adult, is supposed to prevent the child from acting in the direction of the first valence. Thus there exists a conflict situation of the first type (Fig. 7).

The relations are rarely so simple. Generally there is the prospect not only of reward for abstinence, but of punishment for indulgence. Furthermore, as a rule the first valence

---

[1] Charlotte Bühler speaks of "an age of defiance." The fundamental processes underlying the defiance reaction may well be of a general nature. They are not, of course, to be explained merely in terms of the age level itself. Our observations and experimental investigations of infants appear to indicate that the defiance reaction represents an expression in the social sphere of a very general psychological law, equivalent to the proposition "action equals reaction."

increases in strength with the passage of time. It is often easy to resist for a brief period but difficult to hold out over a longer one. The following special example, although simple, represents the topology of a whole group of similar situations. A child learning to swim attempts the full length of the pool; his goal is to swim one hundred meters. This goal attracts him exceedingly. At certain distances along the edge of the pool there are ropes to which he may hold. The child has rested on them in earlier

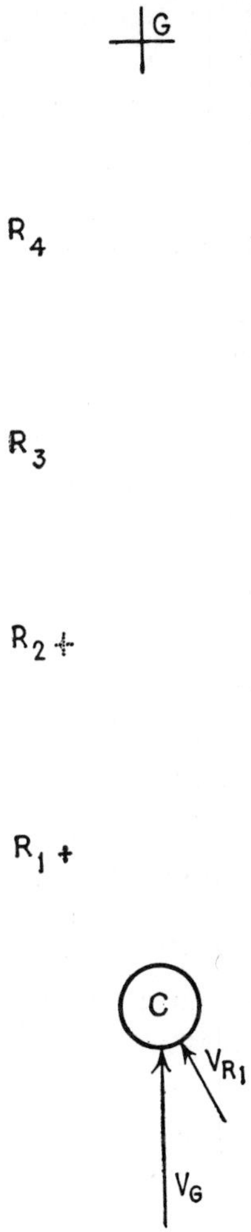

FIG. 29.

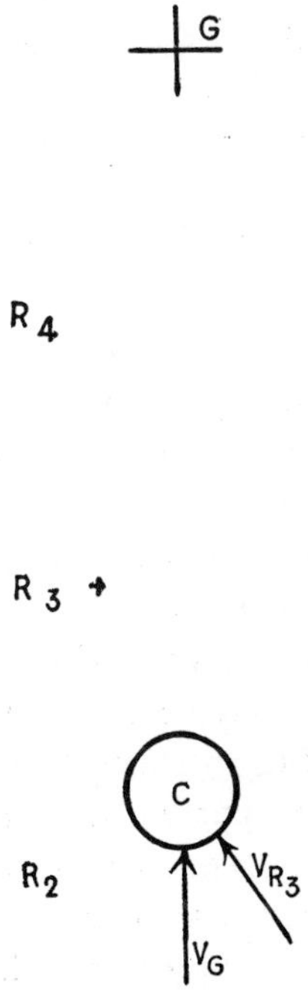

FIG. 30.

attempts. He now faces the problem of swimming past all these attractive resting places to the end of the pool.

In this case the topology of the psychological situation corresponds quite well to that of the physical-geographical.

The child is attracted by the resting place immediately in front of him (R_1, Fig. 29), and at the same time by the desired but distant goal (to swim one hundred meters). As the task grows increasingly difficult and the fatigue of the child increases, the danger that he will yield to the attraction of the nearest resting place becomes ever greater (Fig. 30).

From a certain distance the attraction of the final goal itself generally increases in strength as it is approached. The ultimate behavior will differ according to the relative strengths of the vectors and the condition of the child.

In promising a reward for abstinence from an activity during a definite period, one has also generally to reckon with the existence of a series of attractions tempting toward a transgression of the prohibition. The child receives the reward only when it has successfully steered past all these attractions.

Reward, Punishment, and Genuine Transformation of Interest

Having completed our general discussion of the structure of the situation underlying reward and punishment, we may now turn to a problem closely related both psychologically and pedagogically. We have previously indicated that utilization of reward and punishment becomes an acute problem only when one desires a form of behavior not prompted by natural inclination. In such cases there exists together with these two possibilities of bringing about the desired behavior a third, namely awakening an interest, producing an inclination. This possibility is one particularly stressed by modern pedagogy. The problem arises as to how the situation involved is to be characterized psychologically. A penetrating discussion of this important and theoretically very interesting problem would require much space. Here I must perforce restrict myself to a few remarks.

Interest in an object or activity not previously interesting may be awakened in many ways: by example, by imbedding the task in another context (for instance, carrying out arithmetic problems by playing salesman), and by a variety of other methods.   Not infrequently interest in an object depends upon the personality of a definite teacher.

The question naturally arises as to whether these situations are essentially different from those involving prospect of reward or punishment.

At first sight, and indeed from a psychological point of view, it might appear that the situation in which, for instance, the child calculates only because he likes to play at selling is similar to that of reward.   The activity of calculating possesses a negative valence, but playing at selling, the goal behind it, leads the child to calculate.   The situation would thus correspond to that of Fig. 21.

Such cases doubtless exist.   In them, however, the psychological essential of the third mentioned possibility, transformation in valence of the *thing itself*, is not attained. The characteristic topology of the reward situation remains unaltered: the negative valence of calculating persists unchanged, and there merely arises next to it a second positive valence.   Thus fundamentally there has occurred no true transformation in the valence of calculating.

From the psychological point of view, however, one can scarcely begin to speak of an interest pedagogy unless the valence of the activity in question is successfully and truly changed.

The objection is easily raised that in practice such a shift in valence of the thing itself is rarely attained, that in any case one must always add something to the situation in order to bring about the transformation of interest.   Without ignoring the great practical difficulties involved, and without intending to imply that such a transformation of valence may always be achieved, I should still like to emphasize that the "addition" of new moments may have effects other than those just indicated.

If an activity, undesired in itself, is related to something else that the child likes (*e.g.*, a primer is decorated with pretty pictures), the pleasant and the unpleasant, though standing next to each other, may remain unconnected.   There exist, however, imbeddings of a task or activity of such a sort that the meaning, and together with it the valence, of the task completely changes. A child that does not like a certain food eats it without ado if the goblin on the end of the spoon is to be buried, or if the spoon, as train, is to enter the station of the mouth. In such cases the original action, eating, becomes a dependent part of a more inclusive activity whole and eventually merely a superficial layer of the other activity. It is a fact fundamental to the psychology of action and need as well as to that of sensation that the psychological reality, and the effect of such dependent parts, is primarily determined through the *whole* in which they are imbedded.[1]

It is because of this condition that imbedding a separate task in another mental sphere (*e.g.*, taking an activity from the sphere of school tasks into the sphere of action for a practical purpose) may radically change the valence of the activity.

Whether or not establishment of another connection actually leads to a transformation of valence thus depends essentially upon whether there has thereby been created a true whole, a dynamic Gestalt, or merely a summative conglomerate.[2] Between summative togetherness and the completely unified whole of a strong Gestalt, in which parts completely lose their independence, there exists a continuous transition (dynamically weak Gestalten). Indeed this is of essential significance for our problem of the transformation of interest. One would expect that for a child taking no joy in learning to write the alphabet, a change of valence would occur more quickly when he is allowed as soon as possible to write meaningful communications in sentence form than when he is provided with a primer with decorative drawings bordering its pages.[3] For in the first

[1] For references, see K. KOFFKA, Psychologie der optischen Wahrnehmung, *Handbuch der normalen und pathologischen Physiologie*, 1931, **12**, 2 Hefte, 1215–1271; and KÖHLER, *Gestalt Psychology*, Liveright, New York, 1929. For an especial experimental investigation of wholes in behavior and in systems of needs, see BIRENBAUM, Das Vergessen einer Vornahme, *Psychol. Forsch.*, 1930, **13**, 218 ff.

[2] Cf. the concept of *Und-Summe* in M. WERTHEIMER, *Psychol. Forsch.*, 1921, **1**, p. 47; 1923, **4**, p. 301.

[3] Here lies one of the chief advantages of the "global" method of reading and writing developed by Decroly.

case the letters lose their psychological separateness more readily.

If, however, separate letters constitute too great a difficulty for the child, the writing of each letter will become an independent task and the structural transformation of the meaning of the total activity will be hindered.

Change in valence of a task or of an activity thus becomes possible when one imbeds the "same accomplishment" (externally regarded) in another behavior whole or in another mental sphere. (It is thus important, *e.g.*, that a given piece of work be part of the preparation for a birthday celebration, that some other work be for this or that teacher, and so on.) Pedagogically applied this means that for the small child the *total atmosphere* of the school is not only important but possesses almost a constitutive significance for the dynamics of the separate activities.

We have contrasted transformation of interest in the thing itself with situations involving reward and punishment. To neglect the existence of transition cases would, however, be both false and too schematic. Both threat of punishment and the prospect of reward may in definite instances and to a certain degree lead to a transformation in valence of the thing itself. Threat of punishment may make less valued the forbidden object. Reward may lead the child to regard the thing not at first wanted as something to be valued for its own sake.

This spread of valence from reward and punishment to the thing itself plays a role particularly in the young child, corresponding with the general weakness of functional boundaries between his mental systems.[1] Reward and punishment, when they are externally tacked on, may thus act as a simple strengthening of command or prohibition even though they possess for the child no understandable justification. With older children, however, transformation in valence of the thing itself occurs only when the command or prohibition is recognized as actually justified; when, that is, the behavior is brought into relationship with some whole which attracts or repels the child as something valuable or worthless. Resort to threat of punishment or

[1] See Chap. III.

promise of reward to support a command or prohibition is expressive of the fact that the command or prohibition is not factually justified or not sufficiently so.   Thus in fact the threat of punishment acts antagonistically to transformation in valence of the thing itself.   This opposed effect is clearest when the arbitrariness, lack of factual justification of the reward or punishment, is combined with an unjust accusation of a particular child.

CHAPTER V

EDUCATION FOR REALITY[1]

On the subject Education for the Present I do not wish to discuss the certainly very interesting questions of the position of the aims and methods of Montessori education in the social, economic, and political total situation of the present, nor what education has to perform in this respect. I wish, rather, to inquire into education for present-day life essentially in a *psychological* sense.

I remember a conversation with a Montessori teacher. She told of a student who, in her sixth semester, did not yet know what she ought to study, and added: "In a child that had gone through the Montessori system that would be impossible."

Those who know the Montessori system will understand what was meant by that. The teacher was, she thought, speaking of a person who oscillated between various possibilities and desires and was unable at the right moment to carry out the right act. She fails in the face of the present because she is unable to choose among the things the world offers and to reach a clear-headed decision. The child in the Montessori school learns precisely and primarily this: to decide himself, and to choose freely between possibilities which are given him. This is doubtless one of the most positive aspects of Montessori education.

The American student usually has, as a result of the total environment in which he has grown up, the ability to decide, to stand with both feet on the ground of reality, in higher degree than the German student; the present-day German student in greater degree than the student before the War. Desirable as

[1] From *Die Neue Erziehung*, 1931, No. 2, pp. 99–103. An address given in February 1931 at a convention on problems of the Montessori method. This does not imply that the author would defend the orthodox Montessori method.

this attitude is, it has, nevertheless, a danger to which attention may again be drawn today: the present in which one lives very easily becomes all too narrow, the mode of life [*Praxis*] all too superficial, the level of aspiration all too low, the facts all too naked.

Those familiar with the discussions of the Montessori problems will see at once a relation to the question of the atrophy of imagination through suppression of play. I do not wish to discuss the demand to nurture the imagination of the child because imagination in itself is something beautiful. Even a quite realistic consideration of the requirements for life in the present must recognize an intrinsic problem in this demand.

Extension of Psychological Life-Space and -Time

This becomes still clearer when the question of education for the present is subject to discussion.

If one starts out from the psychology of the small child, one has at first to regard this task as downright paradoxical. It is, indeed, a chief characteristic of the young child, say of the six-months-old infant, to be essentially the present and nothing but the present. With a variation of Hegel's dictum one might say, "The child *is* essentially present." [*Das Kleinkind ist wesentlich itzt.*] The world of the child is not only spatially small (the cradle, the events of the nursery), but also temporally only slightly extended. His units of action are small in scope and of brief duration. Past and future play little part, and that only for short periods, in his psychological environment. *The demand for a life in the present is hence realized to extreme degree in the young child.*

The related demand for *independent decision* in the present is, in a certain sense, also realized to extreme degree in the infant. The infant acts in accordance with his momentary needs: what does not taste good to him he does not eat; if one attempts to compel him he spits out the porridge.

An education for the present seems here to be in no sense necessary. The pedagogical task seems, rather, to be precisely the opposite, extension of the narrow horizon of the present in spatial (including social) and temporal directions. For today Goethe's saying is still valid—"Who cannot give an account of three thousand years remains in the darkness of inexperience, can live only from one day to another."[1]

This development in spatial-temporal extension rests, so it might seem, essentially upon the fact that the child, through experience, learns to survey ever larger relations. The adult would then have the task of furthering and accelerating this natural process. It is today common property of pedagogical theories (although this demand is represented in variously radical degree and the practical tasks are still extremely great) that such a leading out from the narrowness of the child world is not possible by the simple procedure of acquiring and retaining knowledge but presupposes the autonomous activity and productivity of the child as a natural basis.

But a pedagogy that sees in the extension of the psychologically present life-space of the child only an *intellectual* problem overlooks a quite decisive consideration.

The extension of the child world beyond the momentary present into the future consists partly, to be sure, in the fact that the perceptual wholes in which the world is presented are gradually extended, that the intellectual survey becomes more embracing: the child experiences, for example, that some time after the lightning, the thunder comes; that he is scolded when he upsets a cup. In many respects more fundamental, however, is the development of *action wholes;* the child no longer strives solely for present things, not only has wishes that must be realized at once, but his purposes grasp toward a tomorrow. When he is somewhat older, not only events several months past but also events several months in the future play a considerable role in present behavior. The *goals* which determine the child's behavior *are thrown continually further into the future*. A decisive extension of the psychologically present life-space of the child is based upon this temporal displacement of goals.

[1]   Wer nicht von drei Tausend Jahren sich weiss Rechenschaft zu geben
Bleib im Dunkel unerfahren, mag von Tag' zu Tage leben.

This presents, however, a pedagogically important problem. When the perceptual space of a child is extended from his crib to the room and the street, from hours to days and months, it is still, chiefly, a spatial (social) or temporal extension within the same level of reality. But the action goal that reaches out into the future is at the same time somewhat more *unreal*. It is something that comes out of the realm of wishes and dreams, as a rule an ideal goal, that does not yet possess so full a reality as a present event. A far-ranging wish goal brings, at the same time, an extension of the life-space in another dimension; it signifies a reference to another, an unreal level of the psychological environment, and this reference is usually, indeed, more pronounced the more distant the goal. Even in adults the bold, far-seeing plan stands close to Utopia and fantasy, and there is danger of diversion into unreality.

Levels of Reality and Unreality

A word on the difference between levels of reality and unreality.[1] Considered from the point of view of psychological dynamics, unreality, the land of dreams and air castles, presents a soft and easily movable medium. It is characterized by the fact that in it one can do whatever he wishes. Unreality is not limited to things of thought:[2] an action may also be unreal. The child in the kindergarten who has been forbidden for some reason to draw, watches the other children draw or strokes the crayons. The mere *gesture*, the phrase, and in a certain sense even the substitute (compensatory) act belong no less to the level of unreality than do dreams.

The stratification into levels of greater and less degrees of reality is a general property of the psychological environment of the person. The adult flees into unreality when the level of reality becomes too tense and disagreeable. Of the greatest significance for his whole behavior, and a basic fact for

[1] Cf. DEMBO, Der Ärger als dynamisches Problem, *Psychol. Forsch.*, 1931, **15**, 1–144; HOPPE, Erfolg und Misserfolg, *Psychol. Forsch.*, 1930, **14**, 1–62; LEWIN, above, pp. 145–153.

[2] There is also a realistic thinking.

pedagogy, is the degree of reality of the stratum in which the center of gravity of the life of a particular individual lies.

In the child the strata of reality and unreality are still only slightly separated. His thinking, for example, shows traces of magic. To what extent and in what way the separation of reality from unreality is brought about is a crucial question for the life of the child. That this separation occur in a clear and clean-cut way is one of the most essential pedagogical postulates. This is not merely an overcoming of the child's magic-animistic view of the world and certainly not an essentially intellectual process. The separation derives chiefly, rather, from the sphere of action and rests upon the experiences of the child concerning anything that does not go as he wants it to.

There are essentially two general conditions upon a basis of which reality as a psychological fact for the child is formed: (1) the will of *another person;* and (2) the resistance of *things* against his own will.

Social Fields of Force

In the infant the forces of the psychological environment are determined essentially by *his own needs*. By a process of development (which I cannot here discuss more fully) in the course of the first year of life a psychological environment is formed, the attractions and fears, the possibilities and difficulties of which are determined for the most part, not by the child's own needs, but by the fact that the child lives in the *social field of force* of other persons. The will of the parents and comrades induces for the child certain goals, valuations, friendships, and enmities. It is, above all, through these spheres of power of other people that reality and unreality are separated for the child.

Almost always the will of an adult is the strongest and hardest reality in the child's life. Indeed, there exists in the adult, thanks to the actual superiority of his sphere of power, the natural inclination to make his wishes the decisive principle of reality for the child. Pedagogically expressed, the child has to obey.   The more a pedagogy is based on obedience the more this outside will becomes the supporting scaffold of the child's reality.   Even in such cases reality and unreality are separated for the child, indeed the separation is then usually fairly simple.   Self-control in the face of reality is also learned by the child in this way; but this discipline rests upon the fact that the adult leads the child.   A constraint situation is established, the most striking expression of which is the harness or halter for kindergarten children that one still sees occasionally on the street.   If, in such a situation, the sphere of power of the adult, his position of authority, should for any reason collapse, the structure of the level of reality on which the life of the child rests psychologically must also collapse.   This occurs when the child becomes independent, usually at the latest, with puberty.   Such a collapse is usually bad for the child especially because the constraint situation in which he has lived is not only an inimical pressure but at the same time the crutch of his existence.

The child lived in a present which, thanks to the immediate relation of his goals and values to those of the adult, reached formally, to be sure, far beyond the narrow situation of the moment, and in which he arrived at a separation of reality from unreality.   But the level of reality collapses because it lacks a fundamental relation to his own needs. What that means becomes clear when one considers the other conditions upon which reality and unreality may be psychologically separated, namely, the resistance of things to the execution of one's own will.

Objective Barriers

The second way to the separation of reality and unreality, the child's experience of objective difficulties in attaining the goal chosen by himself, is in many respects pedagogically opposed to the first; that is, an intensive experience of a reality independent of his own wish occurs only when the wish for the goal is strong.   The formation of a recognized stratum of objective realities and necessities, which is certainly pedagogically desirable, presupposes the existence of a total situation in which the child has the possibility to set himself goals and to act freely according to his own needs and his own judgment. *Objectivity cannot arise in a constraint situation; it arises only in a situation of freedom.* Intensive needs of the child's own and freedom to set goals are pedagogically not an inhibition but a necessary condition to a happy separation of reality and unreality.

To be sure, it is necessary that the child who has chosen his own goal be not spared the difficulties of attaining it, neither the difficulties conditioned by social life nor those of physical materials. On the other hand, these difficulties should not be so overwhelming that the child gives up entirely setting goals of his own or flees out of the all too disagreeable reality into unreality.

We know how precisely this consideration, free choice of occupation on the one side, self-control on the basis of the special structure of the materials of the occupation on the other side, belongs to the fundamental principles of Montessori education. That the particular difficulties due to the nature of the material used frequently become visibly clear may permit the child to experience the objectivity of the difficulties in an especially fortunate way. Thus one may hope that the barriers to the attainment of a goal, which are usually not understood by the child and hence easily slip into the realm of the indeterminate, the fearful and uncanny, the unreal, may be used in a construction of a clear level of objective reality. For the child in the kindergarten to follow even for some hours his own individual rhythm I believe to be entirely appropriate for most children; since the rhythm of psychological needs in respect of satiation and satisfaction varies so unpredictably from child to child, from day to day, only if the child can actually follow his own needs can we expect that strong tension toward the goal, which constitutes a favorable condition for the development of a marked level of reality.

Even later it remains important that certain intervals of occupation according to one's own choice and own rhythm be provided. Although, to be sure, the incorporation in the social group becomes in many respects more dominant and the question of the formation of an objective level of reality within the personal relation acquires an increased importance, the conditions become much more complicated by reason of multiple imbedding. Thus one of the pedagogically most difficult problems is to give a functionally proper place in the psychological life-space of the child to that middle level between psychological reality and unreality which is commonly called fantasy and which is related in the most intimate way to, for example, the gesture and artistic expression of all sorts. For the requirement of a clear and clean-cut separation of reality from unreality and of a life in the level of reality cannot mean that the level of unreality is to be banished entirely from the psychological life-space of the child or that any functional connection between the planes of psychological reality and unreality is to be destroyed. For the breadth of the present life-space and the adequacy of realistic behavior depend in a far from unimportant degree upon the kind and depth of the relations between these levels.

Freedom and Responsibility

Education for the present cannot mean an education for living in a momentary situation. The problem of the extension of the psychological life-space of the child, which reaches beyond intellectual and didactic problems, is related most intimately to the psychological separation of the levels of reality and unreality. The development of a level of reality which shall provide a sound basis clear through to adulthood requires that the free life-space of the child be not too small. The separation of reality and unreality seems usually to occur earlier in proletarian children; but we know that this is not always an advantage, that an all too hard environment leads to stunting. Analogously, an early separation of reality and unreality is produced by the construction of an authoritative, obedience-demanding, constraint situation; but the arbitrary and over-done separation of these levels carries with it the danger of concealed substitute satisfactions and a later collapse of the whole level of reality. Only in a sufficiently free life-space in which the child has the possibility of choosing his goals according to his own needs and in which, at the same time, he fully experiences the objectively conditioned difficulties in the attainment of the goal, can a clear level of reality be formed, only thus can the ability for responsible decision develop.

CHAPTER VI

SUBSTITUTE ACTIVITY AND SUBSTITUTE VALUE

Experimental studies of the dynamic laws of the behavior and structure of personality have forced us to consider more and more complicated problems. Instead of investigating the single psychological systems which correspond to simple needs and desires, we have to deal with the interrelationships of these systems, with their differentiation and transformations, and with the different kinds of larger wholes built up from them. These interrelationships and larger wholes are very labile and delicate. Yet one must try to get hold of them experimentally because they are most important for understanding the underlying reality of behavior and personality differences. In doing this we often find facts which Freud first brought to our attention, thereby rendering a great service even though he has not given a clear dynamic theory in regard to them. One such fact is that of substitution.

Freud uses the concept of substitution extensively to explain both normal and abnormal behavior. Moreover, sublimation, which is closely related to substitution, is according to him an important foundation of our whole cultural life. We find substitution in very different forms. There is, for instance, the man who dreams of a palace and brings a few pieces of marble into his kitchen. There is the man who cannot buy a piano, but who collects piano catalogs. Again we find the delinquent boy who knows that he will not be allowed to leave his reform school but who asks for a traveling bag as a birthday present. And the little boy who threatens and scolds the larger boy whom he cannot beat on the playground. These and a hundred other examples make us realize how important and far reaching the problem of substitution is in regard to psychological needs as well as with reference to bodily needs such as hunger and sex. The greater the need, the stronger seems to be the tendency to substitution. Even the great field of children's play has a peculiar relationship to substitution, either of objects or of activity.

Everyone recognizes, I believe, that at present we have no theory which really explains the dynamics of substitution. Freud avoids giving a definition of substitution and, according to the opinion of prominent psychoanalysts, he develops no real theory for it.

If one asks about the necessary and adequate conditions for the appearance of substitute action and about its effects, one meets a paradoxical fact. Substitute actions arise often in situations in which one cannot reach a certain goal, situations in which a psychobiological tension exists. Let us take an example from the work of Dembo on anger. The subject who takes part in the experiment has been trying for a long time to throw rings over a bottle, but without success. At last in tears she goes to the door and slings the rings over some coat hooks. Another example is that of the subject who cannot reach the flower which is her goal. She suddenly grabs another flower which stands in a vase nearby.

These events, which at first appear quite understandable, seem less simple when considered from the standpoint of the dynamics of the situation. Obviously the substitute action springs from the tension system which corresponds to the original action. One would expect, therefore, that the tension system of the original action would be discharged through the substitute action, either completely or in part. Yet in many cases the person only becomes more dissatisfied and more emotional as is clearly evident in the experiments we have made. But if the main system is not discharged through the substitute action it is not easy to understand, from the standpoint of dynamics, why the substitute action should arise at all.

For the investigation of this and other dynamic questions we have carried on a series of experiments with adults, feeble-minded children, and psychopathic children. I shall give a few of the results of these experiments.

If one tries to define the range over which substitution may occur, one meets with great difficulty. If, for example, in experiments on the effect of a prohibition, one takes a doll away from a child and the child begins to make doll clothes, one would call this a substitute activity. But if the child begins to play with a train, one is not sure. One person would say that it is a substitute activity and another that it is not, that the child would have played with the train even if the doll had not been taken away. How similar must the original and the subsequent action be in order that one may say surely that the latter is a substitute action? Another example: If the subject throw the rings, not over the bottle, but over a block which is nearby, it is probable that this is a substitute act. But if he playfully puts the rings first over one arm and then over the other, or if he spins the rings on the floor, are these substitute actions or simple restless actions?

It is impossible to escape this difficulty by limiting the concept of substitution to acts which are very similar in content to the original action; for, without doubt, there are substitute actions which are very dissimilar in form to the original act. We know, for example, from the work of Fajans, that a doll may be a real substitute for a child who has been unable to reach a piece of candy. Or the child may accept his mother's sympathy as an equally genuine substitution. On the other hand, we shall see that two actions can be very similar, without one serving as a substitute for the other. In regard to examples from psychoanalysis it is important that the similarity of two facts is not sufficient evidence for the statement that one is a substitute for the other. Whether a substitute is present or not cannot be decided from the *external* appearance of the events. It is necessary in each individual case to see whether the two facts have a certain *dynamic* connection.

From the dynamic point of view one can speak of substitution only in cases in which the substitution is connected with the tension system corresponding to the original goal, that is, only if the substitute action springs from this original system.

According to this dynamic point of view, one finds an unexpected relation between substitution and the use of *tools* or other means of reaching a goal. If one wishes to give information to someone and the telephone is out of order, one sends a telegram; if the child cannot take a direct path to his objective, he tries to reach it by a roundabout route. In all such cases, in which the carrying out of an intention is changed according to environment, a new action springs from the psychological system which corresponds to the original goal.

Experiments have shown that indeed we find a fluid transition between the use of new tools or new ways and the special substitute action. If, for example, the subject uses a stick to place the rings over the bottle, this use of tools changes the meaning of the task so that we have a new task. If we use the concept of substitution in a broad sense, we can speak of the use of tools from the psychological point of view as a substitute goal or substitute action. We shall return to the question of similarity later. At first we shall speak of substitution only when the new action arises from the original tension system and when, at the same time, the new goal is sufficiently different from the original goal. It is necessary to distinguish between different kinds of substitution. But here we shall limit ourselves to the question of whether, and if so under what conditions, a substitute action brings substitute satisfaction.

We have tried experimentally to determine whether a tension system can be discharged through a substitute action. We know from the work of Ovsiankina that if an activity which has been begun is interrupted there is a strong tendency to resume it as a result of the tension system which corresponds to the quasi-need of completing the task. In our experiments on substitution the subject, after the interruption of the first activity, receives a second task which seems to serve as a substitute for the first activity. If, for example, the original task is to make a dog out of plasticine, the second task might be to make another animal or a ball out of plasticine. If one interrupts the telling of a story, the subject might be asked to draw a picture for the conclusion; or if the subject is interrupted in the drawing of some picture, he may be asked to complete the picture by telling a story.

We have investigated cases in which the relationship between the original and substitute activities lies in the action on material of the same kind and cases in which the *content* of the activity is similar but the *material* is different. If the second activity actually has value as a substitute, the tension system of the original interrupted activity must be discharged wholly or in part. Therefore, the subject will resume the original task less often if the second task has substitute value and can bring about a substitute satisfaction. And, on the other hand, the subject will resume the original task more often if the second task has no substitute value. In some cases the experimenter does not give the second task directly, but creates a situation which offers the possibility of spontaneous substitution.

Lissner[1] found, in fact, that there are cases in which the second activity has substitute value and the resumption of the original activity occurs less often. It was soon clear that not only was the similarity of the two tasks important for the substitute value, but also the *degree of difficulty* of the substitute action. For example: if after the interruption of the task of putting mosaic blocks together the second task of making a mosaic pattern was easy, the resumption was 100 per cent, that is, the substitute value was zero; but if the second task of mosaic pattern was difficult, the resumptions dropped to 42.[2] In order that a greater degree of substitution may correspond numerically to a higher percentage, we shall give the results in terms of nonresumption. According to this notation, the above case of easy substitute action has a non-resumption value of 0 per cent; and the difficult substitute action has a value of 58 per cent. Another example: the original task which the subject has to do is to make a little dog out of plasticine. The second task is to make another animal.

[1] K. Lissner, Die Entspannung von Bedürfnissen durch Ersatzhandlungen, *Psychol. Forsch.*, 1933, **18**, 218–250.

[2] *Ibid.*, p. 231, Table 4.

If the second animal is something easy to make, like a snake, the substitute value is smaller (15 per cent) than if it is difficult (70 per cent). We can say, therefore, that the substitute value of the second task is the stronger the more difficult the task. The difficulty of the task is very important for substitute value because it is related to the standard which the person sets for himself. The substitute value is, therefore, related to what we have called the level of aspiration.

Whether or not the substitute action in a particular case is in direct dynamic *contact* with the original task is very important for the substitute value. We find very little substitute value if the two activities are psychologically *separated* through special circumstances of the situation. Such isolation can sometimes be realized by having the experimenter say at the time of interruption: "Now we shall do an entirely new task." With the same task, the substitute value can be strong if one develops the substitute out of the original task. In a particular case the percentage of nonresumption in a situation of isolation was 15; whereas in a situation of contact between the two tasks, the percentage was 57.[1]

The great significance of the kind of connection between the two systems corresponding to the original and substitute tasks shows up, above all, in experiments with feeble-minded children. Köpke and Zeigarnik find with so-called *Hilfschüler* (retarded children of moron level) seven to eight years old the following facts: if one gave no substitute action, the feeble-minded in all cases resumed the interrupted activity; that is, the nonresumption was 0 per cent. With normal children a year younger nonresumption was 18 per cent. If one gave a substitute task the nonresumption in the case of feeble-minded was 5 per cent; whereas in the case of normals it was about 70 per cent. This means that the substitute value of an action which was very strong for the normals was negligible for the feeble-minded. Köpke increased the similarity between the original and the second activity to identity. For example, if the original task was to draw an animal on red paper, the

[1] *Ibid.*, p. 240, Table 8*a*.

second task was to draw the same animal on green paper. Or, if the original task was to build a bridge, the second task was to build another bridge like the first. In this case, the non-resumption by feeble-minded children was never more than 20 per cent. This very significant numerical result appears to conflict with other experiences. One often sees that the feeble-minded child, if he cannot reach a goal, is easily satisfied with an achievement short of his aim. Gottschaldt has observed the same thing in special experiments. If a feeble-minded child wants to build a high tower of blocks and finds difficulties, he is comparatively easily satisfied with a substitute action, such as building a small tower or some other simple structure. That the feeble-minded child is easily satisfied with substitute actions can be further seen in cases like the following. A young feeble-minded child wishes to throw a ball very far. He does not succeed, but he is happy because he made such a vigorous movement. The feeble-minded child has a tendency to be satisfied with a gesture if the real action is impossible. Lazar has a special term for such children; he calls them "gesture children." Thus, there are doubtless many cases in which the feeble-minded child is much more easily satisfied with a substitution than a normal child. On the other hand, our experiments show that in some cases the substitute value is much less with feeble-minded children than with normal children. In order to clear up the contradiction between these two kinds of cases, we must study the nature of the psychological systems in feeble-minded children. Certainly, all cases of feeble-mindedness have not the same psychological nature. I shall speak only of the most common type.

At present, the general assumption is that feeble-mindedness not only is a defect of intelligence, but also indicates a difference in the make-up of the personality. On the whole, however, one cannot yet define this type of personality. We have worked on this question in recent years in different ways, and I shall try to give a short description of the theory that has resulted.

From the dynamic point of view, the difference between persons is based on three points. The person, dynamically, is a totality of systems. First, one can distinguish the structure of the totality, that is, the *degree* of differentiation of the systems and the *kind* of differentiation of systems in this totality. The one-year-old child, for example, is dynamically not so differentiated into separate systems as a thirty-year-old man. In the child we do not have so many systems. The connection between different things is closer, and we do not have such markedly differentiated strata between the periphery and the center. Second, with the same structure the dynamic *material* of the systems may be different. The systems can be more or less rigid, more or less fluid, and so forth. For this kind of difference also we can use the example of the child and the adult. It seems that the possibility of changing a given system is easier in the child—in most cases—than in the adult. The elasticity or the rigidity of the systems seems to be a very basic and important characteristic of the whole person. The third point is the differences of *content* which correspond to the different systems. With the same structure and same material, the content may be different. This third point seems determined chiefly by the history of the person. For example, the content of the systems of a four-year-old boy among the ancient Greeks was quite different from that of a four-year-old in New York City today.

For the most common kind of moron, according to our experiments, it seems to be typical that the psychological systems are comparatively *rigid*, not easily flexible. I shall not enumerate all our evidence for this theory, which is based upon experiments on satiation, will, memory, attention, and intelligence in the feeble-minded.[1] It may be sufficient to show that from this kind of psychological material, we can understand even the paradoxical facts of substitution in morons. From the dynamic point of view, this kind of child is defined as a person who has a less differentiated structure, like that of a younger child. But the systems are not so flexible as in the young normal child: they are more fixed. The smaller degree

[1] For a more complete statement of the theory of the person here sketched, and of the experimental evidence upon which it is based, see below, Chap. VII.

of differentiation is the explanation of what we generally call the *infantilism* of these morons. But it is clear that these feeble-minded are not the same as the younger normal children.

If we accept the theory that the systems are more rigid, then, in the first place, we can explain the results of the simple interruption experiments in which no substitute task was given; the fact, namely, that the feeble-minded resume the interrupted task in 100 per cent of the cases. This abnormal frequency of resumption is a consequence of the fact that a tension system, once it is built up, stays unchanged without being diffusely discharged. This experimental result agrees with the observations of daily life that feeble-minded children are often extremely stubborn and that it is relatively difficult for such a child to change his goal after he has set himself toward it. This well-known stubbornness is a result of the rigidity of his psychological systems.

We do not, however, find 100 per cent resumption if the child is brought after the first task to a totally different situation. On the contrary, the resumption then occurs much less often than with a normal child. In such cases in our experiments, we find again a rather extreme result, namely, 20 per cent resumption.

The reason for the nonresumption in this case is again the rigidity of the psychological systems. The new psychological situation is so rigid that it cannot be changed readily enough for a connection with the old situation to be brought about. It is typical of this kind of feeble-minded that they cannot do two things at the same time. They are either totally in one situation or totally in another. The theory of rigidity of the systems enables us, therefore, to explain why there is in some cases an abnormally high degree of resumption, in other cases an abnormally low degree of resumption. In a similar way, we can use this theory to explain the paradox which we have mentioned before.

The question whether the substitute action has substitute value presents itself in respect to the psychological, dynamic systems as follows: One system corresponds to the original task; and one corresponds to the second task. If the completing of the second task, that is, of the substitute activity, is to have substitute value for the first system, then the two systems must be so connected that the discharge of the second system at the same time discharges the first system; that is, the two systems must be one dynamic whole. In normal children, the systems are fluid enough so that the similarity of the two tasks suffices to effect a special kind of connection between the two systems. When the subject receives a second similar task, the first system changes so that the new system will be a dynamical part of the old. These two systems appear to be not entirely dissolved into one, undifferentiated whole; but we have one unitary system with a dynamic wall between the two parts. If one part is discharged, then, according to the strength of the inner boundary, the whole system may be discharged.

When the feeble-minded child receives the second task, the first system remains, as a result of its rigidity, unchanged; and for the second task a separate system is established. So it happens that the discharging of the second system does not discharge the first; that is, the second task has no substitute value.

If this theory is right, it must be possible to set up, in feeble-minded children, a substitute satisfaction if we find a way to develop the second task out of the original system. In fact, this often happens when the child spontaneously proceeds from the original activity to a substitute, as in the experiments of Gottschaldt and in the cases about which we have spoken before. We have only one system. Therefore, the substitute value must be particularly great. As a result of the rigidity of the systems we do not have in these cases the differentiation of the whole system into two parts, slightly separated from each other, as are those of normal children. Therefore, the substitute action will discharge the whole system in the feeble-minded child more completely than in the normal child. So it happens that with normal children we can bring about rather easily a substitute action, but the substitute value is not perfect.

With feeble-minded children either we have a complete separation of the two systems so that a second activity has no substitute value, or, if the two tasks are connected at all, the substitute satisfaction is perfect. Such all-or-none functioning in feeble-minded persons is important not only in substitution but in other fields (*e.g.*, in intelligent acts).

Besides the degree of connection and the previously mentioned degree of difficulty of the second task, the degree of reality and unreality of the substitute action is important for the substitute value. The substitute often does not occur in the form of a real action, but in the form of an air castle or a *daydream*. In many cases of substitution, speaking or *gesture* takes the place of a *real* act. Has this kind of substitute real substitute value? This question is also important for the theory of dreams and for substitution in psychopathic cases. It is not easy to make experimental investigations upon the effect of this unreal substitution through speaking and thinking, in place of real action. Mahler has made experiments of this type: a piece of handwork was interrupted and the subject had to think how he would complete the work; or if a person could not reach a goal he was asked to tell a fairy story in which he attained his goal. This field is very complicated and I can discuss only a part of it. Mahler found that, in general, the substitute value is stronger the more real the substitute action is. But what degree of reality an action has cannot be determined by the kind of substitute action alone, but always by observation of the relationship between the substitute action and the original action in a particular case. Mahler found that one must distinguish between the *inner goal* and the *outer goal* of an activity and that the degree of reality of the second task, and with it the substitute value, is the greater the more nearly the substitute action approaches the inner goal of the original action. In tasks which have the character of an intellectual problem it is generally not enough for the discharge of the tension that the subject find the solution in thinking; it is important that he express the solution in reality. In this way it is shown that social factors are very important in determining the real or unreal character of an event. Only when it is possible for the subject to inform the experimenter of the solution of the substitute task is an adequate discharge of the original system possible. For only in case of social recognition is the degree of reality sufficient.

The question of unreal substitution has a close relationship to certain problems of play. According to the theory of Piaget, the child's conception of the world has a mystical character. For the child, name and thing, fantasies and reality, lies and truth are not clearly separated. One must ask whether for psychological needs also an unreal event can give real satisfaction to the child. Sliosberg, who has carried out comprehensive experiments on this question, found that it is impossible to make the general statement that the unreal can be substituted for the real. Whether a child is satisfied or not when one gives him make-believe candy for real candy, paper scissors for real scissors, depends in each case on the special character of the situation. We must, as Koffka has said, distinguish between the play situation and the serious situation. The play situation is not so rigid; one may call it "loose." Certain kinds of substitution are possible only in a play situation, in which objects have not so fixed a character as in a serious situation. In the serious situation the child usually refuses the play substitute. It is interesting that the opposite is also true. The child in the play situation will often refuse a real action as a substitute for the play action. Experiments show that for adults also the possibility of a substitute depends upon the looseness of the whole situation.

An important factor for the substitute value is the momentary intensity of the need. The experiments of Sliosberg show that the child more easily accepts the plasticine scissors, for example, after he has played long enough with the real ones. Generally, the stronger the need the less the substitute value of a substitute action.

On the other hand, the tendency for substitute action, without doubt, will increase as the tension of the need increases.

This was particularly clear in the experiments of Dembo, in which the strong affective tension leads to such nonsense action as throwing rings over the coat hooks. Dembo has shown that such spontaneous substitution is always a result of a conflict situation and has given a dynamic theory of how the substitute goal receives its positive valence. We know that if a certain goal exists for a person, this goal works as a psychological field which induces a derived valence in certain other objects. For example, if one wishes to wrap up something, then, suddenly, paper and string assume a positive valence. Köhler has spoken of the directed state of the situation in the use of tools. Dembo has shown that an inducing field exists, which gives valences as means for reaching the goal; moreover, if the tension is strong enough, other goals are induced which have a certain relation to the original goal.

In the beginning we saw that, as far as psychological systems are concerned, a surprising relation exists between substitution and the use of tools. Now we see also that from the point of view of the psychological environment the use of tools and substitution are closely related because both are induced by the same inducing field. Finally, we can formulate our main results in regard to nonspontaneous substitution: the substitute value is the greater the more the substitute action corresponds, not to a new goal, but to another way of reaching the original inner goal.

SUMMARY OF EXPERIMENTS ON SUBSTITUTION

Figures indicate percentages of nonresumption

Original Task	Experiments without Substitution	Experiments with Substitution	
I.		Second task is:	
		Easy	*Difficult*
Mosaic	10	0	58
Plasticine (dog)	20	15 (snake)	70 (ball)
II.		Original and second task are:	
		Isolated	*Connected*
Mosaic		15	57
III.			
Normal children 7 to 8 years	18	68	
Feeble-minded 8 years	0	5	
	(New situation)	(Second task nearly identical with first)	
	80	14	
IV.		Goal of the original task is	
		Reached	*Not reached*
Different tasks	40	77	
	25		25
		Telling	
Figuring on paper	25	100	
Paper box	25		19
V.		Thinking	
		With telling	*Without telling*
Figuring	17	14	0

CHAPTER VII

A DYNAMIC THEORY OF THE FEEBLE-MINDED

During the last few decades, advances in pedagogy, of which Decroly's penetrating work constitutes not the least, have been decidedly influenced by study of the behavior of abnormal children. Psychopathology has continually gained in significance for psychology, particularly for psychological theory. Yet a true understanding of the psychopathological processes themselves is often peculiarly difficult. The following discussion attempts to develop the fundamentals of a dynamic theory of feeble-mindedness. We are aware that we are presenting only the outlines of a theory. This is so of necessity since we shall consider exclusively one relatively frequent type among the many, dynamically perhaps quite varied, kinds of feeble-mindedness. And the experiments upon which the theory is based have been carried out on only one particular degree of feeble-mindedness. Yet at present in a psychological investigation of the varied types of personality, it seems to me most important to attempt as strict as possible a theory of the dynamic relation between the different behavioral manifestations of one type, and then to determine which of the dynamic concepts thus evolved are applicable to the general problem of personality differences. Such a course seems more fruitful than to continue suggesting new classificatory divisions for the entire range of types. Without doubt, however, a dynamic theory of feeble-mindedness must at the same time deal with the basic problems of a general *dynamic theory of the person.*

It is common knowledge that feeble-mindedness is not merely an "isolated disease of the intellect" but involves the total personality.[1] We have, however, progressed little beyond this first general insight. In particular we lack a positive characterization of this peculiarity of the total personality.

As I see it, a truly penetrating experimental investigation of the intellectual processes of the feeble-minded remains to be achieved. Determination by test procedures of deficient accomplishment in certain fields, important as this is in itself, has thrown little light upon the nature of the underlying processes. Nor has it illuminated the differences between them and the intellectual processes of the normal individual. As in other branches of psychology here also insight into the nature of the processes involved can only be won by pushing beyond mere concepts of achievement. Moreover, certain performances, social behavior for instance, may upon occasion be better achieved by the feeble-minded than by a person of normal intelligence.

If one attempts to transcend the concepts of achievement and to inquire into the nature of the psychological processes themselves, he is of course first forced to consider what distinguishes the intellectual activity of the feeble-minded from that of the normal person.

The Act of Insight in the Feeble-minded

In an attempt of this sort one is confronted by unexpectedly great difficulties.

Investigations of the last twenty years have established at least the outlines of the fundamental nature of intellectual activity, especially of creative thinking. Dynamically the act of insight consists in a *reorganization of the field* (Köhler[2]), closely related in many respects to the transformation of so-called ambiguous figures. In the fields both of perception and of thought there is a shift in the totality of internal relations. Forms that appear at first as isolated totalities become

---

[1] Indeed Binet was keenly interested in the problem of the character of the feeble-minded; cf. A. Binet et T. Simon, L'Intelligence des imbéciles, *L'Année psychologique*, 1909, **15**, 1 ff.

[2] Köhler, *Intelligenzprüfungen an Menschenaffen* (*The Mentality of Apes*), and Das Wesen der Intelligenz, *Kind und Umwelt*, Berlin, 1930.

part of a unified whole. Dependent parts become independent or unite with originally dependent parts of other wholes to form new wholes. Briefly, the structure of the field as regards its grouping into wholes undergoes a transformation, usually an abrupt one. In the causation of this transformation definite directed forces play an essential role.

If, proceeding from this theory of intelligent activity, one asks wherein the peculiarity of feeble-minded thinking lies, he must first establish that acts of insight in the feeble-minded appear throughout to have in all fundamental properties the *same nature* as in the normal individual. It is certain that the feeble-minded see wholes and that these wholes are not less pronounced.[1] It cannot be maintained that the feeble-minded do not engage in intelligent activity or that the process as such is less intensive. Moreover the "Aha-experience" typical of the act of thinking undoubtedly occurs in the feeble-minded. Indeed, they appear often to experience it more intensively and to rejoice in it more than do normal children. Morons and imbecile children may experience jokes and enjoy them keenly. Equally with the normal child and the anthropoid, the act of insight in the feeble-minded consists in a transformation of the whole relations in the field.

There remains then this difference, quite an external one from the dynamic point of view: the transformation of field structure typical of the experience of wit or of intelligent activity in general is not occasioned in the feeble-minded by the same events which produce it in normal children of the same age. It is caused by other events, the so-called easier tasks, or more primitive jokes. The only qualitative distinction that seems to have been pointed out between the process of the two groups is that the feeble-minded think more concretely and perceptually.[2]

FORMULATION OF THE EXPERIMENTAL PROBLEM

During the last three years we have attempted to gain insight into the peculiarities of the feeble-minded, not by the direct

[1] We shall see later that it may plausibly be maintained that they are even more pronounced.

[2] *Cf.* W. ELIASBERG, Die Veranschaulichung in der Hilfsschule, *Zeitschr. f. exper. Päd.*, 1926, **27**, 134–145.

route of investigating intelligence, but by experimental investigations in the spheres of will and needs. In many ways these spheres are more directly related to the deeper peculiarities of personality than are intellectual processes. If then feeble-mindedness be an expression of a peculiarity of the total personality it seems not unlikely that through such investigations insight may finally be obtained into the causes of the intellectual difficulties themselves.

One major difficulty in reasoning from the results of intelligence testing to the problem of dynamic differences is the fact that in testing procedures individual differences are determined by means of activities the psychological nature and general laws of which are not sufficiently known.[1] We have, therefore, utilized throughout those experimental procedures in which the underlying processes and their laws are best known to us. For similar reasons we have first investigated relatively light rather than pronounced degrees of feeble-mindedness. This is apparently contrary to the general principle that investigation should begin with differences as crass as possible. Our present approach has been guided by the following consideration. If one uses the same procedure with idiots as with normal children it is very probable that the difference in psychological situations created for normal and for idiot children will be so great that completely different dynamic relations will exist. It may well happen, for instance, that for the one a difficult conflict may arise, whereas for the other none may ensue. Only when truly *psychologically* comparable situations exist may one compare differences in behavior in more than an external way or consider such differences in the same type of activity as the effects of dynamic differences of the person.

The experimental subjects consisted of pupils from different schools for the defective in Berlin, ranging in age from six to twelve years. The majority were classed as moron, a few as imbecile. Control experiments were carried out by the same experimenters on normal children of various ages.

[1] *Cf.* Lewin, *Die Entwicklung der experimentellen Willenspsychologie und die Psychotherapie*, Hirzel, Leipzig, 1929, pp. 28.

The experiments chiefly concern: (1) the process of satiation, (2) the expression of an unsatisfied need (resumption of an interrupted action), and (3) the substitute value of a substitute (compensatory) action. The selection of experiments was naturally guided by certain working hypotheses. We shall first present briefly the results of the experiments on satiation.

PSYCHICAL SATIATION IN FEEBLE-MINDED AND NORMAL CHILDREN

The children were asked to draw moon faces continuously (Fig. 1; "The moon, the moon, the moon is round; it has two

FIG. 1.

eyes, a nose, and mouth"). A moon face was copied for the child on a sheet of note-book paper. The child then had to draw moon faces "until he had enough of it." He was free to stop at any time. But the situation in itself contained, as in the experiments of Karsten,[1] a weak pressure toward continuing to draw. (The experimenter must of course endeavor to maintain this pressure as equal as possible with different children.) According to the general laws of psychical satiation, of which the fundamentals are known from the experiments of Karsten and Freund,[2] the initially positive or neutral valence of the task gradually changes with repetition into indifference and finally into a negative valence. In these experiments breaking off generally did not occur immediately upon reaching the satiation point. The child usually worked for a while after the satiation point had been reached until the activity acquired a certain degree of negative valence. After stopping, he was asked by the experimenter if he would not like to continue, drawing anything he chose (free drawing). If so, paper and pencil remained at his disposal for as long as he wished to go on.

One is accustomed to attribute to the feeble-minded a pronounced inclination toward repetition and at the same time

[1] A. KARSTEN, Psychische Sättigung, *Psychol. Forsch.*, 1928, **10**, 142 ff.

[2] A. FREUND, Die psychische Sättigung im Menstruum und Intermenstruum, *ibid.*, 1930, **13**, 198 ff.

small persistence in working. Since satiation, as we know, is closely connected with the dynamics of needs, it appeared important to determine its course with the feeble-minded. The task presented no special difficulties to the nine- to ten- and to the ten- to eleven-year-old feeble-minded. Only the eight- to nine-year-olds drew decidedly fewer moons than the normals of equal age.

The result in the main is as follows (Table I): the total duration of the satiation experiment (moon faces plus free drawing) is on the average shorter with the eight- to nine-year-old morons than with normal children of equal age (41 as against 58 min.). Times for individual children of the normal and feeble-minded groups, however, overlap considerably. The average time (59 min.) of the nine- to ten-year-old morons is the same as that of the eight- to nine-year-old normals, and shorter, but not decidedly so, than the average of the nine- to ten-year-old normals (75 min.). The average of the ten- to eleven-year-old feeble-minded (77 min.) is almost identical with that (79 min.) of the normal nine- to ten- and ten- to eleven-year-olds.

Considering the notion of little persistence and capacity for concentration on the part of the feeble-minded, it is surprising that at least in the case of the nine- to eleven-year-olds

TABLE I.—PSYCHICAL SATIATION IN NORMAL (N) AND RETARDED (R) CHILDREN

Age, years		Satiation time, minutes			Satiation point, minutes	Moons per minute	Number per 100 minutes of	
		Moons	Free drawing	Total			Pauses	Other activities
8 to 9	R	33	8	41	27	4	30	20
	N	55	3	58	35	8	8	8
9 to 10	R	56	3	59	30	7	30	17
	N	55	20	75	27	7	15	3
10 to 11	R	75	2	77	40	7	23	21
	N	45	33	79	35	8	7	8

no essential difference in total time exists. Even when the comparison is made between times at which satiation first clearly appears, the averages show surprisingly good agreement. In the three age groups of the feeble-minded this satiation point occurs on the average at 27, 30, and 40 min. respectively; in the groups of normal children at 35, 27, and 35 min.

The times required for total satiation in such activities by normal and subnormal children thus appear on the whole not to differ essentially.[1] The *course of satiation*, however, shows certain typical differences. One is first struck by the fact that with the ten- to eleven-year-old morons nearly the entire time (75 min.) is taken up with the drawing of moon faces, and that after satiation of this activity they refuse almost without exception to continue with free drawing.[2] Normal children, on the other hand, are satiated with drawing moon faces much sooner (after 45 min.). Yet all of these children were ready to continue with free drawing. Thus on the average the feeble-minded of this age displayed more persistence in one and the same activity than did the normal children. Once satiated, however, they would have nothing more to do with any part of the sphere.[3] They showed much more frequently, however, small technical variations (in respect, for instance, to position or serial order of drawings).

Together with the tendency toward variation, a typical manifestation of satiation is the appearance of secondary actions, that is, actions which are carried out on the side without interruption of the major activity. In frequency of secondary

[1] One may refer the quicker satiation of the eight- to nine-year-old feeble-minded to the fact that the task was more difficult for them than for the normal children. The feeble-minded drew on the average only four moons a minute as against eight for normals of the same age. According to Karsten, other things being equal, satiation is more rapid with more accentuated central tasks—and the more difficult tasks here must be so regarded.

[2] This refusal may also have been influenced, on the part of the feeble-minded, by a fear of failing in free drawing.

[3] The eight- to nine-year-olds show externally the opposite: the feeble-minded go over earlier than do the normal into the decided variations of free drawing. The same holds with the six-year-olds. I incline to believe, however, that no actual contradiction exists when dynamic questions are considered (see below)

actions there appears to be no important difference between the normal and the feeble-minded. With the feeble-minded, however, and in all three age groups, there occur much more often *pauses for rest* and *interposed actions*, which definitely interrupt the main activity. The number of pauses for rest per 100 min. in the feeble-minded, grouped by age, is 30, 30, and 23; in the normal, 8, 15, and 7. The corresponding values for interposed actions are 20, 17, 21 for the feeble-minded; 8, 3, 8 for the normal children.

As a general result of the satiation experiments we find that in ages eight to eleven there exist between normal and moron no significant differences in rate of satiation of the total complex (drawing moon faces plus free drawing). Typical differences do occur, however, in the course of satiation: conflict between the wish to continue drawing and the beginning of satiation leads in the feeble-minded to many more pauses for rest and interposed actions. That is, the moron child is either definitely engaged in the task in hand or he interrupts this activity *completely* by a pause or a shift to another occupation. The course of satiation in the normal child is far more continuous. He responds to the conflict in more elastic, yielding fashion. He more readily finds a way, with the aid of secondary activities or by other means, to steer through the conflict without externally giving up continuation of the task. The behavior of the feeble-minded is much more abrupt, more "either-or."

The cause of the more elastic behavior of the normal child may be sought in his readier survey of the possibilities of satisfying the demands of the experimenter, thus enabling him really to evade the actual task. Although in point of fact this greater insight plays a role, a purely intellectualistic interpretation would be false. The elastic and inelastic behavior of the two groups proceeds quite directly and without particular deliberation.[1]

[1] Of greater importance, rather, is the fact that the feeble-minded much more readily feels himself inadequate to the social situation, that he fails to stand above it.

I am constrained to believe that a much more fundamental property of the feeble-minded is here operative; namely, a functional rigidity, an immobility of the psychic material, which itself constitutes the true cause of the intellectual difficulties. Before going into this theory the experiments on resumption of interrupted actions and on substitution will be briefly presented.

RESUMPTION OF INTERRUPTED ACTIONS. SUBSTITUTE VALUE OF SUBSTITUTE ACTIONS

If on any pretext one interrupts the execution of a task in which a subject has become inwardly engaged, occupies him in another way, and then after completion of this second task finally leaves him to himself for a short time (say half a minute), the subject ordinarily returns spontaneously to the first task within this period. We know from the work of Ovsiankina[1] that this resumption is very frequent in certain situations and with certain tasks even when the subject knows that a resumption is not in line with the wishes of the experimenter.

Köpke has carried out similar experiments with eight- to nine-year-old feeble-minded[2] and with seven- to eight-year-old normal children (Table II). The frequency of resumption with normal children was 79 per cent (in good agreement with the figures of Ovsiankina); with the feeble-minded under the same conditions 100 per cent. After finishing the second task, the 31 feeble-minded children investigated returned without exception to the interrupted one, and within 30 sec. Thus in the feeble-minded the tension system corresponding to the interrupted action worked itself out with an astonishing regularity in a resumption of the task. We shall discuss the reasons for this later.

Proceeding from the work of Lissner[3] and Mahler,[4] Köpke used a similar technique in the investigation of substitute value.

[1] OVSIANKINA, Wiederaufnahme unterbrochener Handlungen, *Psychol. Forsch.*, 1928, **11**, 302 ff.

[2] Twenty-five of these children were classed as morons, six as slightly imbecile

[3] K. LISSNER, Die Entspannung von Bedürfuissen durch Ersatzhandlungen, *Psychol. Forsch.*, 1933, **18**, 218–250.

[4] W. MAHLER, "Ersatzhandlungen verschiedener Realitätsgrades," *Psychol. Forsch.*, 1933, **18**, 27–89.

TABLE II.—SUBSTITUTE VALUE OF SUBSTITUTE ACTIVITIES IN NORMAL (*N*) AND
RETARDED (*R*) CHILDREN

Age, years		*n*	Frequency of resumption in per cent		*n*	Frequency of resumption in per cent	
			Without substitute	With substitute		Identical substitute	Concealed valence
7 to 8	*N*	34 (I)	79	33			
8 to 9	*R*	31 (I)	100	94	15 (III)	100	16 (VII)
7 to 8	*N*	15 (II)	80	33			
8 to 9	*R*	10 (II)	100	90	13 (IV)	93	0
8 to 9	*R*				6 (V)	86	
	R				8 (VI)	80	
12 to 13	*R*	16 (IX)	80	20			

n = number of subjects
( ) = procedure used

Lissner gave her subject as second activity a task similar to the interrupted one in content or in type of material. It became clear that the substitute value of the second activity (which we shall name the substitute action) for the main activity varied according to the nature, difficulty, and mode of presentation of the second action. The greater its functional substitute value the greater is the relief of the need for completion of the main action and the more complete is the discharge of the tension system corresponding to it. One can therefore test the substitute value by determining how much less often the subject returns to the main activity when a substitute rather than a completely heterogeneous action is interposed.

Comparison of eight- to nine-year-old feeble-minded with seven- to eight-year-old normal children gave the following result.   Under conditions[1] in which the substitute action had such a high substitute value with the normal children that the percentage of resumption sank from 79 (in experiments without a substitute action) to 33, the resumption with the feeble-minded sank only from 100 to 94.[2]   With the feeble-minded the substitute value was thus almost zero.   Köpke then gradually increased the similarity of the main and substitute activities until they were practically identical: for the task "paint an animal" was substituted the task "paint the same animal again on another sheet of paper"; for "build a bridge out of stones" was substituted "build the same bridge out of stones."   In spite of this extremely high similarity the substitute value remained low (resumption remained at 86 to 100 per cent). In these cases, however, resumption was not so prompt, taking place only after 3 to 4 min.

These experimental results accord with certain observations of daily life.   Once a feeble-minded child has in mind a definite goal he often shows a peculiarly rigid fixation on it.   It is extremely striking with what rigidity these children often insist on carrying out a definite action in precisely one way and exactly "now," and how difficult it is to sway them from their preference even with conditions under which a normal child of the same or somewhat younger age would be relatively easily moved.   Thus the *will* of the feeble-minded often appears stronger, certainly more *rigid* than that of the normal child.

This peculiar rigidity of the will expresses itself not only in facing momentary goals but also in so-called habits.   Feeble-minded children frequently impress one with their pronounced stereotypy[3] and pedantry, far exceeding the commonly observed pedantry of normal children.   Thus their shoes must stand

[1] Tasks were used which as far as possible were adapted in degree of difficulty to the capacities of the children.   Examples: to model an animal out of plasticine, to assemble an automobile out of paper strips, to build an automobile out of rods and rings.

[2] In other words: whereas only 2 out of 31 feeble-minded children did not return to the original task, 33 of the 49 normal children did not resume it.

[3] *Cf.* L. M. TERMAN, *The Measurement of Intelligence*, Houghton Mifflin, Boston, 1916, p 203.

before the bed in exactly one way; the buttons on a piece of clothing must be fastened in one definite order; the child is extremely suspicious of new foods, and even when hungry he may refuse at supper time a food generally eaten at lunch.

In contrast to these experiences, which agree with the experimental results on substitution in the feeble-minded, are others which seemingly imply the opposite. The circumstance that tricks and diversions for instance are likely to be more effective with the feeble-minded than with the normal child is due, perhaps, to his lesser intellectual capacities. But the feeble-minded child is much more readily satisfied with an incomplete solution of a task, indeed often a pure gesture appears to suffice. If he finds it difficult to throw a ball far, he may be quite satisfied in raising his arm as though to throw in a forceful manner. To illustrate further, the masculine gestures of many of these children have in high degree the function of real acts.[1] Lazar characterizes such children as *Gestenkinder*.[2] Also the experimental findings of Gottschaldt[3] show that the feeble-minded are relatively easily satisfied with completing a simpler task at a lower level of aspiration when the original task is too difficult.

Experimental results and observations of daily life thus testify with equal impressiveness to an apparent contradiction: on the one hand the feeble-minded show an especial rigidity and tendency toward fixation which makes the occurrence of substitute actions, in the functional sense, very difficult; on the other, there is revealed a pronounced tendency toward substitute actions and a tendency to be readily satisfied with them. Not only is this true of two different groups of children. Both extremes are characteristic of one and the same child.

The theory to be discussed below attempts to penetrate to the essential dynamic factors involved and seems to point to a

---

[1] *Cf.* G. WEISS, Kindertypen in aufgabefreien und aufgabegebundenen Situationen, *Zeitschr. f. Kinderforsch.*, 1930, **36**, pp. 343 ff.

[2] These are by no means always feeble-minded children.

[3] GOTTSCHALDT, *Ber. d. V. Kong. f. Heilpäd.*, München, 1931, 130–143.

way of solution of this and a series of other paradoxes typical of the feeble-minded.

GENERAL THEORY OF THE DYNAMIC DIFFERENCES
AMONG PERSONS

As previously mentioned, the problem of feeble-mindedness is one of individual differences. If these individual differences are regarded from a dynamic point of view the following general considerations arise. As a dynamic system the individual is more or less unitary and more or less self-contained (closed).[1] Differences may derive from a diversity of (1) *structure* of the total system, (2) *material* and state of the system, or (3) its meaningful *content*.

Differences in Structure of the Person.

Degree of Differentiation. One of the most fundamental dynamic differences between small child and adult is the degree of differentiation in their various psychical regions and systems. The fact that various life-spheres (profession, family, friendships with definite persons, and so on) as well as different needs are much more differentiated in the adult than in the one-year-old child scarcely demands extensive demonstration. In the adult it is generally not difficult to distinguish more peripherally and more centrally located regions. The young child shows far less pronounced *stratification*. Thus in this respect he is a much more unitary system, dynamically a stronger Gestalt. A topological representation of the functional differences of the total personality in respect to degree of differentiation corresponds to the differences between Fig. 2 *a* (child) and Fig. 2 *b* (adult).

Types of Structure. Together with differences in degree of differentiation, there certainly exist between different individuals important differences in the type of differentiation. The total structure may for instance be relatively harmonious or inharmonious. The dynamic connections between various

---

[1] LEWIN, Zwei Grundtypen von Lebensprozessen, *Zeitschr. f. Psychol.*, 1929, 113, 220 ff.

part systems of the person are by no means equally close. Great individual differences exist with reference to *the way* this delimitation of relatively closed subordinate wholes occurs: which parts are more strongly and which parts more weakly developed, whether the degree of demarcation among the subordinate wholes is relatively uniform or whether separate parts of the personality are particularly isolated. The phenomenon of division of personality is an example of a very special type of structure.

Differences in Psychical Material and in State of the Systems.

Differences in Material. Diversities in structure (in degree of differentiation and in type of structure) do not exhaust

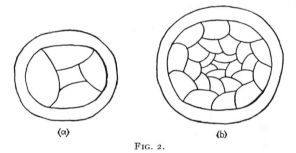

(a)   (b)

Fɪɢ. 2.

the possible differences within the personality. Thus with identical structures, the *ease* with which they *change* may differ decidedly. Further, the shifting may occur suddenly or gradually. In this connection one may speak of a varying dynamic softness, elasticity, hardness, brittleness, or fluidity of the psychical material.

On the whole the infant must be characterized as not only less differentiated but also as more yielding.[1] Among children of the same age there appear to exist great differences in material. The special properties of one's psychical material

[1] Certain facts, such as the strong fixation of the small child on certain habits, appear to speak against the hypothesis of a generally greater plasticity at this age. I prefer, however, from general biological points of view, to maintain the hypothesis of easier mobility of the psychical material and believe that I can otherwise explain the opposed facts (see pp. 228ff.).

must constitute a very deep individual peculiarity of the person and play a decided role in heredity.

If differences in ease of structural change within the system are indicated by variation in thickness of the boundaries separating its various parts, the differences between small child and adult correspond in general to those between *a* and *b*, Fig. 3.

States of Tension in the Systems. Along with the material properties must also be considered properties of the state of the systems, especially their state of tension. In the satisfaction of a need, for instance, this state of tension may change slowly or rapidly. It is also quite probable that together with the diversity of momentary states there exist also enduring differences in the average tension in the systems of the total person. (By material properties in the broad sense we mean to include

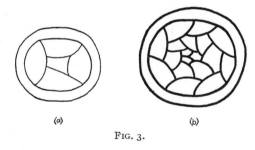

(a)   (b)

FIG. 3.

the properties discussed in the present as well as in the previous three paragraphs.)

The material properties of the different systems within the same individual are by no means completely uniform. The systems of the plane of unreality possess a greater degree of fluidity,[1] and important differences may exist between young and old part regions of the person. In so far, therefore, as we speak of individual differences in the material constants of the person as a whole, it is necessary to compare *homogeneous* parts within the total person.

[1] *Cf.* J. F. Brown, Die dynamischen Eigenschaften der Realitäts-und Irrealitätschichten, *Psychol. Forsch.*, 1933, **18,** 1–26.

Differences in Content of Meaning of the Systems.

Even though the structure and the material properties of two individuals are the same, the content corresponding to the systems may be different and constitute decisive psychological differences of the person. Even though their structure and material properties should be approximately the same, a four-year-old boy in the Russian steppes and one in the Chinese quarter of San Francisco would show important personal differences since the content of their goals and ideals, the meaning of their different spheres of life, are different. In higher degree than material properties and structural plan, these diversities of content depend upon historical influences.

A DYNAMIC THEORY OF THE FEEBLE-MINDED

Theoretical Considerations

In returning from general discussion of the possible dynamic differences among persons to the problem of the nature of the feeble-minded (to, *i.e.*, a relatively frequent type of the feeble-minded) the following is to be considered.

Degree of Differentiation.

The feeble-minded child of, say, eight years is in general less differentiated than the eight-year-old normal child brought up under otherwise similar conditions. Not only is his level of intelligence lower but on the whole it is to be designated as more primitive, more infantile. In respect to structural plan, aside from other differences of structure, the feeble-minded is to be designated as less differentiated. In this respect he resembles a younger normal child (Fig. 4).

The complex of phenomena ordinarily designated as infantilism may be due chiefly to this small degree of differentiation. The greater concreteness of thinking may also be related to this primitiveness in the sense of lack of dynamic differentiation.[1]

Material Properties.

Even though a feeble-minded child corresponds in degree of differentiation to a younger normal child he is not to be

[1] See below, pp. 222ff.

regarded as entirely similar. We conceive the major dynamic difference between a feeble-minded and a normal child of the same degree of differentiation to consist in a greater stiffness, a smaller capacity for dynamic rearrangement, in the psychical systems of the former (Fig. 4).

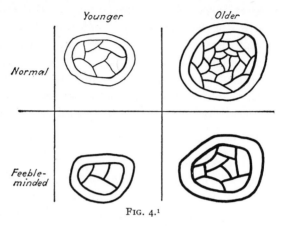

FIG. 4.[1]

Application in Outline

That on the whole the feeble-minded is to be characterized as dynamically more rigid, less mobile, is attested by a large number of observations.

Pedantry and Fixation of Volitional Goals.

As previously mentioned, it is striking with what inflexibility and pedantry[2] the feeble-minded is accustomed to cling to a fixed goal or habit.

In part this inflexibility of the feeble-minded is an expression of his helplessness. Mishaps occur to him oftener. He finds more frequently than the normal child that he cannot trust the world in which he lives. It is far more difficult for him to survey a new situation and to see through it adequately.

[1] As in Fig. 3 increase in thickness of the boundary lines represents decrease in ease of structural change within the system.

[2] By pedantry is meant the tendency to insist upon strict regularities and to develop inflexible habits to an unnecessary degree and under inappropriate circumstances.

Therefore he inclines, as does the normal child in situations of helplessness, to try ways which are well known to him, to cling to means which he trusts. To this extent pedantry also may be a secondary effect of his smaller intellectual capacity, his lesser mastery of the world.

This explanation however seems clearly insufficient. Pedantry in the feeble-minded is very often to be observed even when the child certainly feels neither helpless nor overwhelmed. Rather there seems to exist here a very deep and primary rigidity, which manifests itself not only in well-worn habits but also in new volitional goals. This fixation on the first chosen goal led without exception in Köpke's experiments to resumption of the interrupted goal.

Paradoxes of Substitute Value.

The assumption of a relatively difficult rearrangement of psychical systems in the feeble-minded permits us to account for the paradoxical results of the substitution experiments.

If one inquires into the dynamic assumptions that must be fulfilled in order for a substitute activity to have substitute value, the following is to be established with reference to the inner psychical systems. Let the uncompleted primary task be designated A, the substitute task, B. Satisfaction of the primary task (dynamically, discharge of A) by the completion of the substitute action (*i.e.*, by discharge of B) occurs when, and only when, the two systems A and B are so related that the discharge of B brings with it an immediate discharge of A. That is to say, A and B must be relatively dependent parts of one dynamic whole (Fig. 5) and cannot therefore be mutually isolated systems (Fig. 6). Only when the structure is as represented in Fig. 5, where A and B are, dynamically, relatively weakly bounded parts of one total system, can the substitute action have substitute value.[1]

---

[1] The discharge of A by B may be, other things being equal, more complete and thus the substitute value of the second action higher, if the total system A and B is bounded from other systems by a strong common outer wall. In this case the state of tension of A-B is less dependent upon that of the neighboring systems.

Actually Lissner[1] found that the substitute value depends significantly upon the type of transition from the first to the second activity. If the second activity is introduced by the experimenter as, so to speak, an entirely new experiment the substitute value is, other things being equal, much less than when the second activity is developed out of the first. The investigations of Zeigarnik[2] and Birenbaum[3] have already shown the fundamental importance of the interconnections of psychical systems for their tension and discharge (directly or by the discharge of other systems). They have also indicated the means by which one may experimentally produce definite relations between whole psychical systems.

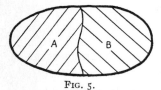

FIG. 5.

FIG. 6.

In the situations utilized in the substitution experiments of Köpke, a certain degree of similarity between the two tasks was adequate to bring about a sufficient connection between the two systems. When these children were presented with a substitute task sufficiently related to the initial one, the system which arose did not seem to be completely separated but appeared rather to grow out of the first or at least to develop in close connection with it. Occasionally such a close connection between the two systems first arose only during the course of the work.[4] As a rule a structure similar to that of Fig. 5 results.

That the psychical systems be easily susceptible of re-formation is an additional requisite under the conditions given for the

[1] K. Lissner, *ibid.* p. 240. Table 8.

[2] B. Zeigarnik, Über das Behalten von erledigten und unerledigten Handlungen, *Psychol. Forsch.*, 1927, **9**, 1–85.

[3] G. Birenbaum, Das Vergessen einer Vornahme (isolierte seelische Systeme und dynamische Gesamtbereiche), *Psychol. Forsch.*, 1930, **13**, 218–284.

[4] See Birenbaum, *op. cit.*, concerning the course and conditions underlying the formation of such totalities.

construction of such a totality on the basis of similarity and thus also for the existence of substitute value. If the capacity for transformation be small, the building of such totalities under the previous conditions will occur with difficulty, if at all. System B, corresponding to the second task, will then be more likely to appear as an independent system (corresponding to Fig. 6). If not it will unite with A to form a dynamic unity only with greater difficulty. The substitute value will be small. Actually Köpke found this to be the case with feeble-minded.

At the same time it may be predicted from our basic assumption concerning the slight mobility of the psychical material of the feeble-minded that with them, under certain circumstances, the substitute value must be greater than with the normal, rather than less. For instance, if with the feeble-minded one should succeed in bringing the second task into dynamic connection with the first, the relative difficulty of transformation of the system must give it a particularly high degree of unity, thus resulting in a high substitute value. This might be attained by developing the second task out of the first. We have already referred to the seemingly paradoxical fact that along with instances of extreme difficulty of substitute satisfaction there occur in the feeble-minded others in which substitute satisfaction appears readily. In the cases mentioned by Gottschaldt, when the first task was too difficult for the child he *spontaneously* turned to easier tasks. On failing in the construction of a high tower he contented himself with a lower one. There is much indicating that in such spontaneous growth of the second task out of the first the two activities dynamically are unseparated. If, however, the tension systems are not divided, there exists actually only one tension system. Thus the substitute value will be high; higher, indeed than with the normal. This inference is supported by a consequence adduced from our fundamental assumption, a consequence which we must consider somewhat in detail, since it is of essential significance for the specifically intellectual problem.

Material Properties of Systems and the Formation of Wholes.

In normal individuals if there occurs spontaneous substitution, for instance of the type of substitution of resignation,[1] the new goal in general is dynamically not completely identical with the old. The original goal is not wholly transformed into the new one, but often maintains a certain independence, for example an "ideal goal." In such cases there frequently develops in normal children a dynamic structure similar to that of Fig. 5: one relatively unitary total system arises in which are distinguishable two, although weakly divided, part systems. That is, a wall exists between the two part systems even though it is a weak one functionally. Discharge of the one system will therefore cause a substantial though not a complete discharge of the other (in so far as a deeper transformation does not occur during discharge).[2]

If the systems are particularly rigid in respect to their material properties, such a differentiation of one total system into two weakly divided parts would less easily occur. If

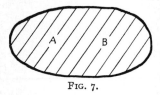

FIG. 7.

the forces in question are strong enough two separate systems, *A* and *B* (Fig. 6), are more likely to result, or *A* and *B* will remain completely undivided (Fig. 7). In these cases a very high substitute value (externally viewed) must ensue because there exists a dynamically undifferentiated system, a strong Gestalt, and because therefore each discharge of tension must directly embrace the whole system.

From this dynamic rigidity of systems and its effect on the formation of differentiated total systems the paradoxes of substitute value may be derived as necessary consequences. Thus, in general, is to be understood the either-or behavior so characteristic of the feeble-minded in a variety of fields. This

---

[1] See DEMBO, *op. cit.*

[2] It frequently does. *Cf.* Hoppe, Erfolg und Misserfolg, *Psychol. Forsch.,* 1930, **14,** 1–62.

either-or characteristic rests upon the fact that in the feeble-minded, because of their psychical material properties, we encounter, in higher degree than with the normal, strong dynamic Gestalten. That is, we encounter in higher degree unitary, internally undifferentiated systems which, in so far as they are separated, are separated completely.

There is a relative lack of weak Gestalten, those organizations in which two or more part systems constitute a dynamically connected unity although at the same time remaining separated to a greater or less degree.

One of the fundamental properties of the feeble-minded is, in my opinion, the paucity of continuously graded transitions between absolute separation and absolute connection in more inclusive dynamic wholes. This state of affairs makes clear why in so many fields one finds in the behavior of the feeble-minded extreme apparent contradictions.

Material Properties and the Psychical Environment.

In surveying the consequences of a person's dynamic material properties for experience and behavior, one must remember that these properties are characteristic not only of the internal psychical systems but equally of the psychical environment and of its changes, in so far as the latter are psychologically conditioned.[1] Not only such facts as valences of environmental objects and events but also the meaning and structural peculiarities of the perceptual field depend significantly upon psychobiological factors of the individual concerned and are not completely or univocally determined by the objective stimulus factors. Thus not only the content and momentary state of needs and interests, but all dynamic properties of the person, the rigidity and unchangeability of his systems, make themselves felt in the structure and changes of the psychical environment. Ordinarily, however, in treating particular objects or

[1] The principle that within the dynamic world of a definite individual is to be included not only his inner psychical systems and motorium but equally his psychical environment is one that has been repeatedly emphasized but so far insufficiently needed. *Cf.* W. Köhler, *Gestalt Psychology*, and Lewin, *Vorsatz, Wille und Bedürfnis.*

situations, one refers to the degree of fixation of their valence rather than to the transformation of tense or discharged psychical systems.

Regarded from this conception of the psychical environment, the behavior of the feeble-minded reveals the same either-or structure, as effect of the general rigidity of the psychical material. We mentioned above that the retarded pupils returned, without exception, to the interrupted task. From the standpoint just developed we should speak of a strong fixation of valence on the uncompleted work. This valence, however, will only remain effective under the conditions of the previous experiment as long as the feeble-minded does not leave the immediate psychological environment of the task. Under the given conditions,[1] allowing the child to carry out the second task (interrupting task) on another table suffices to reduce almost to zero the frequency of returns to the first task. The behavior of normal children contrasts decidedly with this. The situation may be formulated thus: in higher degree than the normal the feeble-minded is *either in the one or in the other situation*. Separate situations are in much higher degree opposed closed wholes, and the feeble-minded acts according to the field forces of these closed situations.

From the point of view of a psychology of the will, difficulty of transformation [*Umstrukturierung*], the effect of which upon the intellectual processes we are to consider immediately, signifies a *deliverance* of the person to the mercies of the momentary situation. According to the circumstances, this may have externally different effects. It may, for instance, appear as helplessness, as incapacity to find a way out. (The frequency of seductions to stealing, or within the sexual sphere, may well be closely related to this situation.) Under other circumstances the small changeability and relatively strong segregation of the situation result in great persistence and energy in the pursuit of a definite goal, to a particularly high concentration. On the other hand, if even a small change in the situation is

[1] Under other conditions the feeble-minded also may very well return to tasks which are not present.

occasioned by an external influence, it will constitute a much more profound interference. For in these persons the changed situation must, in much higher degree, tend to appear completely closed, supplanting entirely the facts of the first situation. That is to say, the formation of two or more simultaneously existent stratified situations will be much more difficult than in the normal individual. As a matter of fact the feeble-minded are thus generally extremely sensitive to distractions.

As previously mentioned in connection with the satiation experiments, this either-or characteristic results much more frequently in the introduction of pauses by the feeble-minded. Thus they completely interrupt their work more often than do normal children.

The peculiar resoluteness and *obstinacy* of the feeble-minded have already been referred to. An essential role in their determination is played by the facts just discussed, namely, the more difficult formation of relatively separated systems and the occurrence of less weakly connected but relatively separated situations. These are very intimately related with the great difficulty encountered by the feeble-minded when he is forced to *remain in a conflict situation.*

The characteristic conflict situation before decision[1] is a state of suspension in which the situations corresponding to various possible decisions are sufficiently present but must at the same time be kept sufficiently apart. On account of the reasons mentioned, the maintenance of this state of suspension is peculiarly difficult for the feeble-minded, and his obstinacy may be associated with this tendency toward univocal, dynamically closed situations.

The same difficulty in maintaining stratified situations makes it hard for the feeble-minded to dissimulate. This is expressed in most varied ways. In play for instance it often gives the total behavior of the feeble-minded an uncommonly appealing appearance of moral rectilinearity.

Helplessness and fear may prevent the feeble-minded from escaping a conflict out of which a normal, more mobile child

[1] See Chaps. III and IV.

would find a way with relative ease. If, despite all tendencies to the contrary, the child is forced by superior circumstances to remain in an unresolved conflict he generally suffers very acutely. Strong emotional reactions or suppressions result.[1]

Intelligence Defects.

In these considerations we have achieved an approach to the understanding of feeble-mindedness in its proper sense, that is, the intellectual processes of the feeble-minded.

As we have previously mentioned, the act of insight consists essentially in a change in the whole-relations in the field. Two initially quite independent facts become dependent parts of an interconnected whole; an originally unitary whole splits into relatively independent parts; or, by far most frequently, a re-formation of the field occurs such that parts of different wholes simultaneously become loosened and combine with other parts to form new wholes. Such re-formation of the whole-relations may be favored by objective shifts in the field (for instance, decreasing the spatial distance between banana and stick in Köhler's experiments). It is most particularly dependent, however, upon the general dynamic psychological properties of the given field, or of the particular person.[2] *This means then that an insufficient general mobility of the psychical systems must hinder the occurrence of intellectual acts*, that is, the occurrence of certain transformations of the structural unities in the field.

That the same material properties of the person hitherto discussed are of extreme significance for ease of intellectual activity will become even clearer upon consideration of certain

[1] Dembo has shown that generally anger is connected with the presence of an outer barrier creating a situation without escape for the person concerned. This enables us to see the relation of anger and helplessness, which may be of particular significance in the understanding of the feeble-minded.

[2] This state of affairs, illustrated by the difficulty of achieving insight with too great a stage of tension, is related, among other things, to the fact that forces working toward shifting of whole-relations can effect little if the total system is dominated by strong forces maintaining a condition of equilibrium. We will refer later to another circumstance working in the same direction.

rather complicated re-formations typical of intellectual acts and their difficulties.

Rupp[1] mentions several examples of typical difficulties in drawing by the feeble-minded, which seem to me to be particularly significant in the present connection. If a feeble-minded

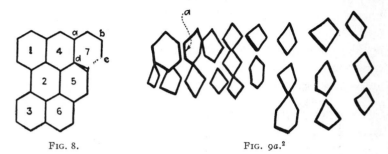

Fig. 8. Fig. 9a.[2]

Figures 9a and 9b show clearly this isolation of the smaller wholes of the given pattern. The line a in both figures is an example of doubling a line, a condition which results from the inability to see the line simultaneously as part of the two different wholes.

child is presented with a honeycomb pattern (Fig. 8) of which the cells 1, 2, and 3 are given, and asked to continue in the sequence 4, 5, 6, 7 . . . , he encounters great difficulties which can be shown not to be manual. Frequently there occurs a loosening up and isolation of the individual cells (Fig. 9a). If we inquire into the cause of this isolation of the cells, or as we may say, the Gestalt disintegration (see above), we find the following. The child may have proceeded as far as cell 7, and have drawn lines a, b, and c. What now is the situation with regard to line d? For the child at work on cell 7 it is

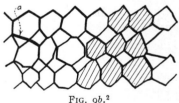

Fig. 9b.[2]

[1] H. Rupp, Über Optische Analyse, *Psychol. Forsch.*, 1923, **4,** 262–300.

[2] Figures 9a and 9b are from Rupp, *op. cit.*, p. 267, Figs. 4c and 4, respectively. The cross-hatching in Fig. 9b was intentionally inserted afterward by the experimenter in order to bring out the structure of the drawing.

obvious that the cell must possess a boundary line below to the left. This line is however also the upper right boundary of cell 5. The line d is thus simultaneously a dependent part of two different wholes and indeed has a quite different character in the two. Further, in such constructive activity it is necessary at the moment of actual drawing to perceive the separate line as a relatively independent whole. Thus, fundamentally, one must see with sufficient clearness three wholes: d as, (1) an independent line (to be drawn, for instance, in a definite direction from a definite point), (2) a dependent part of cell 5, and (3) a dependent part of cell 7. The situation is closely

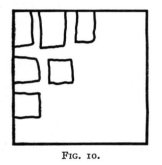

Fig. 10.

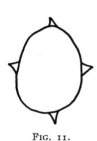

Fig. 11.

related to that of conflict with substitution previously described. The drawing can succeed only when the different characters of d in the two wholes are sufficiently differentiated and clearly appreciated. If, at the time, the child is dominated only by whole 5 or 7 and if d is sufficiently fixated as belonging to the already completed whole 5, as constituting its upper right boundary, then in bounding cell 7 he will be constrained to draw a new line, its lower left boundary.

A similar situation occurs when, instead of solving the task of dividing a square into smaller ones by drawing parallel lines through the entire figure, the feeble-minded solves it by making a row of smaller squares as in Fig. 10. It plays a role, together with two other factors, when in the copying of the Binet rhombus the figure is reproduced as a circle with added corners (Fig. 11).

The cause of difficulties of the feeble-minded in such intellectual tasks thus rests upon the fact that in the feeble-minded there is a much greater tendency toward the formation of strong Gestalten, that is, of unities whose subordinate parts are extraordinarily closely bound together and which as wholes are relatively completely separated. Thus from the same dynamic properties which have revealed themselves as essential foundations of the processes of need and will, we may deduce the intellectual defects of the feeble-minded. We shall recur later to the connection between the degree of differentiation of the person and the appearance of strong Gestalten.

Rohrschach[1] found that on presentation of ink-blot figures the feeble-minded gave decidedly fewer whole answers. Beck[2] confirmed this finding and discovered a small yet decided correlation between mental age and the tendency to give whole answers, that is, to describe the unclear field as a whole.

From this tendency to proceed from parts rather than from wholes an objection might be developed against our thesis of the special importance of the *strong* Gestalt in the feeble-minded. I shall therefore deal briefly with this question.

It must first be made clear that the thesis, "*X* tends to perceive wholes in greater degree than *Y*," is in this generalized form absolutely meaningless. Even though there existed persons who perceived only a "mosaic of points," they would be perceiving wholes. One can only meaningfully distinguish what particular wholes will be perceived with given constellations of stimuli. For example, the whole answers of normal children with Rohrschach by no means referred to the piece of paper with the ink blot but only to the ink blot. Yet they are not considered as part answers.

Here we may leave it open whether type of instruction or any other factor is responsible for the preference of these wholes in description. Certainly one may say that it is frequently harder for the feeble-minded, even as for the younger normal child, to sufficiently see through extended situations. This is indeed one of the most frequent difficulties in the solution of intellectual tasks. *Extension* is here essentially to be conceived in the sense of a property of structure; it would be completely misleading to assert that the small child or the feeble-minded see only parts and no wholes. It can no longer be doubted that small children, primitive people, and animals depend to a

[1] H. ROHRSCHACH, *Psychodiagnostik*, Bern, 1921.
[2] S. J. BECK, The Rohrschach Test as Applied to a Feeble-minded Group, *Arch. Psychol.*, No. 136, 1932.

particularly high degree upon the total character of situations. Rather the objective temporal and spatial extension of that which will be experienced by a young child as one connected situation, or as one relatively closed whole within a situation, often fails to correspond with that which would appear to the adult as the total situation or a special whole within it.   This objective extension of the total situation is occasionally greater with the small child, very frequently however less than with the adult.   The child's greater difficulty of surveying extended situations derives above all from the fact that with the adult the maximal degree of differentiation of wholes appears to be higher.   That is to say, with the adult more complexly stratified yet clearly differentiated wholes may develop as subordinate wholes.   This means, however, that the small child by no means sees only parts, but that with him, on the contrary, strong Gestalten play a much more dominating role.   It may scarcely be doubted that in this respect the feeble-minded stands closer to the younger child.

Concreteness.

Because of the slighter mobility of his psychical systems and his greater difficulty in developing and changing Gestalten, one is enabled to understand why the feeble-minded requires other conditions than the normal individual in order to achieve a reorganization of the field, an intellectual Aha-experience. There remains the further question as to whether the specific concreteness and primitiveness of their way of thinking is to be understood in terms of these same considerations.

Primitiveness of thinking may perhaps be referred to the tendency toward development of strong Gestalten.   From this one might infer that the general Gestalt characteristics play a relatively greater role with the feeble-minded.   Yet rather than tracing this peculiarity of the feeble-minded directly to the rigidity of his systems it is probably more correct to refer it to his smaller degree of differentiation as a person, to which we have already referred.   Indeed the tendency to concreteness and primitiveness appears to be a general feature of the child-like or otherwise undifferentiated person. It may thus be the effect of that structural property which the feeble-minded has in common with the young child (see page 209).

One will probably have to recognize in the tendency toward concreteness more than merely the primitiveness of the younger child. For this difficulty concerning abstract thinking still appears pronounced in the feeble-minded at an age at which the normal child of equivalent mental age no longer shows this peculiar concreteness. Our general groundwork indicates a way in which this peculiarity of the feeble-minded may be derived.

Concreteness of thinking and action in the feeble-minded signifies chiefly, as previously mentioned, that every object and event derives its meaning in peculiarly high degree from the present situation, that it is not a separable part of the situation. Thus abstraction, by which one generally means construction of groups according to certain factual relations of the individual objects, is rendered more difficult. In addition to emphasizing in general the dependence of the particular object on the actual situation, the thesis of concreteness implies that certain types of group construction are especially hindered. These are the types of grouping which are not directly in the level of reality, but more imaginal, conceptual, unreal. This condition may be related to very specific properties in the structure of the feeble-minded.

Compared with the total behavior of normal or even of certain psychopathic types of children, that of the particular kind of feeble-minded which we are considering strikes one by its relative lack of imaginativeness. This does not mean that the feeble-minded child has no ideas. Not infrequently he possesses a good and accurate memory for concrete facts. But his thinking and play as well reflect a poor imagination. He lacks a certain richness and a particular kind of mobility characteristic of imaginative play.

This lack of imagination on the part of the feeble-minded is revealed in the above mentioned investigations of Rohrschach[1] and Beck,[2] utilizing the Rohr-

[1] H. ROHRSCHACH, *op. cit.*, pp. 94 ff.
[2] S. J. BECK, *op. cit.*, p. 72.

schach ink-blot figures. From the fact that the figures relatively seldom were described as in motion, Beck concludes, "This finding indicates that the feeble-minded have very little capacity for creative fantasy." Just what psychological processes play a role here is, as Rohrschach himself emphasizes, rather unclear.

We regard the dynamic basis of the peculiarity of imaginative behavior as consisting in the relation of these occurrences to levels in the psychological environment and in the person, levels we have designated by the term unreality. Differences in degree of reality determine a dimension in the psychological life-space[1] and in the person. The levels of unreality stand, for example, in close relation to dreams, play, and ideal goals. *The degree of their development, their position in the whole structure of the person, and the type of connection between these levels of reality and unreality appear to me to be of fundamental significance for the total character of a person, in particular for his imagination and creativeness.*

We know from the investigation of Brown[2] that the dynamic properties of the levels of unreality are characterized by especial fluidity. If now relatively small mobility of psychical systems is characteristic of feeble-mindedness it is understandable that those psychical levels which in the normal individual are characterized by a particularly high fluidity will suffer particularly in the feeble-minded. Thus the consequence of a relative lack of development of the levels of unreality must be a lowered imaginativeness in total behavior, an increased concreteness of thinking.

Whether one must speak only of a lack of development and relative nonfluidity of the levels of unreality or whether the function of these levels within the total person is displaced can be determined only from a precise investigation of the particularities of development of levels of unreality in the feeble-minded. In the normal child formation of levels of different degrees of reality is the effect of a differentiation from beginnings in which the planes of reality and unreality cannot actually be separated. An investigation of the corresponding development in the feeble-minded should yield important

[1] See Chap. IV, p. 145.
[2] J. F. BROWN, *op. cit.*

information concerning the general problem of the development of different parts of the total person and perhaps furnish also an important practical instrument for the differential diagnosis between feeble-mindedness and late development.

This suggestion leads us to the consequences for the development of the feeble-minded which result from our basic assumption.

Infantilism.

One of the most tangible peculiarities of the feeble-minded is his retardation in comparison with normal children of like age, that is, his infantilism. The slow development of the feeble-minded child occurs by no means only in the intellectual sphere.[1] The fact of retardation is so central that, for instance, the difference in intelligence between normal and feeble-minded can roughly be characterized by its degree, that is, by mental age. It is scarcely to be doubted that the feeble-minded behaves in many respects like a younger child, not only with regard to intelligence but also with reference to the breadth of his mental horizon, his store of knowledge, his attention,[2] his emotional instability.

In a theory of infantilism one must keep in mind that retardation is not a specific peculiarity of the feeble-minded but also occurs frequently, for instance, in psychopathic types, especially the sensitive and impulsive.

Dynamically retardation may be related especially to a *smaller degree of differentiation* of the total systems of the psychical person, be it in all parts or in certain important spheres. We have, accordingly, to state as one of the most essential facts concerning the feeble-minded that the rate of differentiation of the total person, or of important spheres, is smaller than with the normal individual.

[1] Wallin (*Clinical and Abnormal Psychology*, Houghton Mifflin, Boston, 1927) reports the later appearance of the first tooth and the later closing of the fontanelle; Morgan (Physiological Maturity of Feeble-minded Girls, *Tr. School Bull.*, 1926, **27**, 23, 231 ff.), that menstruation occurs later with feeble-minded.

[2] Binet, indeed, attempted to bring differences of intelligence in direct relation to processes of attention.

Inquiry concerning the dynamic conditions upon which the rate of differentiation of such a total system depends leads us to the following considerations. Differentiation is certainly a function of the conditions of the environment as well as of the individual peculiarities of the person. At present we cannot answer the question whether one may properly speak of an inherited predisposition for a faster or slower rate of differentiation. The question, however, as to the relation existing between material properties and rate of differentiation of a system may well be raised.

Two systems, A and B, may be equal in respect to their degree of differentiation and their type of structure, yet differ with regard to their material properties. Further, in both cases the forces effecting differentiation may be equally strong and similarly directed. (For our present purpose it does not matter whether these are inner forces of the system or forces of the environment.) In such a case one may say unequivocally that a high functional *rigidity* with respect to changes must *hinder differentiation* of the total system. If, then, the material properties of the feeble-minded are to be characterized as particularly immobile, the direct deduction may be made that his development must, other things being equal, be slower.[1]

This derivation of the rate of differentiation from material properties agrees very well with the fact that the difference in development (measured in years of mental age) between a feeble-minded and normal child does not remain constant with change in age but in general increases. Indeed, this increase is so decided that the intelligence quotient remains constant or actually decreases. Naturally it is very possible not only that the slower rate of differentiation rests upon peculiarities of material properties but that the forces effecting differentiation are also relatively weak.[2]

[1] A more precise dynamic derivation would have to proceed from the relation between the strength of the forces pressing toward re-formation and of those necessary for the reorganization of a definite material.

[2] It is quite conceivable that there are instances in which the material properties of different persons correspond in the rough and only the forces effecting differentiation differ. In such cases also infantilism must result.

One may not, however, assert that in general differentiation of a system occurs the more readily the more fluid the system. We are concerned with the problem of an enduring, or in any case a relatively stable differentiation. If the total system is very fluid momentary differentiation may occur relatively easily, but the slightest force will again alter the structure so that development of a differentiated permanent structure of the total person does not result.[1] Such dynamic relations seem to us to be characteristic of the infantilism of certain *psychopathic* types.[2]

It is thus understandable why from the pedagogical point of view work with the milder grades of feeble-minded is often more fruitful and satisfying than work with psychopathic children. Single advances in differentiation may occur much more slowly with the feeble-minded and of course there are with them also frequent relapses, but the construction in general seems to possess a higher degree of stability.

Thus the favorable condition for enduring differentiation of the total psychical systems of a person is neither a maximal nor minimal but rather an optimal degree of material rigidity, varying according to the strength of forces working toward differentiation.

It must be emphasized at this point that not only too great inflexibility but also too great fluidity of the system must lead to feeble-minded types of behavior. It might be worth-while to test the applicability of such a dynamic characterization to the so-called erethetic feeble-mindedness.

Degree of Differentiation, Susceptibility to Influence [Beinfluss-barkeit], *Intellectual Mobility*.

The connection just discussed between material properties and rate of development seems to me to speak quite forcibly for the correctness of our fundamental thesis. On the other hand, there are several kinds of facts related to degree of differentia-

[1] With a completely fluid system, differentiation in the sense of an enduring structure would be impossible (we never encounter the state of completely stable equilibrium in a living being). Such a complete fluidity in an organism could be as little admitted as complete rigidity.

[2] *Cf.* LEWIN, Filmaufnahmen über Trieb- und Affektäusserungen psycho-pathischer Kinder.

tion which are difficult to see through, dynamically. We do not wish to neglect pointing out these difficulties.

Several Theoretical Difficulties. As mentioned, the young normal child is to be considered as a relatively slightly differentiated as well as a relatively soft, mobile system. Yet there can be no doubt that in many respects the small child appears to be more fixated, pedantic, yes, even more difficult to influence than an older child or indeed the adult. Not only the feeble-minded but also the small child demands with striking rigidity to sit on "his" chair while eating. If for some reason or other it does not please a one-year-old child to eat, it is generally much harder to move him to do so than it is an older child. Thus even though one wishes to continue holding to the thesis of greater mobility of the child (in itself quite probable[1]) it becomes apparent that behavior quite closely related to the fixation and rigidity of the feeble-minded may occur under circumstances in which an immobile material is not to be thought of.

One might consider reconstructing the theory so as to place at the center lack of differentiation rather than material properties, or one might attempt to dispense altogether with the assumption of a difference in material. The question of whether slight mobility is to be given a primary or secondary significance would not disturb us greatly, since in a dynamic theory dealing always with the totality of the properties of a system such questions are no longer seen as of much importance. Aside from special difficulties, however, a theory that would restrict itself to differences in degree of differentiation cannot be regarded as sufficient fundamentally. According to such a conception the feeble-minded would be conceived of as entirely similar to a person with slower development. Such a view is, however, undoubtedly false. Furthermore infantilism, that is, a smaller degree of differentiation, admittedly occurs with types which are not to be designated as feeble-minded.

[1] Compare the concept of plasticity, for instance, with C. Bühler, *Kindheit und Jugend.*

Another difficulty is connected with the problem of differentiation. Failure in the face of differentiated tasks involving comprehension, as for instance in drawing, in retention of rows of numerals, and similar tasks,[1] is found not only with feeble-minded but also with small children. Yet one might reason that their relative mobility should rather facilitate the formation of differentiated perceptual fields.

Our present experimental findings and insight into the general dynamics of the connection between psychical systems are not sufficient to yield a complete answer to the problems here in question. But the distinctions between degree of differentiation, degree of communication among part systems,[2] and the degree of their changeability have shown themselves so fruitful to us in recent years in the characterization of individual differences in such diverse spheres and in such varied connections that I should like to add a few considerations with reference to the solution of the difficulties involved.

In beginning, it should be emphasized that the relatively small differentiation of the feeble-minded follows from our fundamental thesis. Therefore the feeble-minded must show certain characteristics of the normal younger child, namely those which are specific effects of lack of differentiation.

Further, general observation seems to me to speak for the view that the degree of rigidity with the feeble-minded goes significantly beyond the occasional fixation observable in younger children.

Above all, however, one must inquire into the real dynamic meaning of fixation in the normal child.

Pedantry in the Normal Child. Whatever pedantry in the small child, for example, his wish always to sit on the same chair at table, may signify, it is by no means characteristic of the

---

[1] *Cf.* H. ROHRSCHACH, *op. cit.;* S. J. BECK, *op. cit.;* W. PETERS, Die Entwicklung der Wahrnehmungsleistungen beim Kinde, *Zeitschr. f. Psychol.*, 1927, **103**, 129–184.

[2] Through these concepts, particularly that of the degree of communication, the complex of facts referred to by E. R. Jaensch in the distinction between integrated and disintegrated types can probably be comprehended in sharper dynamic concepts.

entire young child of, say, less than one year. At this age the child is still quite insensitive to unusual situations of certain kinds. One can, for instance, take him on trips with fewer difficulties than a child of three or four. The child of three or four years already lives in a world of commands and prohibitions. A very definite must is often attached to certain things and types of behavior. This meaning is particularly stressed and held to by the child, probably in connection with the development of initial islands in a firm level of reality. This connection is, however, not always easily transparent to the adult, and often it is infected with magical features.

It is very possible that the pedantry of the feeble-minded is similarly based. Yet when some connection is not rationally transparent to him the feeble-minded must incline the sooner to magic ideas and fears. The question of material peculiarities here can only be answered by means of a comparative investigation of the degree of fixation under otherwise equal psychological conditions.

Susceptibility to Influence. In other cases in which the child appears to be influenced with greater difficulty the younger he is, the relations seem to be essentially different. If the hungry infant refuses his nourishment because he does not like its taste, there often remains only the possibility of brute force. The six-months-old child who does not savor his porridge turns his head away, purses his lips together, and eventually spews it out.

With the very small child the adult has fundamentally only a few methods of psychological interference. He can attempt to divert the child, to better his emotional state, or try to provoke a contrary action on the part of the child by apparent withdrawal of the object in question. The varied possibilities of encouragement and persuasion applicable to an older child are lacking.

Does there exist actually a greater dynamic rigidity of the psychical systems of the small child? To me such an interpretation appears false. The situation in question is as a whole to be characterized as one in which there exist for the child pronounced inclinations or disinclinations, that is, definite dominating field forces, together with an attempt by the adult to change the child. Under certain conditions this change is more difficult to effect in the small than in the older child. If one is to understand the basic dynamic factors operative it must be emphasized that it is only under very definite conditions that the smaller child is harder to change. The primitive method of diversion becomes generally ineffective with somewhat older children. One must then state that *under certain conditions the small child is harder, under other conditions easier to change than the older child.*

This paradoxical situation seems to be directly related to the lack of differentiation of the small child. In a higher degree than older children or adults the small child is a dynamic whole. The different parts of the total system are still so closely connected that in a peculiarly high degree the small child engages with his entire person in everything that he does. At the same time this unity means that the inner psychical and the bodily systems of the total person are particularly closely connected and that the dynamic boundary between person and psychological environment is relatively weak.[1] This means, for instance, that in the small child the needs of his person alter directly the character of his psychological environment and also that a change in the psychological environment affects more directly and strongly the total state of the person.

This wholeness and the slight firmness of the wall between person and environment have a double consequence for the ease with which the child may be influenced. If, by one means or another, one succeeds in altering the psychological environment of the child, then the small child is exposed with fewer defences to the changed environment. On the other hand, the total picture of the environment of the small child conforms much more directly to his own momentary state and under certain conditions it will be more difficult to bring about such

[1] See Chap. III.

an alteration.[1] For instance, if the small child is angry, the whole world is momentarily flooded with anger. If one is not successful in evoking an occurrence strong enough to change the character of the whole situation. the child will remain relatively unchangeable.

The greater wholeness of the total system leads here also to an either-or effect, similar to that which we have discussed as resulting from the rigidity of systems. Thus *in a certain respect there exists a functional equivalent between greater material rigidity and greater wholeness of the total system*. Both material rigidity and slight differentiation must favor the origin of stronger Gestalten, thus leading to an either-or effect.

The feeble-minded combine both a relatively high material rigidity and a specially small degree of differentiation of the total person[2] (which, as we have seen, may itself be conceived as an effect of rigidity on development), which must work in the same way with regard to the either-or effect. Actually in the feeble-minded one may observe in a striking manner the above discussed paradox of susceptibility to influence: under certain circumstances he is influenced with ease, under others with particular difficulty. This circumstance may have played a role in Binet's classification of the feeble-minded into rebellious and tractable types.

Differentiation of the Person and Mobility of Comprehension.

The fact that in certain respects it is easier to gain access to an older child is related further to the greater differentiation of the older child's worlds of perception and experience. Under objectively equal conditions, the degree of differentiation of the experienced environment appears to stand in closest connection with the degree of differentiation of the person concerned. This connection is apparent in the early development of the perceptual world[3] and also in the later development

---

[1] Further, the special organization of the social field is naturally of particular significance for susceptibility to influence.

[2] Relative immobility of systems does not necessarily mean that these systems are not in communication with each other. Reformability and degree of communication are to be distinguished even though not independent of each other.

[3] Cf. K. KOFFKA, *The Growth of the Mind.*

of perceptual achievements.[1] Together with the thorough structuring of a factual sphere, there grow generally the differential characteristics of the features of individual facts in the sphere and thus, at least to a certain extent, the possibility of more differentiated distinction.[2]

From the greater differentiation, the greater wealth of inner levels, there must thus result for the given person a greater richness of ways of conceiving and observing, in so far as other forces do not work antagonistically. The result of this situation is that a second person finds comparatively more spheres from which he may attempt to evoke a change in the existing way of comprehension. Even without the influence of someone else, the more differentiated person will have more possibilities of differently conceiving a given situation if the strength of the field forces do not impose a definite conception. If, for any reason, the total situation is unsatisfactory (if, for instance, access to a goal is barred, as in the detour experiments), a change in conception, a re-formation of the field, will occur, other things being equal, earlier in the more differentiated child. Whether this re-formation of the field occurs as the most painless evasion of the difficulty or as creative insight may depend upon the kind and degree of differentiation with respect to the factual sphere concerned and upon other personal peculiarities. In any case a certain degree of differentiation of the person will facilitate the restructuring of the field necessary for intellectual insights. In general it will make possible a greater richness of differing modes of behavior.

Thus under certain conditions and to a certain extent there exists a functional equivalence between a higher degree of

[1] Cf. W. PETERS, *op. cit.*

[2] It would lead too far afield to enter here into the problem, not wholly a simple one, of the cause of this relation. In any case an important role is played by the fact that the world picture of a more differentiated person is itself more differentiated (according to the lack of dynamic separation between the psychical person and the psychical environment). The individual perceptual fact thus acquires a position in a completely structured whole. I incline to believe that in addition a general relation between the maximal degree of structural detail in a perceptual picture and the degree of differentiation of the receptor is of decided significance.

differentiation of the total system and a greater mobility of the person in the face of a given situation or task.   There exists, that is, an equivalence between a specific characteristic of structure and a definite material property.

The same conclusion is reached as the result of the following considerations.   Let A and B represent total systems of similar material properties and with equal (medium) degrees of communication.   Further, both systems contain part systems a and b respectively, which in themselves are as similar as possible. A is on the whole, however, less differentiated than B.   Under these circumstances, because of the greater diversity of part systems in B, there will exist many more possibilities of a change of b than of a through inner shifts in the total system.

Such re-formation through inner forces occurs in voluntary changes of conception [Auffassung].   The tasks of voluntary concentration and attention, tasks, that is, in which a change or maintenance of field structure is to be brought about by inner means, are therefore (at least within certain limits[1]) easier for a person of higher degree of differentiation.   It requires little demonstration to establish that possibilities of influencing the separate part systems are significantly raised if the difference in differentiation of the total system consists not only in the number of part systems but (as actually occurs in the development of the child) also in qualitative differentiation within the total system.   In particular, the development of levels of reality and unreality, of levels, that is, differing in material properties, contributes richer possibilities dynamically.

It is quite possible that a determining role in the intellectual weakness of the feeble-minded and in their poor capacity for voluntary concentration, is played by precisely this smaller differentiation of the total system in consequence of the associated *slighter secondary mobility*.   Indeed it may here be more important than the direct effect of the material rigidity of the system.

---

[1] The danger of spontaneous changes in the part systems seems to constitute an antagonistic factor.

If our conception of a certain equivalence between higher degree of differentiation and external mobility be correct, then under certain conditions, even with the feeble-minded, a greater mobility of actual behavior should make itself noticeable with an increase in age. Even though the actual material properties do not change, or, indeed, though the change with age is in the direction of greater rigidity, yet a sufficiently faster advance of differentiation should increase the wealth of possible varieties of behavior. I incline to believe that the development of the slighter degrees of feeble-mindedness confirms this conclusion throughout. In any case the absolute advance of intellectual achievements on the part of the feeble-minded becomes fully understandable from this point of view.

The functional equivalence between greater material rigidity of the systems and a greater wholeness of the total system in respect to (1) the formation of strong, relatively undifferentiated Gestalten (systems), and (2) the secondary mobility of behavior is one of the major causes of the normal child's increase in intellectual achievement with age.[1] This occurs without increase in fluidity of the psychical systems, but rather despite a more probable gradual stiffening. This equivalence explains, further, why (because of a slighter differentiation of the total system) the feeble-minded, in spite of his greater material rigidity, is so similar to the younger child in susceptibility to influence, in intelligence, and in many other respects.

With these considerations the sketch of a dynamic theory of the feeble-minded is outlined in its main features. It scarcely need be emphasized that an abundance of detailed questions remains to be discussed or that a theory which attempts to proceed from the totality of dynamically possible differences of the person as a whole must raise a host of problems to be answered only by experiment and by comparison of very different individual types. But before theoretical penetration has achieved a certain degree of maturity it is often impossible

---

[1] As additional important factors the increased store of knowledge and abilities and, above all, the greater differentiation of the world picture are to be mentioned.

even to formulate the questions which should be answered by experiment.

Senile Dementia.

We refrain from consideration of the different kinds of mental disease or the effects of brain injuries which sometimes are accompanied by a kind of rigidity reminiscent of the behavior of the feeble-minded. Certainly the cause of behavioral rigidity may vary. Not only, as we have seen, is the degree of differentiation of the total person of influence, but the encapsulation of certain part systems remains a possible causal factor. The work of Dembo[1] on anger has shown, furthermore, that increase in state of tension may, under certain conditions, lead to greater momentary unity and primitiveness of the total behavior and may result in a certain fixation and weakness of intelligence which appears rather feeble-minded. The question as to whether a change is actually one of *material* property (the systems' mobility) must therefore be raised each time.

It cannot be questioned that dynamic mobility of the psychical systems is related in the closest fashion to the total biological constitution of the person concerned. We do not wish here to make definite assumptions concerning its relation to any specific biochemical, endocrine, or growth processes. We shall, however, briefly consider a general biological change in the total person which agrees peculiarly well with our fundamental thesis. This is the change designated as *senile dementia*.

The great material plasticity of the normal small child gives way, generally at least, to greater firmness. That with increasing age this development may lead finally to decided rigidity, lack of mobility, and inelasticity scarcely demands extensive demonstration. It has previously been pointed out that this progressive stiffening of the system's material properties is cut across by an increasing differentiation of the total person. In respect to intellectual achievements by far the most apparent initial effects of the combined processes are the increased structuration of the field of experience and the

[1] T. Dembo, *op. cit.*

greater intellectual mobility associated with differentiation. Should stiffening, however, proceed faster than differentiation with increasing age intellectual mobility of behavior must decrease and in cases of high degree of material immobility lead to appearances of feeble-mindedness. In this respect the effect must be particularly striking if, with age, instead of increase in differentiation there occurs an impoverishment of structure, a loss of part systems.

There exist, moreover, great individual differences in the tempo, extent, and age limits of enduring differentiation as well as in the tempo and extent of stiffening of the psychical material. In concrete instances one must lay most weight upon how the different part systems of the person individually behave.

In general if a stiffening of psychical material occurs with age and if the type of feeble-mindedness here considered is characterized by relative rigidity, then it follows not only that the process of differentiation must proceed more slowly, as discussed above, but also that it must *cease earlier*. This conclusion agrees very well with observation. "The mental development of the feeble-minded is not only slower than that of the normal individual, it also ceases earlier and begins to decline earlier."[1]

The theory here propounded thus permits a surprisingly unified view not only of those individual differences which are related to differences of the person in the feeble-minded, in the normal, and to a certain extent in the psychopathic, but also of those resting upon *development in age*. Further, it permits us to deduce the fundamental similarity of one type with other age levels of a different type and to comprehend in a unitary fashion a great multiplicity of kinds of behavior in very different fields, which, taken separately, are very diverse, often apparently contradictory.

---

[1] R. PINTNER, Feeblemindedness, in CARL MURCHISON, *Handbook of Child Psychology*, 1st ed., 1931, Chap. XIX, p. 611. Pintner supports this assertion by reference to a number of investigations by various authors who used large numbers of subjects, in some cases over periods of ten years,

Finally, I do not wish to neglect pointing out that the theory here presented attempts to avoid *methodologically* those difficulties which all classificatory divisions, however different in detail, must contend with and because of which these divisions are in certain respects so unsatisfactory. These difficulties of all classifications appear by no means only in psychology but in every science. They seem to be superable only when in the characterization of individual differences of the total person one passes beyond classificatory to constructive methods. We have made such an attempt. The constructive theory here presented does not lead to a distinction of three, four, or five pure types and their transitions, but, proceeding from certain basic dynamic concepts, contains from the beginning a principle for the construction and deduction of an endless variety of personal differences.

SUMMARY

Proceeding from comparative experimental investigations on normal and feeble-minded children of psychical satiation, resumption of interrupted actions, and substitute value of substitute actions, a dynamic theory of a definite type of feeble-mindedness has been developed.

The behavior of the feeble-minded is deduced from certain dynamic material properties of the psychical systems, which themselves imply specific structural peculiarities of the total person with respect to its degree and rate of differentiation and special kind of structure. The effects of these peculiarities of the person in the fields of intelligence, attention, will, and so on, have been discussed, and finally their relations to the structure of the person of the normal small child and of the senescent.

CHAPTER VIII

SURVEY OF THE EXPERIMENTAL INVESTIGATIONS

The following synopsis is designed to give the reader a very brief survey of our experimental investigations. It is planned, above all, to orient those who wish to go on to a closer acquaintance with these investigations. The description is therefore essentially from the systematic point of view. It may be desirable, however, to introduce it with a few historical remarks.

HISTORICAL REMARKS

The point of departure for *Untersuchungen zur Handlungs- und Affektpsychologie* [Investigations in the Psychology of Action and Emotion] was the investigation of the measurement of the will and the fundamental law of association,[1] the original aim of which was to make more precise Ach's attempts to measure the will. This investigation showed that the fundamental law of association (apart from other defects) errs in its basic dynamic concepts in so far as it treats couplings or other constraining forces as constituting also reservoirs of energy or tensions. Also it became clear to me that the phenomena occurring in these experiments were by no means so simple as was customarily assumed, but quite complicated and unstable. It was evident that one had to look for the simpler and essentially stabler phenomena of will psychology in facts which were generally considered especially complicated.

There followed a series of investigations in the field of the psychology of perception. In one of these[2] I attempted to

[1] K. LEWIN, Das Problem der Willensmessung und das Grundgesetz der Assoziation, *Psychol. Forsch.*, 1922, **1**, 191–302; **2**, 65–140.

[2] K. LEWIN and K. SAKUMA, Die Sehrichtung monokularer und binokularer Objekte bei Bewegung, und das Zustandekommen des Tiefeneffektes, *Psychol. Forsch.*, 1925, **6**, 298–357.

derive the perception of depth from certain constellations of forces in different layers of the perceptual system. The investigation of the reversal of spatial position[1] treats a problem which stands in the closest relation not only to the structure of the perceptual field but also to the problems of the will.

Fortunately I experienced Max Wertheimer's teaching in Berlin and collaborated for over a decade with Wolfgang Köhler. I need not emphasize my debts to these outstanding personalities. The fundamental ideas of Gestalt theory are the foundation of all our investigations in the field of the will, of affection, and of the personality. In the few articles in which the problems of general Gestalt theory are not explicitly discussed, this is solely because they have become the self-evident foundation of experimental practice.

Historically the first experimental investigation of the series on the structure and dynamics of the personality and of the psychological environment is that of Zeigarnik.[2] All later experimental investigations are built upon this. It was an attempt to break a first path through a primeval forest of facts and assumptions, using as compass concepts the practical utility of which was still wholly untried. The coincidence on the part of B. Zeigarnik of unusual conceptual clearness with great psychological acuity in the judgment of particular cases made this attempt possible.

Among the later experimental investigations a similar fundamental significance attaches to Dembo's investigation[3] of anger as a dynamic problem. She shows, by means of a self-critical investigation versatile in attack, that even rather complicated problems (success and failure, level of aspiration, substitution or compensation, reality and unreality, conflict, social relations, changes in the structure of the person), problems which at first seem to lie beyond any possibility of a dynamically strict and yet experimentally demonstrable presentation, are capable

[1] K. Lewin, Ueber die Umkehrung der Raumlage auf dem Kopf stehender Worte und Figuren in der Wahrnehmung, *Psychol. Forsch.*, 1923, 4, 210–261.

[2] Über das Behalten erledigter und unerledigter Handlungen, *Psychol. Forsch.*, 1927, 9, 1–85.

[3] Der Ärger als dynamisches Problem, *Psychol. Forsch.*, 1931, 15, 1–144.

of such a presentation with the aid of a constructive psychology. Her investigation is an impressive illustration of the fact that in a dynamic theory of psychological processes the problems of the environment and of the person are inseparably bound up together. It turned out that the investigation of this emotion extended itself necessarily to an investigation of certain environmental structures. In this research the utility and fertility of topological concepts for the presentation of complicated environmental structures was demonstrated for the first time. The reader will naturally miss the quantitative evaluation which is an essential component of Zeigarnik's and of all the other researches of the series. But according to my experience the thorough quantitative investigation of a field can always be obtained with some persistence if only the qualitative analysis is sufficiently advanced. A quantitative elaboration of some of the questions attacked by Dembo is already at hand, namely: the problem of success and failure and level of aspiration by Hoppe, Fajans, Rosenfeld; the problem of substitution (compensation) by Köpke, Lissner, Mahler; the problem of reality and unreality by Brown, Mahler, Sliosberg; certain social fields by Wiehe. I hope that the last-named investigation may have a fundamental significance for a broad field of social psychology.

SYSTEMATIC SURVEY

One may distinguish roughly two meanings of the question "Why" in psychology:

1. Why, in a given momentary situation, that is, with a given person (P) in a certain state and in a certain environment (E), does precisely this behavior (B) result? The problem is thus to represent the behavior (event) as a function of the momentary total situation $(B = f(PE))$.

2. The more historical question: Why, at this moment, does the situation have precisely this structure and the person precisely this condition or state?

It is important to separate these two questions more clearly than is done, for example, in association psychology and in

Freud's theory. The center of gravity of our experimental work lies, as a rule, in the first kind of why. In experimental practice, to be sure, these two kinds of problems are often so closely related that the creation of a sufficiently unequivocal situation requires a certain historical structure of the experimental situation.

In accordance with our general conceptual and methodological assumptions nearly all of our investigations treat not only questions of *individual differences* but problems of general *lawfulness*. The center of gravity lies, as a rule, in the problem of the general laws.

As regards content, no action is referred either to the person on the one side or to the psychological environment on the other; or yet to a more-or-less combination of both factors. Rather, each action is referred to the momentarily obtaining structure of such a person in such a psychological situation. Nearly all the investigations are therefore occupied with both problems. The following classification thus indicates merely the center of gravity of the problem formulations.

General Laws of the Psychological Systems

Tension Systems (Need, Purpose).

Ovsiankina, The Resumption of Interrupted Activities.[1] This article contains proof that the effect of a purpose or intention is the formation of a quasi-need, that is, dynamically, of a tension system. This tension system drives toward discharge and causes activities which serve the execution of the purpose. The technique of the experiments was essentially as follows: an activity was interrupted, and after a certain interval a situation of relative freedom for the subject was created. There resulted a frequent resumption of the interrupted activity (Table I).

The influence of the following factors, among others, upon the frequency of resumption were investigated: (1) the kind of activity; (2) the phase in which the activity was interrupted;

[1] *Psychol. Forsch.*, 1928, **11**, 302–379.

(3) the duration of the interruption; (4) the nature of the act of interruption; (5) the presence or absence of the uncompleted task at the end of the interruption; (6) the attitude and character of the person.

TABLE I[1]

Duration of interruption, minutes	CI						DI						
	RI	TR	R	R?	NR	R in per cent	RI	TR	R	R?	NR	R in per cent	R + TR in per cent
0 to 2	3	..	18	..	..	100	3	..	15	..	..	100	100
2 to 4	..	..	14	..	..	100	..	..	19	..	1	95	95
4 to 8	..	..	8	..	..	100	..	1	17	..	5	74	78
8 to 20	..	..	3	..	..	100	..	1	13	..	4	74	78
20 to 40	..	..	1	..	..	100	..	..	5	1	..	92	92
Over 40............	..	..	..	..	..	...	..	..	2	1	..	83	83
Indeterminate.......	..	..	..	..	..	...	..	1	..	..	5	...	...
Total..............	3	..	44	..	..	100	3	3	71	2	15	79	82

[1] Ovsiankina, *op. cit.*, Table I, p. 326.

The left half of the table under the heading *CI* includes the experiments with interruptions occurring as though by chance. The right half with the heading *DI* lists the experiments in which the first task was interrupted by asking the subject to do another (disturbing) task. In the first column the duration of the interruption is given in minutes. The six following columns show the number of cases of *RI* (refusal to be interrupted), *TR* (tendency to resume), *R* (resumption), *R?* (questionable resumption), *NR* (nonresumption), and *R* in percentage (total percentage of resumptions), according to the duration of interruption. In calculating the percentage of *R*, the instances of *R?* are counted as one half.

The proof that the resumption (or as the case may be, a repetition of the activity) fails to occur as soon as the tension system is discharged by the attainment of the goal is important for the character of the quasi-needs as tension systems. It is shown that a substitute satisfaction can have the same effect and, further, that the presentation of the half-finished work of another person does not, as a rule, cause a tendency to completion.

Zeigarnik, On the Retention of Completed and Uncompleted Activities.[1] Zeigarnik attacks the same problem as Ovsiankina but with another technique. If a purpose or intention cor-

[1] *Psychol. Forsch.*, 1927, **9**, 1–85.

responds dynamically to a tense system, it is to be expected that the state of tension of the system should be evident not only in the tendency to completion of the activity but also, for example, in its better retention. Zeigarnik finds, indeed, that *memory* for uncompleted activities is much better (Table II). She proves that it is not the shock effect of the interruption that is the cause of this better retention but rather the state of the psychical systems involved at the time when the subject is asked to recall. The influence of the following things, among others, was investigated in detail: (1) the structure of the task (an activity with a definite end as against a continuous activity); (2) interest in the task; (3) the attitude of the subject toward the experimenter; (4) the differences among children, adolescents, and adults.

Zeigarnik shows that the tension systems may be destroyed by sufficiently strong variations of tension in the whole person (affective variations produced naturally, Table III, and artificially); and that in a fatigued state (owing to the then occurring fluidity of the systems) no sufficiently stable systems arise. Zeigarnik attacks the important question of the firmness of form of nontense systems. (This question is directly investigated in an unpublished work of Kaulina and plays an essential part in that of Schwarz.) The structure of the more comprehensive system totalities is shown to be essential; only when the single psychological systems are sufficiently separated are completed activities better remembered than uncompleted.

Birenbaum, On the Forgetting of an Intention.[1] It is shown that intentions or purposes which correspond to a main task (or to a central need) are almost never forgotten. With the less important purposes such, for example, as writing the name (or the date) on the sheet of paper used for the main task, the forgetting (nonexecution) depends essentially upon whether and if so how the system corresponding to the purpose is *imbedded* in that of the main task or main goal.

Birenbaum treats of the factors which determine whether a newly arising system is dynamically a relatively independent

[1] *Psychol. Forsch.*, 1930, **13**, 218–284.

TABLE II.[1]—THE RATIO OF THE RETAINED UNCOMPLETED TO THE RETAINED COMPLETED ACTIVITIES $\dfrac{RU}{RC}$

Rank Order of Subjects

Rank $\dfrac{RU}{RC}$	Subject	Activities				Arithmetic mean by groups			
		ΣR	RU	RC	$\dfrac{RU}{RC}$	ΣR	RU	RC	$\dfrac{RU}{RC}$
1	Wd.	7	6	1	6				
2	Be.	9	7	2	3.5				
3	St.	13	10	3	3.3				
	Jf.	8	6	2	3.0	9.1	7	2.1	3.5
5	M.	8	6	2	3.0				
	Eu.	12	9	3	3.0				
7	Pl.	7	5	2	2.5				
	Paj.	9	6	3	2.0				
	Gin.	9	6	3	2.0				
10	Hf.	6	4	2	2.0				
	Pt.	15	10	5	2.0				
	Ml.	12	8	4	2.0	10.8	7	3.8	1.9
	Dm.	11	7	4	1.75				
14	V.	11	7	4	1.75				
	Git.	11	7	4	1.75				
16	Dm. E.	13	8	5	1.6				
	Ml. R	15	9	6	1.5				
	Jn.	10	6	4	1.5				
19	Rm.	15	9	6	1.5				
	Gld.	10	6	4	1.5				
	Jic.	10	6	4	1.5				
	Ml. E.	12	7	5	1.4	13.3	7.8	5.5	1.4
23	Kür.	19	11	8	1.4				
	Hn.	12	7	5	1.4				
25.5	Glk.	16	9	7	1.3				
	Jnk.	14	8	6	1.3				
	Gl.	12	6	6	1.0				
28	Wlt.	12	6	6	1.0	11.3	5.7	5.7	1.0
	Schn.	10	5	5	1.0				
30.5	Sim.	11	5	6	0.8				
	Fr.	9	4	5	0.8	9.0	4.0	5.0	0.8
32	Sim. H.	7	3	4	0.75				
Arithmetic mean.....		11.1	6.8	4.25	1.9				

ΣR = number of retained activities.
RU = number of retained uncompleted activities.
RC = number of retained completed activities.
RU/RC = ratio of retained uncompleted to retained completed activities.

[1] Zeigarnik, *op. cit.*, Table I, p. 9.

TABLE III.[1]—$\dfrac{RU}{RC}$ FOR EXCITED SUBJECTS

Subject	RU	RC	$\dfrac{RU}{RC}$
I	3	4	0.75
II	4	5	0.8
III	6	7	0.9
IV	7	9	0.8
V	4	4	1.0
VI	2	4	0.5
Mean	4.3	5.5	0.78

[1] Zeigarnik, *op. cit.*, Table 28, p. 70.

TABLE IV[1]

	Task	E	SE	F	Per cent E
Before Critical Task	1. Match task A	36		1	97
	2. Match task B	37			100
	3. Match task C	36		1	97
	4. Match task D	36		1	97
	5. Match task E	36		1	97
	Mean: Tasks 1 to 5	36.2	0	0.8	97.6
Critical Task	6. { I. Favorite poem or II. Draw a pentagon or III. Write cities }	10	11	16	27
After Critical Task	7. II or III or I	13	8	16	35
	8. III or I or II	16	4	17	43
	9. Guessing a name	16	5	16	43
	10. Word building	16	6	15	43
	11. Outlining a figure	8	5	24	22
	12. Monogram	7	5	25	19
	Mean: Tasks 7 to 12	12.7	5.5	18.8	34.2

E = number of subjects who executed intention.
SE = number of subjects who subsequently executed intention.
F = number of subjects who forgot intention.
[1] Birenbaum, *op. cit.*, Table 2, p. 238. A series of five match tasks (different, but of the same general character) is followed by one radically different in content (the critical task, No. 6 above), which is then followed by a heterogeneous series.

whole or a dependent part of a more comprehensive regional system. The special structure of the total system and the degree of its wholeness [*Ganzheitlichkeit*] (in the sense of a stronger or weaker dynamic Gestalt) may be to a large extent experimentally determined by means of the temporal structure of the event and the internal relations of its content (Table IV). Under certain circumstances the structure of the total system may be changed after the event. The tension of the single systems, as well as the structure of the total system (and hence the frequency of forgetting) is found to depend, further, upon the general state of tension and the affective state of the whole person.

Substitution.

The question of the discharge of the psychical systems through substitute or compensatory activities forms the chief problem in the investigation of the following.

Lissner, The Discharge of Needs by Substitute Activities.[1] Lissner investigated the conditions under which a substitute activity has dynamic substitute value for the original activity (Table IVa). The nonresumption of interrupted activities after the insertion of a substitute activity was used as a criterion of substitute value (see Chap. VI, page 180). The substitute value of a difficult performance was found to be considerably higher than the substitute value of an easier performance (see page 248). The substitute value increases with the similarity between the original and the substitute task. The degree of connection between the systems involved plays a decisive role.[2] Köpke investigates this question comparatively on feeble-minded and normal children.

Mahler, Substitute Activities of Different Degrees of Reality.[3] Mahler, with a similar experimental technique, studied the question of dynamic substitute value especially for substitute

[1] *Psychol. Forsch.*, 1933, **18**, 218–250.
[2] LISSNER, *op. cit.*, Table 8, p. 240.
[3] *Psychol. Forsch.*, 1933, **18**, 27–89.

TABLE IVa.[1] — THE DEPENDENCE OF THE SUBSTITUTE VALUE UPON THE DEGREE OF DIFFICULTY (MEASURED IN WORKING TIME[2]) OF THE SUBSTITUTE ACTIVITY AND UPON ITS SIMILARITY TO THE ORIGINAL ACTIVITY[3]

Task	Puzzle					Riddle					Translation				
	Original activity	Similar		Different		Original activity	Similar		Different		Original activity	Similar		Different	
		easy	hard	easy	hard		easy	hard	easy	hard		easy	hard	easy	hard
n............	44	13	11	9	11	43	13	11	9	10	39	11	10	9	9
Working time mean in seconds...	194	70	<687	32	<323	340	211	<744	223	<600	399	312	<693	236	<550
Mean variation...	76.7	37.4	370.4	22.8	101.2	119.2	73.2	289.5	145.8	222.3	124.9	84.8	187.5	55.6	181.2
Substitute value: $\dfrac{RWS}{RS}$[4]		1.8	2.2	1.3	1.5		1.4	3	0.9	1.3		2.3	2.8	1.2	1.4

Substitute value comparison diagrams:
Puzzle: 1.8 < 2.2 > 1.3 < 1.5
Riddle: 1.4 < 3 > 0.9 < 1.3
Translation: 2.3 < 2.8 > 1.2 < 1.4

[1] Lissner, op. cit., Table 6, p. 237.

[2] As a measure of the difficulty of the activity we use the time required for its execution. In the case of the original activity also time may be used as a measure of difficulty, even though these activities are interrupted before completion. The interruption occurred at almost exactly the same point in the execution with the different subjects. The riddle task was regularly interrupted after ten words, the translation task at a certain point in the text. Even in the case of the puzzle the mode of work was sufficiently similar to permit the selection of a rather precisely defined point for interruption.

[3] The difference between the arithmetic means for easy and hard substitute activities is, without exception, great both absolutely and in comparison to the original activity. The fact that the mean variation is considerable is due to the magnitude of the individual differences and does not impair the characterization of the substitute activity as easy or difficult. If one compares original activity and substitute activity for the same subject, the following is to be noted. The easy substitute activities are executed more quickly than the original activity in 59 out of 64 cases (even though the original activity is not completed). The difficult substitute activities, on the other hand, require a longer time than the original activity in 59 out of 62 cases.

[4] The summary of the substitute values in this table shows particularly clearly and without exception that (1) the substitute value of the more difficult substitute activity is greater than that of the easier; (2) the substitute value of similar substitute activities of the same degree of difficulty is greater than that of dissimilar substitute activities; (3) the substitute value of easy similar activities is greater than that of difficult dissimilar activities; (4) the difference between the substitute values is greatest between difficult similar and easy dissimilar substitute activities.
The substitute value is expressed as the ratio of the frequency of resumption of the interrupted activity when no substitute is given (RWS) to the frequency of resumption of the interrupted activity when a substitute is presented (RS).

activities of varying degrees of reality (thinking; talking; actual doing) in adults and children (Table V). On the whole, substitute activities of higher degrees of reality have greater substitute value. The relation of the substitute act to the inner goal of the original activity nevertheless remains of decisive importance. Substitute satisfaction occurs only when this inner goal is in sufficient degree attained by the substitute activity (Table VI). Mahler investigates the difference between problem tasks and realization tasks and shows the significance of the creation of a socially acknowledged fact for the degree of reality and the substitute value of the substitute activity.

TABLE V[1]

	Tasks not completed			Tasks completed by substitution (subst. = *acting*)			Tasks not completed			Tasks completed by substitution (subst. = *talking*)		
n	24	24	18	24	24	23	12	12	11	12	12	12
	TSR	*SR*	*RI*	*TSR*	*SR*	*RI*	*TSR*	*SR*	*RI*	*TSR*	*SR*	*RI*
Per cent	19	33	28	17	4	15	58	8	9	25	0	24
ΣR in per cent	65			29			67			42		
$\dfrac{RAN}{RAS}$	2.2						1.6					

SR = spontaneous resumption.
TSR = tendency to spontaneous resumption.
RI = resumed after supplementary instruction.
ΣR = $SR + TSR + RI$.
RAN = resumption of acts not completed.
RAS = resumption after completion of substitute act.
n = number of cases.

The supplementary instruction (used with subjects that did not spontaneously resume, at the very end of the experiment, when numbers of both completed and uncompleted tasks were equally accessible) was as follows: "Now do any one of these tasks." The preference for uncompleted tasks in response to this neutral instruction provided in these cases a further criterion for the persistence of the tension.

In the columns *TSR*, *SR*, and *RI*, the figures indicate the total number of cases of resumption of the different kinds, irrespective of whether the same subject showed more than one kind. In ΣR, however, only one resumption of each resumed task is counted for each resuming subject, even though he may have resumed in more than one way. Consequently it may happen that ΣR is less than $TSR + SR + RI$.

[1] Mahler, Table 4, p. 44.

TABLE VI[1]

	Tasks not completed			Tasks completed by substitution: *Goal of act attained*			Tasks not completed			Tasks completed by substitution: *Goal of act not attained*		
n	24 TSR	24 SR	19 RI	24 TSR	24 SR	24 RI	12 TSR	12 SR	10 RI	12 TSR	12 SR	12 RI
Per cent	27	25	24	4	0	10	42	25	15	50	8	33
ΣR in per cent	60			13			75			75		
$\dfrac{RAN}{RAS}$	4.6						1					

[1] Mahler, Table 6, p. 50.

Success and Failure; Level of Aspiration.

Related to the structure of the psychological systems and the differences in degree of reality is the experimental work of the following.

Hoppe, Success and Failure.[1]   In spite of the great practical significance of this problem we have hitherto known very little about the occurrence of experiences of success and failure and the laws of their operation.   Hoppe shows that the occurrence of these experiences is not a simple function of the result of the activity but depends, among other things, upon the relation of this result to the momentary level of aspiration (real and ideal goal) of the person and upon the ascription of the result of the activity to the self as its own performance. He shows that these experiences are limited to a rather narrow zone of difficulty, which is determined essentially by the limits of the ability of the person.   In quite too hard and quite too easy tasks experiences of success or failure do not occur (Fig. 1).

It is sometimes possible to fix upon different altitudes of the level of aspiration and to compare them for different persons. Thus one can investigate the effect of success and failure on the displacement of the level of aspiration ("real goal," Fig. 2) and the degree of reality of the ideal goal.   These displacements of the level of aspiration, the formation of substitute goals, as well as the tendency to spontaneous interruption after certain

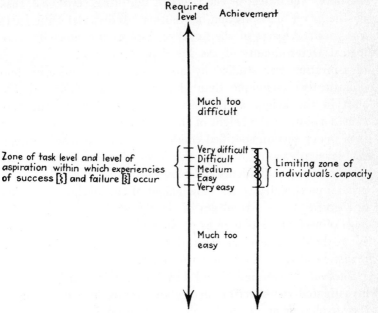

FIG. 1.—(*Hoppe, op. cit., Fig. 25, p. 55.*)

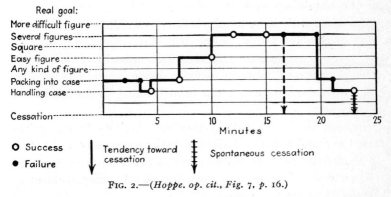

FIG. 2.—(*Hoppe. op. cit., Fig. 7, p. 16.*)

successes and failures, rest upon a definite conflict situation. Close relations were found to obtain between the level of aspiration and the *self*-consciousness of the individual as a social person.   Pronounced and apparently very deep-lying individual differences were found.

Frank, The Effect of the Level of Performance in One Task on the Level of Aspiration in Another,[1] Individual Differences in Certain Aspects of the Level of Aspiration,[2] Some Psychological Determinants of the Level of Aspiration.[3]   The level of aspiration was studied by means of a more objective and quantitative technique than Hoppe's.   It was found that a shift in the height of the level of performance in one task causes a shift in the height of the level of aspiration in another task under certain specified conditions.   The relation between the level of aspiration and the level of performance differs widely among individuals and seems to represent a reliable and general personality trait.   The height of the level of aspiration in a given case is a resultant of the tendencies (1) to keep the level of aspiration as high as possible, (2) to avoid failure, and (3) to hold the level of aspiration in close agreement with a realistic estimate of future performance.

Jucknat, Performance and Level of Aspiration.[4]   Jucknat investigated the effect of success and failure in one field upon the displacement of the level of aspiration in another field. She uses an essentially improved technique for the diagnosis of the obtaining level of aspiration.   The experiments were carried out with some hundreds of school children and showed that success and failure in one field may importantly displace the level of aspiration in another field, upward or downward. This presupposes, however, definite dynamic relations between the two fields and a not too fixed level of aspiration in the second field.

Fajans, II, Success, Persistence and Activity in the Infant and the Small Child.[5]   Fajans investigated success and failure in children of from one to four years and in infants of six months to one year.   She found a very considerable displacement of

[1] *Jour. Exper. Psychol.*, in press.
[2] *Amer. J. Psychol.*, 1935, **47**, 119–129.
[3] *Amer. J. Psychol.*,1935, **47**, No. 2.
[4] *Psychol. Forsch.*, in press.
[5] *Psychol. Forsch.*, 1933, **17**, 268–305.

the level of activity of behavior: characterologically rather passive children can be moved by success to a rather active kind of behavior and characterologically rather active children can be reduced by failure to a rather passive kind of conduct.

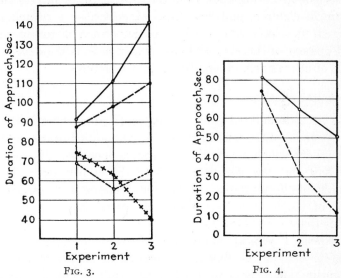

Fig. 3.

Fig. 4.

Fig. 3.—Comparison of the effects of success, encouragement, substitution and failure upon the duration of approach [*Zuwendungsdauer*]. A positively valent object was hung out of reach of the child: his efforts toward it were timed with a stop watch and are indicated as "duration of approach" upon the ordinates. (*Fajans, II, Fig. 7, p. 290.*)

———————Success with concomitant encouragement. Increase in duration of approach from first to third experiment = 48 per cent.
– – – – – –Success. Increase in duration of approach = 25 per cent.
. . . . .Substitute success. Diminution in duration of approach = 6 per cent.
+ + + + +Failure. Diminution in duration of approach = 48 per cent.

Fig. 4.—Effect of success (———————) and failure (– – – – – –) upon the infant. (*Fajans, II, Fig. 2, p. 278.*)

Fajans discusses the relation of success and failure to embarrassment and to going-out-of-the-field. It appears that the attainment of a substitute goal, a consolation, or an encouragement is, for the child, to a rather considerable degree the equivalent of a genuine success (Fig. 3). The quantitative results suggest that the attainment of a goal means psychologically something essentially other in the infant (Fig. 4) than in the young child. This circumstance is confirmed and more explicitly investigated by the following.

Rosenfeld, The Ontogeny of Experiences of Success and Failure.[1] It is shown in what way the experiences of achieving and of non-achieving differ from the experiences of success and failure in children, and how these experiences are related to different developmental levels. An important factor in the development of success and failure experiences is the development of increasingly differentiated goal structures.

Psychical Satiation.

To be distinguished from the above-described questions on the dynamics of the tension system is the question of the conditions under which a new tension system spontaneously arises and how the new goal is related to the earlier goal. This problem has been attacked in the investigations of the displacement of the level of aspiration. A special problem in this field is that of psychical satiation.

Karsten, Psychical Satiation.[2] Karsten investigates the question of how the repeated execution of an act influences the inclination to execute the act yet again. The technique is essentially as follows: the subject must do a certain task repeatedly; he is, however, free to stop as soon as he has enough of it. Karsten used a group of activities as varied as possible. By reason of the repetition, an originally positive valence of the act changes to a negative. Finally the subject tries to go out of the field. The progressive process of satiation is evidenced by such typical criteria as variation, dissolution of the whole (of both perceptual and action unities), inattention, forgetting. Psychological satiation is shown to be different from fatigue although fatigue is frequently a symptom of psychical satiation. The speed of satiation depends, among other things, upon the structure of the task, upon the state of tension of the whole person, upon whether the task involved is of a more peripheral or more central character (both agreeable

[1] *Psychol. Forsch.*, in preparation.
[2] *Psychol. Forsch.*, 1928, **10**, 142–254.

TABLE VII.[1]—CONSATIATION. FIRST DAY, SUBJECT GROUP α

Subject	Sum of the part regions	Number of part regions per third	First third of the part regions			Second third of the part regions			Third third of the part regions		
			Total time		Amount	Total time		Amount	Total time		Amount
			Minutes	Seconds		Minutes	Seconds		Minutes	Seconds	
Tr.	3	1	38	15	569	18	..	476	8	15	70
Ha.	4	1.3	13	30	314	7	45	199	6	45	31
So.	7	2.3	25	30	645	14	30	532	7	..	174
J.	21	7	10	10	357	6	45	188	3	35	56
Fa.	28	9	5	20	130	4	..	40	4	..	78
Mean	..	...	18	30	403	10	12	287	5	55	82

The procedure used in this experiment was to have the subject make strokes in a certain rhythm (3,5) until he would no longer continue even upon slight pressure from the experimenter. He was then asked to make strokes in another rhythm (4, 4), again until spontaneous cessation. He was then asked to make strokes in still another rhythm, again until spontaneous cessation, and this process was continued until the subject could no longer be moved to make strokes in any new rhythm whatsoever. Each rhythm is regarded as a part region. As may be seen from the table, subject Fa. required the satiation of only three part regions before the whole region (i.e., making strokes any way at all) was satiated; whereas subject Tr. required the satiation of 28 part regions before the whole region was satiated. The "thirds" referred to in the table are the results simply of the division of the total number of part regions required for the subject into three equal parts. "Amount" means number of stroke groups executed.

[1] Karsten, Table 5, p. 222.

and disagreeable tasks are comparatively more rapidly satiated than neutral ones), upon the character of the person.

The problem of the *consatiation* [*Mitsättigung*] of neighboring regions is quantitatively investigated (Table VII) as is also the effect of variation upon the satiation of the total region (Table VIII). A condition of satiation is the occurrence of "genuine repetition." Karsten discusses the conditions under which satiation, in spite of many repetitions, fails to occur.

Karsten's results are, in addition, an impressive demonstration of the thesis that repetition by no means always brings with it an improvement in performance such as would be expected from the law of association.

Table VIII shows that with increase in amount of activity necessary to satiate single part regions, the number of part regions that have to be explicitly satiated in order to satiate the whole region decreases.

TABLE VIII.[1]—SUBJECT GROUP α ON THE FIRST DAY

(1) Rank order	Subject	Number of explicitly satiated part regions	Average satiation time per part region
1	Tr.	3——————21 Min. 30 Sec.	
2	Ha.	4—————— 7 Min.	
3	So.	7—————— 7 Min.	
4	J.	21—————— 0 Min. 58 Sec.	
5	Fa.	28—————— 0 Min. 29 Sec.	

(2) Rank order	Subject	Number of explicitly satiated part regions	Average satiation quantum per part region
1	Tr.	3——————372	
2	Ha.	4————136	
3	So.	7————193	
4	J.	21—————— 29	
5	Fa.	28—————— 9	

[1] Karsten, Table 3, p. 217.

Lange, Action Unities in the Occupations of the Kindergarten.[1] Lange investigates the duration of occupations in children of various ages under the conditions of a Montessori kindergarten and the various factors which determine the kind of occupations and cessations of activity.

Problems of the Environment[2]

The properties of the psychobiological environment (E) depend, among other things, upon the state of the person (P) involved [$E = f(P, X, Y \ldots)$]. The valences, especially, are directly related to the state of the tension systems.

General Topology and Dynamics.

Of especial importance for the structure of the psychological environment are (1) the *topological* relations (*i.e.*, the mode of connections of different regions, the presence of dynamic barriers, etc.); (2) the *fields of force* (direction and strength of the forces at the various points of the field).

Fajans, I, The Significance of Distance for the Strength of a Valence in Infants and Young Children.[3] Fajans investigates the special problem of whether the strength of the force corresponding to a valence diminishes as the spatial distance between the valence and the person increases. She used as subjects infants and preschool children who tried to reach a goal object from various distances. She compared the duration of active and passive, direct and indirect, approaches (Fig. 5).

She found, in the case of the infants, a clear diminution in the strength of the field forces with increasing distance but no such diminution (within the investigated distances) with the preschool children. This difference rests in part upon the different magnitudes of the life-space at these different ages, in part on the greater significance of social fields for the older children. Fajans follows up the metamorphosis of "thing" [*sachlichen*] fields into social fields, the structure of the new

---

[1] *Psychol. Forsch.*, in preparation.

[2] A somewhat more thorough survey of the results up to the present concerning environmental forces is found in Chap. III.

[3] *Psychol. Forsch.*, 1933, **17**, 215–267.

environment in embarrassment, the effect of certain conflict situations on expression, and other questions. Methodologically important is the development of special criteria which permit the discrimination of differences in the strength of driving forces from differences in the firmness of barriers. Fajans shows that the strength of these restraining forces is a function of the strength of the driving forces.

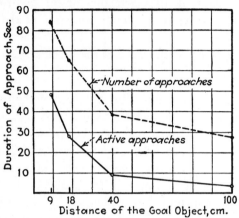

FIG. 5.—In these experiments with infants a positively valent object was hung at eye level as the infant sat upon a table at the horizontal distance indicated from his outstretched hand. The total duration of "active approaches" and "passive approaches" (visual regard) was measured with a stop watch and is indicated upon the ordinates. (*Fajans*, I, *Fig.* 4, *p.* 239.)

– – – – – –All approaches (active and passive).
————Active approaches.

Dembo, Anger as a Dynamic Problem.[1] Dembo analyzes the change in the topology of a situation in which a goal is unattainable (formation of a dynamic barrier between person and goal, formation of an outer barrier) and shows the effect of the obtaining topology on the possible modes of behavior. The decisive significance of the different *degrees of reality*, which are to be represented by a special dimension of the psychobiological life-space (Fig. 6), becomes clear. Besides the topology, the field forces, their distribution and their changes, are investigated. The structure of the fields of force in the *conflict* situation is given, its effect on behavior in the

[1] *Psychol. Forsch.*, 1931, **15**, 1–144.

level of reality (oscillation, various kinds of going-out-of-the-field), as well as the tendency to go into the level of unreality (fantastic solutions). Dembo uses the idea of *inducing fields*

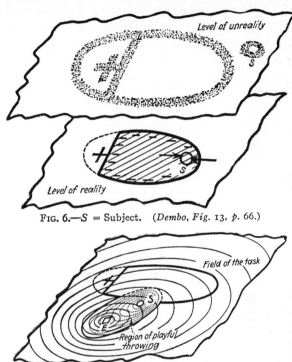

FIG. 6.—*S* = Subject. (*Dembo, Fig.* 13, *p.* 66.)

FIG. 7.—The outer barrier embraces not only the field of the task but also the field of the struggle with the experimenter. (The task here is to throw rings over a bottle. The experimenter intentionally provokes the subject by catching the thrown rings, moving the bottle, etc. The subject immediately takes this up as a *game*, which gives him a basis for conducting a struggle with the experimenter, a basis which, as mere subject, he did not have.) To this extent, then, the field of the struggle with the experimenter corresponds to "a special region of the field of the task." If the subject should succeed continually in getting the upper hand in the struggle the field of the task, its vectors and its barriers, would be annulled in so far as these rest upon the field of force of the experimenter. (*Dembo, Fig.* 17, *p.* 82.)

—————————Field of force of the experimenter.

. . . . .Field of force of the subject.

for the presentation of social power relations and deduces the occurrence and the forms of the struggle between experimenter and subject from the nature of these fields (Fig. 7). She also uses this concept in treating the difficult problems related to the spontaneous occurrence of substitute goals and relates the problem of the substitute goal to that of the use of tools. Dembo follows in detail the process of *destructurization* [*Destrukturierung*] and *homogenization* [*Homogenisierung*] of the field, which is very significant for the dynamics of anger. The experimental findings of this investigation form the essential basis for my analysis of the situation of reward and punishment (see Chap. IV, page 114).

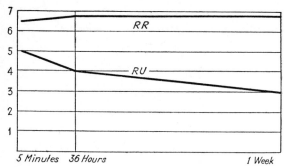

FIG. 8.—*RR* = real tasks retained. *RU* = unreal tasks retained. (*Brown, Fig. 5, p. 13.*)

Reality and Unreality.

Brown, On the Dynamic Properties of the Levels of Reality and Unreality.[1] Brown tests experimentally the assumption that the less real levels are dynamically more fluid than the more real, by investigating the speed of discharge of tense systems which belong to different levels. He makes use of the technique of Zeigarnik and compares especially the discharge of systems which correspond to serious and nonserious tasks.

He finds that tension persists much longer (Fig. 8) in the former, that they thus correspond to dynamically less fluid media. A special experimental arrangement shows that attention or intensity in the execution of the task does not determine this effect.

The question of the differences between levels of reality and unreality also plays a role in the already mentioned works of Lissner and Mahler.

[1] *Psychol. Forsch.*, 1933, **18**, 1–26.

Sliosberg, On the Dynamics of Play.[1] Sliosberg investigates the problem of substitution especially in the play of the child. It is found, among other things, that the substitute value of an object or an action depends essentially upon whether the child is in a play or in a serious situation. The question is discussed whether the close connection between

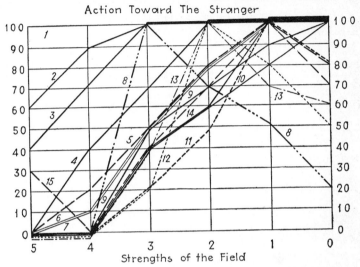

Action Toward The Stranger

Abscissae represent per cent of cases in which the different kinds of action occur at the different strengths of the field

1-Listen to	4-Smiling at	7-Express wishes	10-Staying near	13-Show off
2-Look at	5-Speaking to	8-Give or throw	11-Personal questions	14-Make demand
3-Turning	6-Address to	9-Bodily contact	12-Demonstrate ability	15-Affective reaction

FIG. 9.

reality and unreality which determines the child's magical view of the world (Piaget) is also determinative for the satisfaction of his needs.

Social Fields.

Wiehe, The Behavior of the Child in Strange Fields.[2] Wiehe investigates the significance of a special social field for the behavior of children. The children, sometimes alone, sometimes in the presence of the mother, are brought into a strange

[1] *Psychol. Forsch.*, 1934, **19**, 122–181.

[2] In preparation.

TABLE IX.[1]—ACTION TOWARD THE STRANGER

Behavior		Degree of the strengths of the social field					
		$N = 5$, 21	$N = 4$, 38	$N = 3$, 59	$N = 2$, 52	$N = 1$, 51	$N = 0$, 22
1. Listen to	unh	100 %	100 %	100 %	100 %	100 %	100 %
	h	0	0	0	0	0	0
2. Look at	a	40	10	0	0	0	0
	o sh	30	10	0	0	0	0
	une	30	0	0	0	0	0
	unc	0	20	10	0	0	0
	oem	0	60	30	10	0	0
	d	0	0	30	40	40	0
	unh	0	0	30	50	60	100
3. Turn bodily toward	a	60	30	0	0	0	0
	v w	30	30	0	0	0	0
	une	10	20	0	0	0	0
	w	0	20	30	0	0	0
	he	0	0	40	20	0	0
	o st	0	0	30	30	0	0
	oem	0	0	0	40	60	0
	unh	0	0	0	10	40	100
4. Smile at	a	100	60	30	0	0	0
	o sh	0	20	0	0	0	0
	unc	0	20	50	0	0	0
	c	0	0	20	40	0	0
	oem	0	0	0	40	60	0
	s un	0	0	0	20	40	100
5. Speak to	a	100	80	50	20	0	20
	o sh	0	20	20	0	0	0
	we	0	0	20	30	0	0
	i	0	0	10	0	0	0
	d	0	0	0	0	20	0
	oem	0	0	0	30	50	0
	s un	0	0	0	20	30	80
6. Address to	a	100	90	50	20	0	0
	unc	0	10	20	20	0	0
	i	0	0	30	0	0	0
	d	0	0	0	30	20	0
	oem	0	0	0	30	40	0
	s un	0	0	0	0	40	100
7. Express wishes	a	100	90	50	20	0	0
	v we	0	10	10	0	0	0
	unc	0	0	20	30	0	0
	i	0	0	20	20	10	0
	c	0	0	0	40	60	100
	oem	0	0	0	0	30	0
8. Give or throw something	a	100	100	0	30	50	80
	o sh	0	0	60	40	0	0
	unc	0	0	30	0	0	0
	i	0	0	10	0	0	0
	oem	0	0	0	30	30	0
	s un	0	0	0	0	10	20
9. Make bodily contact	a	100	100	50	30	10	0
	o sh	0	0	30	20	10	0
	unc	0	0	0	0	0	0
	he	0	0	10	30	10	0
	i	0	0	10	10	0	0
	sub	0	0	0	10	10	0
	oem	0	0	0	0	30	0
	s un	0	0	0	0	30	100

TABLE IX.[1]—ACTION TOWARD THE STRANGER.—(*Continued*)

Behavior		Degree of the strengths of the social field					
		5 $N = 21$	4 $N = 38$	3 $N = 59$	2 $N = 52$	1 $N = 51$	0 $N = 22$
10. Stay nearby	a	100 %	100 %	60 %	40 %	20 %	0 %
	o sh	0	0	30	20	0	0
	unc	0	0	10	20	10	0
	up	0	0	0	20	10	0
	oem	0	0	0	0	30	0
	s un	0	0	0	0	30	100
11. Ask personal questions	a	100	100	80	50	0	30
	i	0	0	20	20	20	0
	unc	0	0	0	30	20	0
	s un	0	0	0	0	60	70
12. Demonstrate ability	a	100	100	80	0	20	50
	unc	0	0	10	10	0	0
	sub	0	0	10	0	0	0
	oem	0	0	0	70	50	0
	s un	0	0	0	20	30	50
13. Show off	a	100	100	60	0	30	40
	une	0	0	20	0	0	0
	unc	0	0	20	10	0	0
	oem	0	0	0	70	40	0
	s un	0	0	0	20	30	60
14. Make demands	a	100	100	60	40	0	0
	o sh	0	0	20	0	0	0
	v we	0	0	20	0	0	0
	we	0	0	0	30	0	0
	c	0	0	0	30	0	0
	aff	0	0	0	0	10	20
	oem	0	0	0	0	30	0
	we	0	0	0	0	40	50
	s un	0	0	0	0	20	30
15. Affective reactions	a	70	100	60	30	0	20
	v we	0	0	20	0	0	0
	o sh	0	0	10	20	0	0
	we	0	0	10	50	10	0
	oem	0	0	0	0	60	0
	s un	0	0	0	0	30	80
		30	0	0	0	0	0

a = absent.
aff = connected with affections.
c = confident.
d = discretely.
he = hesitancy.
i = indirect.
oem = overemphasized.
o sh = overshort.
o st = only starting.

p = personal.
sub = substitute activity.
s un = socially unhindered.
unc = uncertain.
une = unemphasized.
up = impersonal.
v we = very weak.
we = weak.
wo = doing with emphasis.

[1] Wiehe, in preparation.

room, or a strange person appears in the child's home. Wiehe distinguishes six different degrees of strength of this strange field. The degree of strength is, apart from individual characteristics of the child and of the strange person, a function of the spatial distance of the strange person, of the duration of his presence, and of his conduct. It is possible to correlate the different degrees of the strength of the field with definite modes of behavior of the child. Surprisingly marked quantitative lawful relations resulted (Table IX). The strongest pressure was expressed by the child's becoming motionless; crying and the tendency to run away, where possible to the neighborhood of the mother or into another field where the child feels itself more at home, correspond to a weaker degree of pressure (Fig. 9). The other activities of the child also showed, with great regularity, an inhibited character under high pressure of strangeness and an overexcited or overemphasized character under somewhat weaker pressure. Only a further reduction of pressure led to natural free behavior.

Structure and State of the Whole Person

Nearly all the investigations described above have also contributed somewhat to the problem of the state and structure of the whole person. Zeigarnik showed the dependence of the single tension upon the fatigue (Table X) and affectivity of the whole person. Birenbaum showed their dependence upon the state of tension (Table XI) of the whole person. In Karsten's investigation the stratification [Geschichtetheit] of the

TABLE X.[1] $\frac{RU}{RC}$ FOR FATIGUED SUBJECTS

Subject	R	RU	RC	$\frac{RU}{RC}$
A	11	6	5	1.2 $(5)^2$
H	9	$(\frac{4}{9})$	$(\frac{5}{11})$	0.98 (1)
S	9	4	5	0.8
F	9	4	5	0.8
K	7	3	4	0.75
Lk	7	3	4	0.75 (1.75)
Ph	11	4	7	0.57
E	12	4	8	0.5 (1.66)
E	6	2	4	0.5
Fr	6	2	4	0.5 (1.5)
Mean	8.7	3.6	5	**0.74**

[1] Zeigarnik, Table 25, p. 66.
[2] The numbers in parentheses indicate the results of the experiment with the same subjects in the fresh condition six months previously.

whole person and the significance of the more central and more peripheral inner psychological strata for the process of satiation became clear. Hoppe, Fajans, and Jucknat treat of the relation between experiences of success and failure and the state and character of the whole person.

TABLE XI[1]

Activity	7 Subjects (naive-excited): basic experiment				The same seven subjects instructed for speed			
	E	SE	F	$E\%$	E	SE	F	$E\%$
1. Match task..............	4	1	2	57	7	...	...	100
2. Draw a pentagon........	3	2	2	43	6	...	1	86
3. Write cities.............	5	2	...	71	7	...	...	100
4. Guess a name...........	3	1	3	43	7	...	...	100
5. Word building..........	2	2	3	29	7	...	...	100
6. Poem..................	3	3	1	43	6	1	...	86
7. Outline................	...	1	6	0	4	...	3	57
8. Names of scholars with one initial.................	5	1	1	71	7	...	...	100
9. Monogram.............	4	1	2	57	6	...	1	86
Mean....................	3.2	1.5	2.2	46	6.3	0.1	0.6	90.5

E = executed intention.
SE = subsequently executed intention.
F = forgotten intention.
[1] Birenbaum, Table 10, p. 271.

Experimental Simplification of the Structure of the Person: Regression.

The above-mentioned investigation of Dembo on anger goes more extensively into the problems of the whole person and of the change in its structure. Anger, for example, can show itself in extraordinarily different, indeed in opposed, ways. Dembo investigates the different kinds of pure emotional expression and emotional behavior, the criteria of emotional intensity, and the dynamics of emotional outbursts. The functional firmness of the boundaries of the strata between the inner psychical systems and the environment is of decisive significance.   The paradoxical circumstance, that superficial emotions lead more readily to emotional expression than the more serious ones, is explained (Figs. 10 and 11).

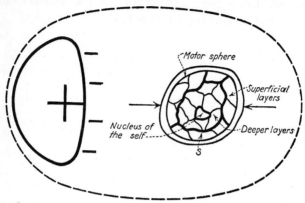

Fig. 10.—Structure of the psychological environment and the person in superficial emotion.   (*Dembo, Fig. 18, p. 109.*)

Dembo follows the change in the finer structure of the person with increasing affective tension, and the displacement of the chief boundary between the inner psychical systems and

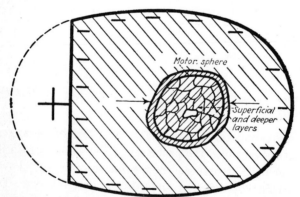

Fig. 11.—Structure of the psychological environment and the person in deeper lying emotion.   (*Dembo, Fig. 19, p. 110.*)

the environment with special reference to the motorium.   The results on de-differentiation, that is, on the changes of the person in the direction of a more primitive, a dynamically less differentiated unity, seem to me of especial significance. This process goes hand in hand with the simplification [*Primitivierung*] of the structure of the environment and is of decisive significance for emotional outburst. There result essential common features between the world picture [*Weltbild*] of the affectively de-differentiated adult and that of the still relatively un-differentiated child. The dynamic homogeneity of the child and the difference in its whole person in emotion and in fatigue are discussed.

Menstruum and Intermenstruum.

Freund, On Satiation in and between Menstrual Periods.[1] Freund investigated the influence of the menstrual and inter-menstrual periods on the speed of satiation for certain tasks. Because of the great individual differences the same subjects were investigated in both conditions. There resulted a very marked difference in the speed of satiation, which held indeed without exception for every individual (Fig. 12). This difference in *inclination* is the more noteworthy since there occurred no regular difference in speed or quality of performance when the same subjects were set definitely limited tasks of the same sort.

Psychopathology.

Some not very systematically executed experiments on psychopathic children seem to show that certain types of these children are more rapidly satiated than normal children of the same age.[2]

It may be of interest, as an example of our way of work, that these individual differences in speed of satiation, as well as the difference in the behavior of the same person in different conditions (during and between menstruation) and, finally, the difference between peripheral and central tasks, may be deduced in unitary fashion.

[1] *Psychol. Forsch.*, 1930, **13**, 198–217.

[2] Cf. Lewin, Trieb- und Affektäusserungen psychopathischer Kinder (Motion pictures of psychopathic children compared with normal and feeble-minded children), *Zeitschr. f. Kinderforsch.*, 1926, **32**, 414–447.

The dynamic concepts (such as degree of structuredness, fluidity, state of tension) which resulted from investigations of the general laws form the foundation of the experimental study of the feeble-minded and the psychopathic child.

Feeble-mindedness.

Köpke. Köpke found essential differences between normal and feeble-minded children in regard to the substitution value of substitute activities (see Chap. VI, page 180).

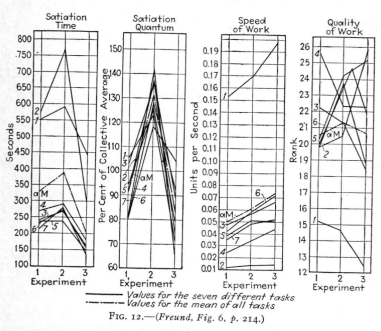

FIG. 12.—(Freund, Fig. 6, p. 214.)

Erfurth, Saathop, and Wöhrmann. Erfurth, Saathop, and Wöhrmann investigated the speed of satiation in normal and feeble-minded children. On the basis of these experiments it is possible to determine more precisely the dynamic characteristics of a certain type of feeble-mindedness (see Chap. VII, page 194). As we noted above, one finds special determinations on individual differences in nearly all the researches of the series.

Modes of Execution, Perceptual and Cognitive Structure
of the Environment

In conclusion three works should be mentioned which do not fit well into the selected grouping. These investigations center about problems for which the nature of the stratum between the inner psychical systems and the physical environment is chiefly determinative, the stratum to which one may refer the motor tasks [*Ausführungshandlung*] and the processes of perception. Since these questions are closely related to problems of which one usually thinks in speaking of experience in learning, a few words on our general position toward the problem of "*experience*" should precede discussion of these investigations.

The results of the investigation of the fundamental law of association[1] are sometimes misinterpreted to mean that I hold "experience" to be unimportant. The articles on satiation, on the effect of success and failure, on lapses in relearning, among others, show that such a conception is far removed from my view. It is only that the effect of experience cannot be sufficiently characterized by means of the concept of association. The effect of experience always consists in the fact that a person (P), upon the repetition of a situation, reacts not in the same way but in another way than that in which he reacted the preceding time. If the behavior (B) is really in both cases the same, it means that the person has remained unchanged. (Thus if $B_1 = B_2$ and $E_1 = E_2$, P_1 must equal P_2 in accordance with the general law: $P = f(BE)$). The effect of experience is always a change of the person or of the psychological meaning of the environment. A theory of experience can consist only in a determination of the various possible changes in the structure of the person, of the environment, and of the forces dominating that environment. I am inclined to doubt that a unitary theory of the whole field of these changes in terms of experience is possible.

---

[1] LEWIN, "Das Problem der Willensmessung und das Grundgesetz der Assoziation." *Psychol. Forsch.*, 1922, **1**, 191–302; 1922, **2**, 65–140.

Schwarz, On Relapses in Re-learning, I and II.[1] Building upon the negative findings of my investigation of association, Schwarz attempted to formulate, on the newly found basis, the conditions under which a change in a repeatedly executed task presents difficulties and to determine what the nature of the errors occurring under these conditions might be. Schwarz distinguishes between errors of confusion and errors of relapsing. He separates the question of the momentary source of the energy for the execution of the task from the form of its expression and especially from its dependence upon constraining forces. He finds that the two kinds of error are dynamically of essentially different nature. Both occur only when, in the learning process, systems of quite definite form have been built up and have also become sufficiently rigid. He treats in detail the question of action unities, their different forms, their genesis, and their change; he further discusses the significance of the valences for the execution of the task.

Forer, An Investigation of the Decroly Method of Learning Reading.[2] Forer compares the retention of children from five to six years old for single letters, words, and sentences. She investigates their memory for (1) these written forms of different extent; for (2) their significance; and for (3) the coordination of written form and significance. In general, it is shown that a group of relatively heterogeneous written forms and meanings is more easily learned than a homogeneous group. The written form of a sentence and of a word are about equally well, that of a letter a little better, retained. But the meaning of a word and the meaning of a sentence are very much better retained than letters; further, words referring to things are better retained than words referring to activities or to properties. The spatial juxtaposition of the written form and the related object constitutes an essential advantage for the retention of children in contrast to that of adults. This difference seems to me to be related to the magical world picture of the child in that, at this age, the written forms designate objects and not concepts.

---

[1] *Psychol. Forsch.*, 1923, **2**, 86–158, and 1933, **18**, 143–190.
[2] *Zeitschr. für Kinderforsch.*, 1933, **42**, 11–44.

Voigt, Precision of Direction at a Distance.[1] Voigt treats the problem of the steering of the execution of a task by the perceptual field. His subjects shot with a light-pistol, without taking aim, at targets of various kinds and at varying distances. He found that within certain distances the angular precision of the shooting increased with the distance of the target (Fig. 13). Voigt investigates exhaustively the dependence of these

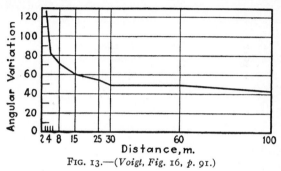

FIG. 13.—(*Voigt, Fig.* 16, *p.* 91.)

results upon the structure of the perceptual field and upon the motor apparatus used (shooting with the right hand, the left hand, and with both hands). He demonstrates the significance of the motor field [*Handlungsfeld*], which embraces in unitary fashion the person and the goal. Voigt also goes into the question of the learning of that sort of activity.

Survey of the Experimentally Handled Problems in Terms of Traditionally Used Key Words

(The names of authors treating a given topic most exhaustively are printed in italics.)

Action, activity (*Handlung*)	Schwarz (wholeness), Voigt (steering), Zeigarnik and Ovsiankina (kinds). On dynamics see Need, Emotion, etc.
Anger (*Ärger*)	Zeigarnik, Karsten, Ovsiankina, Hoppe, Fajans, II, *Dembo.*
Attention (*Aufmerksamkeit*)	Karsten, Dembo, Fajans, I and II, Schwarz, Wiehe.
Attitude (*Einstellung*)	Zeigarnik, Ovsiankina, Karsten, Schwarz, Freund, Brown.
Character (*Charakter*)	Ovsiankina, Hoppe, Dembo, Fajans, I and II, Wiehe.

[1] *Psychol. Forsch.*, 1932, **16**, 70–113.

Compensation   See Substitute.

Conflict (*Konflikt*)   Ovsiankina, Zeigarnik, Karsten, Birenbaum, Hoppe, *Dembo*, Jucknat, *Fajans, I and II,* Rosenfeld, Schwarz, *Wiehe.*

Depth (*Tiefe*)   Lewin and Sakuma, Voigt.

Development (*Entwickelung*)   See Problems of child psychology.

Embarrassment (*Verlegenheit*)   Fajans, II, Karsten, Jucknat.

Emotion (*Affekt*)   Zeigarnik, Karsten, Ovsiankina, Birenbaum, Hoppe, Fajans, II, Dembo, Freund, Wiehe.

Experience (*Erfahrung*)   See Learning, Satiation, Success.

Failure (*Misserfolg*)   See Success.

Fantasy (*Phantasie*)   Zeigarnik, Dembo.

Fatigue (*Ermüdung*)   Dembo, Brown, Hoppe, Mahler.

Force (*Kraft*)   See Structure of environment, Conflict.

Gestalt (*Gestalt*)   See Whole, unity.

Gesture (*Geste*)   Fajans, II, Hoppe, Dembo. See also Unreality.

Goal (*Ziel*)   Hoppe, Dembo, Jucknat (ideal and real goal, level of aspiration), Mahler (inner and outer goal of action), Karsten.

Habit (*Gewohnheit*)   Lewin (measurement of the will), Schwarz, Karsten, Freund, Jucknat, Hoppe.

Hallucination (*Halluzination*)   Dembo.

Ideal (*Ideal*)   Hoppe, Jucknat, Dembo. See also Unreality.

Instrument (*Werkzeug*)   Dembo (substitute), Voigt (steering), Hoppe (ascription of the effect).

Individual differences (*Individuelle Unterschiede*)   Köpke (feeblemindedness), Zeigarnik, Ovsiankina, Karsten, Fajans, II, Freund.

Intention (*Absicht*)   Voigt (significance for steering). See also Purpose, Need.

Lapse (*Rückfall*)   See Habit.

Learning, relearning, forgetting (*Lernen, Umlernen, Verlernen*)   Schwarz, Voigt, Forer, Karsten.

Memory (*Gedächtnis*)   Lewin (measurement of the will), *Zeigarnik*, Schwarz, Birenbaum, Jucknat, *Brown, Forer.*

Need (*Bedürfnis*)   Zeigarnik, Ovsiankina, Birenbaum, Hoppe, Karsten, Mahler, Rosenfeld, Jucknat, Lissner, Freund, Lewin (measurement of the will).

Perception (*Wahrnehmung*)   See Depth.

Persistence (*Ausdauer*)   Karsten, Hoppe, Freund, Birenbaum.

Person, structure of the whole person (*Person, Struktur der Gesamtperson*)   *Dembo*, Köpke, Karsten (stratification) Freund, Hoppe. See also Individual differences, Problems of child psychology.

Play (*Spiel*)   Dembo, Schlossberg. See also Unreality.

Problems of child psychology (*Kinderpsychologische Probleme*)   Zeigarnik, Ovsiankina, Fajans, I and II, Mahler, Wiehe, *Rosenfeld*, Jucknat, Forer.

Purpose (*Vornahme*) — Zeigarnik, Ovsiankina, *Birenbaum*, Brown, Hoppe.

Reading (*Lesen*) — Forer.

Reality (*Realität*) — See Unreality.

Restlessness (*Unruhe*) — See Emotion, Conflict, Satiation.

Satiation (*Psychische Sättigung*) — *Karsten*, Freund.

Satisfaction (*Befriedigung*) — See Need.

Self-consciousness (*Selbstbewusstsein*) — Hoppe, Fajans, II, Jucknat.

Self-control (*Selbstbeherrschung*) — See Conflict, Emotion, Success.

Skill (*Geschicklichkeit*) — Voigt, Schwarz.

Social relations (*Sociale Beziehungen*) — *Dembo, Wiehe*, Hoppe, Jucknat, Fajans, I and II.

Structure of environment (*Umweltstruktur*) — Voigt (connection with steering), Forer, Dembo (concept of the world), Zeigarnik, Ovsiankina, Fajans, I (environmental forces), Zeigarnik, Hoppe, Fajans, II (topology). See also Conflict, Social relations.

Struggle (*Kampf*) — *Dembo*, Wiehe, Karsten.

Substitute (*Ersatz*) — Zeigarnik, Ovsiankina, Birenbaum, Hoppe, Dembo, Mahler, Jucknat, Fajans, II.

Success (*Erfolg*) — Dembo, *Hoppe*, Fajans, I and II, Jucknat.

Superstition (*Aberglauben*) — Dembo.

Unreality (*Irrealität*) — *Brown, Dembo*, Fajans, II, *Mahler*, Hoppe, Forer, Schlossberg.

Valence (*Aufforderungscharakter*) — Ovsiankina, *Karsten*, Dembo, *Fajans, I* (and distance). See also Conflict, Need.

Whole, unity (*Ganzheit*) — Voigt (visual wholeness and performance), Forer (differentiation of word and meaning), Birenbaum, Zeigarnik (wholeness, unity of tension systems), Dembo (structure of the whole person). See also Success, Substitute.

Will (*Wille*) — See Purpose, Need, Conflict.

World, concept of (*Weltbild*) — Forer, Dembo, Hoppe. See also Unreality.

INDEX OF NAMES

INDEX OF SUBJECTS

V

Vagabonding, 125
Valence, 51, 81
  definition of, 175
  dependence on distance, 86f., 166
    on need, 78
  examples of, 118
  induction of, 175
  magnitude as function of distance, 166

Valence, shifts in, 163
  transformation of, by imbedding, 167ff.
Vector, definition of, 81

W

Wholeness, degree of, 247
Will, measurement of, 239
  rigidity of, in feeble-minded, 204
Withdrawal (*see* Going-out-of-the-field)